THE GAUQUELIN EFFECT

A PROOF OF
CELESTIAL INFLUENCE

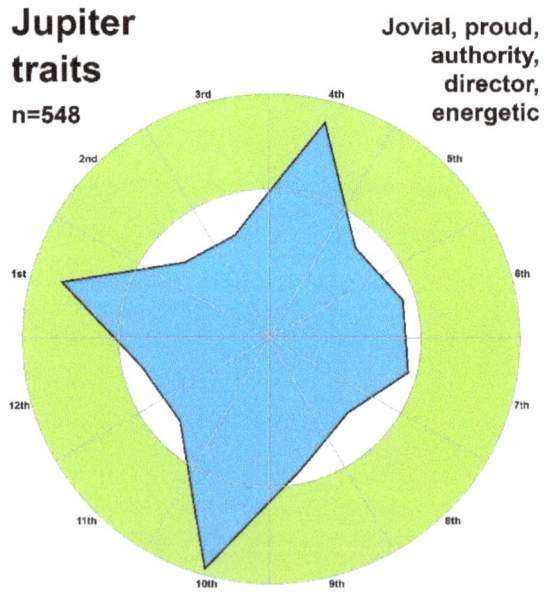

The character-traits of Jupiter

THE GAUQUELIN EFFECT

by

Nick Kollerstrom

M.A. Cantab., PhD, F.R.A.S.

A **New Alchemy Press** publication
www.newalchemypress.com
Copyright © 2023
Nicholas Kollerstrom
The author has asserted his moral right to be
identified as the author of this work.
Any part of this publication may be reproduced or utilized,
but kindly acknowledge the source
ISBN 978-1-7399994-6-9

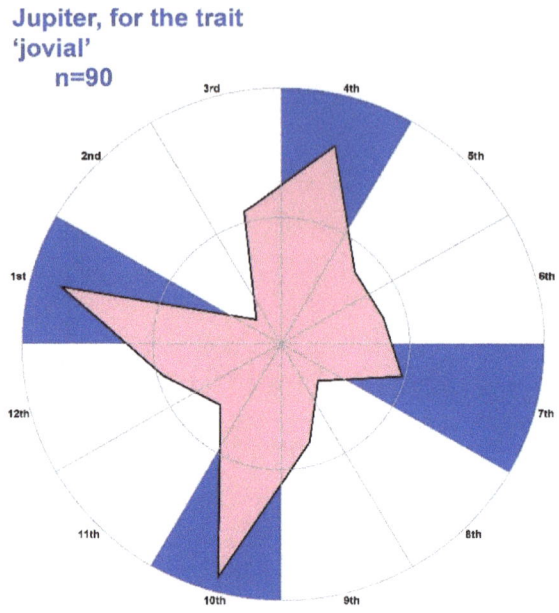

Figure: Is Jupiter jovial?

Thanks to the Urania Trust, for a grant; to Sven Raphael, Ray Murphy, Thierry Graff, Rudolf Smit, Derek Norcott and Graham Douglas; and to Fiona Bowring for cover design.

CONTENTS

Intro by Rob Hand	
Foreword	1
Chapter 1 Looking at the data	12
Chapter 2 How Big was the effect?	27
Chapter 3 So Brief a hope	38
Chapter 4 Sceptics hit back	51
Chapter 5 Ertel: Did Michel cheat?	75
Chapter 6 French Skeptics see the Mars Effect	95
Chapter 7 A Search for 'proof'	112
Chapter 8 A 'Heredity' effect? Not really	133
Chapter 9 Character traits	140
Chapter 10 The Primary archetypes	146
Chapter 11 Venus found	165
Chapter 12 John Addey's dream	173
Chapter 13 Introvert / Extravert	182
Chapter 14 Synastry of Parisien couples	193
Conclusion	202

Introduction

Both those who are for and against astrology (in the broadest sense) as a serious field for study recognise the importance of Gauquelin's work. It is probably not putting it too strongly to say that everything hangs on it.

Arthur Mather, Zetetic Scholar 1979

I would argue that the ground-breaking research of French statistician Michel Gauquelin provides us with compelling evidence for the existence of meaning in our world.

Ray Grasse, The Waking Dream, Unlocking the symbolic language of our lives, 1996, p.266

For nearly forty years, contrary to what skeptics claimed, the Gauquelins had been right. They had found a replicable planetary connection that was also independently replicable by others.

Dean et. al., Astrology Under Scrutiny, 2013, p.128.

The Gauquelins have no way of proving that they did not cheat

George Abell, 'The Mars Effect', Psychology Today 16(7) 8-13.

INTRODUCTION

WHAT THIS BOOK IS ABOUT, AND WHY IT IS IMPORTANT

BY ROB HAND

From the 1960s to the 1990s the research of Michel and Françoise Gauquelin into astrology created an enormous stir in both the astrological community and those parts of the scientific community that believed that the Gauquelins' work impinged upon their subject areas. Most notably these were psychologists and other social scientists, and astronomers. Other disciplines would become involved, but these were the most important ones. There had been a degree of research by astrologers intending to prove that there was "something to astrology." However, these efforts did not rise to the level of attracting interest from mainstream scientific investigators. Although Michel Gauquelin had long been interested in astrology, he and his wife, Francoise, were trained academic psychologists, trained in the scientific method. Their early work investigated previous attempts by astrologers to demonstrate an astrological affect. This investigation yielded nothing that was of interest except for the work of one French astrologer, Paul Choisnard, who applied reasonably sophisticated statistical techniques to an analysis of the placement of planets in the charts of notable professionals in various fields. As it turned out, his sample sizes were too small to be significant, but the work intrigued the Gauquelins, and they decided to replicate it with much larger samples. The measures they took to do this are described in this book. Suffice to say for the present, the results they obtained were statistically significant and particularly related to prominent athletes and the positions of Mars in their birth charts. This was the first discovery of a pattern that is called the "Mars Effect".

While they were at it, they tested other hypotheses stemming from astrological ideas and found them to be wanting. This fact was not

What This Book is About, and Why It Is Important

terribly encouraging to astrologers and the manner in which Mars was distributed in the charts of sports champions was not precisely what astrologers would have expected. However, the key point was that the Gauquelins seemed to have discovered an effect of the kind that one finds suggested by the principles of astrology. There was no reason why the planet, Mars, which is associated with athletes, should have been anything other than randomly distributed in the charts of athletes. Their work found that the distribution was not random. They also applied this technique to charts of other professional groups and found similar non-random distributions with other planets. All these planets were ones that astrologers could plausibly have associated with these professions according to the principles of astrology. To put it simply, the Gauquelins had discovered an effect that did not seem to be possible according to anything but astrology, even though that astrology might be quite different from the astrology conventionally practiced.

As the word got out about this research, there were two different sets of reactions. On one hand, conventional astrologers accepted that something like an astrological "effect" had been discovered by acceptable scientific means. On the other hand, they were disappointed because the effects did not precisely agree with what traditional astrology might have predicted. The other group consisted of philosophers, psychologists and astronomers who seem to have decided in advance that the effects that the Gauquelins had discovered were completely inconsistent with science and scientific philosophy and therefore set upon a program that has lasted to the present day, namely, to prove that the effects that the Gauquelins had found were the result of bad science, bad method, or outright cheating. In September/October 1975 issue of *The Humanist* was published a paper entitled, *Objections to Astrology: A Statement by 186 Leading Scientists*. The original of this paper was signed by persons associated with the magazine, *The Humanist*, of which the principal leader was Dr. Paul Kurtz of the University of Buffalo philosophy department. The paper was circulated among leading scientists in many fields and 183 of these signed the paper including Nobel laureates. The initial signatures were those of Bart J. Bok, Lawrence E Jerome, and Paul Kurtz, all counted among the 186. It is interesting to note that among these first three was a philosopher, a popular science writer, and a genuine astronomer. There were many who did not sign this paper, not because they believed in astrology, but because they believed that the paper was an effort to control free-thinking. Paul Sagan was among these. From this point until the present the battle was on, but it died down somewhat with the death of Michel Gauquelin in 1991.

The most important contribution of Kollerstrom's book is threefold. First, it is a good summary of the history of this whole controversy. Second, it is particularly useful in that it covers in detail much of the work that was done later in Michel Gauquelin's life and adds to it work done by others and especially by Kollerstrom himself. Third, for those who may decide to become involved in this work, there is a veritable treasure trove of bibliography and other sources so that anyone can follow up. Along with this, Nick himself, has written software and assembled databases in a form suitable for modern desktop computers to continue the research. Information regarding all this is provided in the book. Before any would-be researcher becomes discouraged at the prospect of doing research that was originally done on mainframes and powerful minicomputers, the revolution in personal computers is so great that even the average laptop, supplemented by a few external storage devices, is capable of doing this research and there is also software that will assist in the process. Information about all this is contained in this book.

My Personal Relationship with the Gauquelins and Their Research

My first encounters with astrology were through my father in the late 1950s. He studied it because of his discovery of what seemed to be correlations between the movements of stock prices with astronomical phenomena such as eclipses, other phases of the moon, and then gradually began examining correlations with planetary movements. My serious efforts to begin the study of astrology began in the autumn of 1960 when my father provided me with ephemerides, tables, and introductory books on astrology. Very early in these studies my father encountered the work of Michel and Francoise Gauquelin. Although the results in their earlier works seemed to refute many of the tenets of astrology as conventionally practiced, they did appear to support a basic logic similar to that of astrology.

My father passed away in 1963. But I continued my studies through the remainder of my years at university experimenting with various systems but generally studying astrology outside of the normal

My Personal Relationship with the Gauquelins and Their Research

educational apparatus of astrology, such as it was at that time. Most would-be students of astrology would find a teacher who was also a practitioner of astrology and learn that individual's techniques. I mostly read in the literature and experimented with various methods. To be honest I was somewhat appalled but what I found in books describing conventional astrology is practiced in the mid-twentieth century.

In my later 20s my experimentation with astrology continued but at a somewhat reduced level of intensity. This lasted until 1971 when I attended two astrology conferences in New York City and realized that astrology was what I genuinely wanted to do with the rest of my life. From this point on astrology was and has been ever since the primary focus of my life. I do not remember exactly when I first met Michel and Francoise Gauquelin, but it was somewhere in the early 1970s. I was one of the earliest members of the New York chapter of the National Council for Geocosmic Research (at that time the only chapter) and the Gauquelins' research was a frequent topic of conversation. Neil Michelsen was just beginning at that same time to provide astrological services via computer, and he became influential in turning attention to astrological research. I do not recall the exact year when Michelsen turned his attention to the Gauquelin research, but I believe it was still in the 1970s. On several occasions in the next several years the Gauquelins visited his facilities originally in the suburbs of New York and then later in San Diego. They also began to participate in astrological conferences. As a result of this I encountered both of them on several occasions and shared with them my intense interest in their research. In fact, the need to do research and astrology on a scale similar to what Michelsen was able to do with the Gauquelin data was one of the main factors in my becoming involved at a very early point with what were then called microcomputers, later known simply as personal computers. So, in the late 1970s I purchased one of the earliest systems and began learning how to program it. At the time these computers had little memory and not very fast, but I and several others quickly learned what they could do even at the beginning.

However, the development of the personal computer was quite rapid. By the middle 1980s, Neil Michelsen decided to do a test of the relative speeds of the then current model of the IBM personal computer equipped with a math coprocessor and that of a sophisticated minicomputer that he employed in his astrological computing business. In a test of the speeds of astronomical calculations on both computers the personal computer was faster than the minicomputer.

Not too long before Michel's death, in the 1990s Michel was visiting the New England area and came to visit Cape Cod where I lived to give a talk on astrological research. He stayed at my house and visited what was then business *Astrolabe*. [Note: Astrolabe still exists but I am no longer associated with it.] In that visit I became more acquainted with him, and as a result of this and previous encounters I can attest personally to the sincerity and intellectual integrity of his and Francoise' work.

The "Conflict" between Astrology and Science

The reputation of the scientific community in popular culture involves brilliant, disinterested, and hard-working scholars coming together to apply the Scientific Method to a search for the Truth. This is not entirely inaccurate. However, scientists, like other members of professional communities, have egos. They will fight bitterly over disagreements about hypotheses, theories, and research methods. Even though it sometimes gets messy, given enough time agreement is reached and as a result of that agreement, research continues. However, there is a substantial misconception concerning science that is as follows. Science (or the sciences) consists of a series of disinterested and objective research projects into the phenomena of nature, or, in the case of mathematics, logical mathematical studies that lead to a set of conclusions that are forced upon them by their observations. I realize that there are very few scientists, if any, who would accept this naïve view. But the public reputation of the sciences is such that until the advent of sophisticated historical research into the history of the sciences [Note: My Ph.D. program involve the concentration in late medieval and early modern History of Science.] Very few people are aware of the influence of historical pressures, institutional pressures, and important belief systems, both spiritual and otherwise, that have influenced the development of the sciences. This includes many practitioners of the sciences and also most persons involved in Science Education.

The "Conflict" between Astrology and Science

The hypotheses and theories of the sciences do not arise spontaneously out of the phenomena and impress themselves upon the objectively detached minds of scientists. In addition and making the problem worse is the widespread belief among scientists that the sciences, especially the "hard sciences", Physics and Chemistry, are not philosophies. I have personally had several discussions with scientists about their philosophy and they have asserted that they have no philosophy, philosophy not being scientific. Let me point out that the original name for what we now call "the Sciences" was "Natural Philosophy," that is, the philosophy of nature. Personally, I would advocate that the term Science be once again replaced by Natural Philosophy. But even if we assume that there is a distinct break in continuity and structure between the Sciences and other branches of Philosophy, it is far more injurious to the discussion of Astrology and the Sciences, when one understands understood that on top of the Scientific Method as a practical technique for inquiring into Nature, there is an implicit philosophy not widely acknowledged as part of the sciences, which introduces serious conflict with unbiased observation, as well as the willingness to deal with certain kinds of phenomena. This is called Scientism. This term is widely derided in scientific circles as nothing more than a term used to denigrate science. I agree the term it is often use loosely and sloppily. However, below I present a more rigorous definition of "scientism" largely derived from the writings of Huston Smith. This is the understanding of the term scientism that I employ in this paper.

However, in addition to scientism, there is another aspect to the scientific method, which, while no doubt necessary to the pursuit of mature sciences, also causes the sciences to be resistant to change. As a result, until the necessity of change becomes so acute that a fundamental revolution must come about in assumptions about the structure of the world implicit in the sciences, all work in the sciences occurs within a framework. In the philosophy of science these are referred to as 'paradigms'. I will now take up these two different facets of the problem that exists between astrology and the sciences. I will not argue that astrology, as it is, and unrecognized science. But I do argue, that under current conditions it is virtually impossible for astrology to evolve into a recognized science no matter what changes and discoveries are made in astrology.

Let us first look at the problem of scientism. I contend this is far more than a simple attempt to dismiss the scientific method. I assert here and now that scientism, and the scientific method have no connection at all with each other except historically. The following passage is from Huston Smith:

> With science itself there can be no quarrel. Scientism is another matter. Whereas science is positive, contending itself with reporting what it discovers, scientism is negative. It goes beyond the actual findings of science to deny that other approaches to knowledge are valid and other truths true. In doing so it deserts science in favor of metaphysics – bad metaphysics, as it happens, for the contention that there are no truths save those of science is not itself a scientific truth, in affirming it scientism contradicts itself. It also carries marks of a religion – a secular religion, resulting from over extrapolation from science, that is seldom numbered great scientists among its votaries. Science has enormous difficulty dealing with things that cannot be measured (if it can deal with them at all), "the immeasurable is the primary independent source of all reality... Measure is a secondary independent aspect of this reality.[1]

The scientific method itself does not require that problems with which it cannot deal be considered illegitimate questions. They are simply problems with which science cannot deal. Here are categories of problems which both philosophers of science and historical scientists have agreed are not amenable to the scientific method.

1. Values – These include judgments that are generally described as "subjective," such as good versus bad, beautiful versus ugly, morally worthy versus morally unworthy and so forth. While attempts have been made in philosophy to define these terms in ways that are independent of the individual observer, they have been unsuccessful. Marxism, in particular, was an attempt to give an objectively real definition to the concept of value, that is, giving value a quantitative measure that does not depend on the moral or any other philosophy of the observer. The success of Marxism in this respect is highly debatable.

---

[1] Huston Smith, *Forgotten Truth*, 2 ed, NY 1992, 16-17; see also Jnl of the Blaisdell Institute, 1974, IX, 2.

2. Purpose, or Final Cause – Final Causes of the subject matter of the branch of philosophy called Teleology. Does the existence of anything have a purpose or reason for its existence? This is a question to which most religions would answer "yes." But in the sciences, there is simple existence, and while the existence of something, a biological characteristic for example, may after the fact have a useful function in the survival of an organism, that biological characteristic or trait according to science has evolved at random and does not manifest any higher will or intention. All causation is from the past, not the future. The idea of causation coming from the future, i.e. something toward which we are inevitably moving is teleology

3. The Meaning of Life – Do our lives serve a purpose, does life have meaning? This is not considered to be a question appropriate for the sciences. This last issue has particularly powerful consequences for human existence and the importance of life.

All three areas of these should not be considered illegitimate questions simply because the sciences cannot deal with them. It is true that Social Sciences do, but these are not generally regarded as "proper" sciences. The fact that the sciences as currently constituted cannot deal with these questions should make no statement whatsoever as to the validity of the questions. Yet despite these positivistic philosophers of science have designated these questions as "meaningless." Smith's point is very simple. It is not in the realm of the sciences, nor, I would argue, even in the realm of philosophers of science to make this judgment as anything other than personal opinion. This is scientism.

Anyone with any awareness of the nature of astrology can see immediately that astrology deals with all three of these matters, although one could argue that in the cases of one or more of these that discussing them is not necessary for astrology. I believe I can state that the overwhelming majority of those who practice the current forms of astrology would disagree with that statement. However, as you read this book you will discover that what the Gauquelins found does not raise any of these questions. The fundamental question that is raised by virtually all their research is the same: Are there any astronomical variables whatsoever, regardless of whether they are astrological or not, whose correlations with objectively measurable human characteristics are non-random in some important respect? There is no issue of meaning here, nor a final cause, nor of the meaning of life. While scientism in general, a belief system that is extremely pervasive in the sciences, is no doubt influential in creating the tension between any attempt whatsoever to find correlations between astronomical variables and measurable human characteristics, it is especially so in the minds of most scepttics. I consider Scientism to be at best very bad philosophy (in agreement with Smith), and at worst superstition.

The second major problem is the 'paradigm'. This is a much more complex issue than scientism. It is a problem posed by philosophy of science and has largely arisen from the works of Thomas Kuhn. There are those philosophers of science that would dismiss Kuhn's ideas completely, but I believe they are themselves the victims of the paradigmatic assumption, namely, that the sciences operate in a sociological and historical vacuum and that nothing affects the evolution of science except the gradual progression of the application of the scientific method. The word itself is derived from the Greek word for 'model'. The idea is simple enough to express, although it does raise philosophical issues which have been the subject of much debate. I recommend two books by Kuhn. The first is his book on the Copernican Revolution. And the second is his classic *The Structure of Scientific Revolutions*. The book on the Copernican revolution is not a text about scientific philosophy. It is a study of the Copernican revolution and the many changes that are brought about in the basic assumptions and philosophical worldview of astronomers. In this work he does not explicitly describe the paradigm, but rather demonstrates it by a lengthy historical analysis. It is the second work on scientific revolutions that is the revolutionary work, which explicitly introduces the concept of the paradigm. Here is the definition of both paradigm and paradigm shift obtained from Google:

> **Paradigms** are generally defined as a framework that has unwritten rules and that directs actions. A **paradigm shift** occurs when one paradigm loses its influence, and another takes over.

For a general introduction to the scientific philosophy and history of Thomas Kuhn, I recommend the article on "Thomas Kuhn" in the online *Stanford Encyclopedia of Philosophy*.

In the above description of the paradigm, the tricky part is the phrase "unwritten rules." Kuhn's major contribution to the

The "Conflict" between Astrology and Science

philosophy of science was to challenge philosophers and historians of science to make such "unwritten rules" explicit. An obvious example of an explicit aspect of the scientific paradigm is the banishment of themes which are considered entirely subjective. All analyses in the sciences must employ completely objective techniques of analysis and research must be repeatable by anyone else with other databases of the same kind. This set of rules has clearly been adopted by the Gauquelins in their research. One of the problems, however, is the general use of statistics, not by the Gauquelins in particular, but in sciences and the social sciences in general. The following comment is anecdotal, and I cannot cite the source, but I have read it repeatedly. It regards one statistician's ironic comment about the statistical research of the late J. B. Rhine into extrasensory perception, E.S.P. The comment ran along these lines. The main thing that Rhine proved with his use of statistics in researching E.S.P. is that statistics cannot be used to prove anything that people are unwilling to believe. Of necessity the Gauquelins' studies were both statistical and demonstrated things that people were unwilling to believe. One of the valuable functions of this book by Kollerstrom is that it gives a good account of this process as it unfolded and still unfolds. Statistical methods are incredibly complex and the more arcane the material studied by statistical analysis, the more arcane the statistics get, and the more likely it is that people can dismiss the results on the basis of statistical principles that get increasingly "flexible" when dealing with material that scepttics find inherently unbelievable.

One of the concrete problems in the modern sciences is that the old idea of mechanism has become increasingly unable to account for the complexities of nature. It is unarguably proven that there are effects for which there is no known mechanism, at least not in the traditional sense of the word. Consequently, even Physics relies heavily on statistical methods particularly at the cutting-edge. While there are arguments, and disputes about conclusions drawn from their use, there seems to be no particular resistance to the use of statistics in the hard sciences. Astrology is quite another matter.

In astrology the only thing that can possibly be demonstrated is correlation, i.e., that certain phenomena are correlated with certain variable factors in a manner that suggests causation. Now the correlations in quantum mechanics between what could be called causes and effects are very high and reliable. The problem in subjects like astrology and ESP (and research psychology as well) is that they are not quite so high although some of the material in the Gauquelin studies has demonstrated correlations that are impossibly beyond chance, if there is such a thing as chance. But unfortunately, astrology is also *a priori* impossible. Therefore, the sceptics double their efforts to find a fatal flaw in the methodology.

The final resort is cheating. As Nick's book points out there have been several instances of scepttics cheating in their supposed efforts to reproduce the results of the Gauquelin research. Yet at the same time, cheating is a charge that has often been levelled at the Gauquelins. This is clearly not the result of detached scientific minds evaluating objectively and responsibly research information which does not fit a paradigm. Quantum mechanics does not require a clear cause and effect mechanism such as is found in classical mechanics. But astrology must do so before any result can be excepted, if then.

Since the nineteenth century historians have regarded the sciences as engaged in warfare between the rational and the irrational. This has been particularly true regarding religion. In the nineteenth century was written a book by Andrew Dixon White, entitled, *A History of the Warfare of Science with Theology in Christendom* [available online]. This is the classic history of the advance of Reason in the form of Science advancing against Ignorance and Obscurantism in Western history. To be fair it was not written by a historian of science, philosopher of science or even a scientist. But it represents a popular viewpoint. While this book does not go into the subject of astrology, it is only because that was regarded as a settled question by the author. Astrology is "bunk"!

Now we come back to the issue of the paradigm. Astrology is neither a macroscopic type of science in which there are clear mechanisms, nor a type of science like quantum mechanics. Astrology has been heresy in much of society since the "enlightenment." Although such a position can be hardly regarded as one derived from rigorous philosophy, it is nevertheless, generally accepted. It is interesting to note that if one peruses the list of the 186 scientists who signed the initial paper in the Humanist, that there the number of practitioners of the hard scientists was not large. Those who were on the list tended to be older and more traditional in their thinking. Also,

The "Conflict" between Astrology and Science

apparently many people practicing within the hard sciences just did not want to be involved. They had too much else to do to wage war against astrology. I suspect most of them also believe that astrology is a settled question – it is bunk!

In the sciences it has also become a settled issue that there is only one type of existent, those things that can be analyzed as composed of matter and energy, although the latter of these two categories is getting increasingly murky and unclear except possibly mathematically. Astrology can be viewed as implying that there are kinds of information which are also truly substantial and inherent in nature. It also seems to imply that this kind of information is organized into archetypal patterns. Astrology makes no statement about how these might work. But modern philosophy has rejected the idea that there is any kind of archetypal informational principle inherent in the universe. This is called 'Essentialism'. This is a critical term that is hurled at many phenomena that are regarded as questionable, increasingly so in the social sciences. Are there such things as the archetypal male or female and gender, for example and the list could go on. Astrology suggests, but does not rigorously require, that there are archetypal essences which exist independently of any material expression. The problem is that among these archetypal essences are the entirety of the principles of mathematics and logic!

I am not saying that astrology and astrological research has at this point proven anything. Of course, it cannot so long as people are unwilling to be convinced by any amount of evidence. This indicates that among these archetypal polarities that should be dismissed as false is the idea of truth versus falsehood. There are those who believe that all truth is relative. There are also those who believe that consciousness does not exist. I particularly enjoy these because when I hear this my reaction is to say, "Then I can disregard everything you have said because if my consciousness does not exist then neither do you!" Think about that a moment. In other words, for genuine research and astrology to continue we must discard traditional notions of what is possibly true and what is not and rely heavily on dispassionate observation. Even if we accept a paradigm, we must also define it in such a way that it is susceptible to disproof and disproof. There should be more than disbelief.

In conclusion, Kollerstrom's book not only gives the reader a history of events concerning the Gauquelin data. It also provides references and access to tools that enable the reader to continue the work if one chooses. This last part is perhaps the most valuable aspect of the book. But the other parts are essential to understanding what has happened and what directions future research should take. At this point, I am not sure that our primary task is now to produce convincing evidence that will change the minds of sceptics and others of those utterly unwilling to jettison scientism or to expand the paradigm in which they work. According to Kuhn's work, this requires research carried on either by younger researchers or those who are already working within a new paradigm. One must then wait for another generation of philosophers and scientists to begin to accept a new paradigm. But first we must begin to make clear the outlines of that paradigm and its relationship to the prevailing paradigm of naturalistic/materialistic science. Will it add to it or overthrow it?

Bibliography

Kuhn, T. S. *The Copernican Revolution: Planetary Astronomy in the Development of Western Thought.* Cambridge: Harvard University Press, 1957.

Kuhn, T. S. *The Structure of Scientific Revolutions.* Chicago: University of Chicago Press, 1962.

Smith, Huston. Forgotten Truth. 2 ed. New York: HarperCollins, 1992.

White, Andrew Dixon. *A History of the Warfare of Science with Theology in Christendom*, 2 vols. (1896), online at Gutenberg text file.

Rob Hand studied at Princeton University, is the manager of Arhat Media and is the most cited of living astrologers. In the present context his essay 'Astrology as a Revolutionary Science' may be especially recommended.

FOREWORD

IN THIS 21st CENTURY, the entire debate over the Gauquelins' work appears to have fizzled out. It's quite hard to remember, that an international debate went on, involving French, German, British and American scientists, astronomers – and astrologers. Had something been demonstrated? Was human fate linked to the heavens above? Had destiny been demonstrated? Or was it just bad science, a glitch in the statistics, another unrepeatable result, as the sceptics said?

Huge data-bases were collected, tens of thousands of the most famous and eminent people in the last couple of centuries. Did they prove the case ... or was there some flaw in them, were they biased?

All the world got to hear about the 'Mars Effect' which Michel Gauquelin claimed to have discovered, whereby top sports champions would have Mars in particular heavenly positions at their birth more frequently than ordinary mortals: reflecting what MG called in a fine phrase 'the soul of hardened steel characteristic of the true sports champion.'[1] Looking on the web you could be forgiven for supposing that the Gauquelin effect pertained merely to a claim concerning sports champions and Mars – everything else he did has been forgotten![2] But there was a lot more to it than that – in the words of Arno Muller, the German professor of psychology, the work linked

> the serious, meditative Saturn with scientists; the radiant and dominant Jupiter with actors and prominent personages; and the dream-tempting moon with the poets.[3]

Were traditional archetypes reappearing in the 20th century, alive and well?

Michel's story really began in 1951, when he was examining the birthdates of top French physicians. To quote his partner Francoise

---

[1] MG, *Cosmic Influences on Human Behaviour*, London 1977, p.100.
[2] The US *Journal for Scientific Exploration* has an excellent series of eleven articles debating the topic (all online), 1988-2000 which almost solely concern 'the Mars Effect' ie sports champions.
[3] Prof Arno Müller, *JSE*, 'Planetary influences on human behaviour ("Gauquelin Effect")' 1990, 4.1, 85-94, 88.

Foreword

Gauquelin, 'His first significant results, after years of disappointing outcomes with various astrological theories, showed up in 1951 with 576 French Academicians of Medicine.'[4] He describes his eureka-moment:

> Then the breakthrough came when a close friend, who was very interested in my projects of astrological analysis, showed me a work called the 'Index des Membres, Correspondents et Associés de l'Académie de Médicine... Having (painfully) worked out by hand the position of the planets at the hour of birth of each doctor, I made a statistical compilation of my findings.
>
> Suddenly, I was presented with an extraordinary fact. My doctors were not born under the same skies as the common run of humanity. They had chosen to come into the world much more often during roughly the two hours following the rise and culmination of the planets, Mars and Saturn. Moreover, they tended to 'avoid' being born following the rise and culmination of the planet Jupiter.[5]

The Gauquelin thesis can be explained quite easily, on account of the way in which the *primary archetypes* are embedded in the language: Saturn-types are *saturnine*, Jupiter-types are *jovial*, Mars-types are *martial* - and Selene's sphere inspires dreamy poets! The above quote by professor Arno Müller well expresses this. It's not rocket science.

However, the Gauuqelin's work does goes against the grain of modern thought in that it is *inherently elitist*. It only worked for the most eminent persons. But, if schools and academies are aspiring towards excellence, there may be no harm in examining this radically new view of what produces excellence.

Hans Eysenck who was then Britain's top psychologist published a review of a book on the subject, in an academic psychology journal, in which he remarked:

---

[4] FG, 'The G. sectors', APP September 1992, p.27.
[5] This he published in 1955, in *Hommes et Les Astres*. MG, *The Truth about Astrology*, 1983, pp.20-21.

The evidence for the Mars Effect is better than for most of the 'facts' you will encounter in your psychology textbooks.[6]

He was well acquainted with the Gauquelins and various other the people involved. A decade earlier, his quite comparable view had been:

I have read all the criticisms … and I do not think any of these criticisms remain. At the moment this data stands as absolutely impregnable ... which does not mean one cannot improve certain aspects of the work.[7]

The word 'psychology' means something like, science of the soul, from the Greek *psyche* ψυχή the soul, which was the animating breath or spirit; and *Logos* a Greek word meaning the word, intelligence or rational principle, which is in our minds but also in the world. That concept involves the Greek affirmation that the world can be known, because of the logos-principle. The etymology indicates what we are here trying to study.

There is to be sure a materialistic and somewhat rat-oriented view of human nature that would tend to exclude *a priori* everything that we are here concerned to evaluate.

Apart from some concepts developed by Carl Jung, such as introversion-extraversion, there isn't a lot in modern psychology that has a non-pathological significance these days. Dire new arts of human persuasion, control and manipulation are for sure being developed, but in terms of what we would enjoy hearing about I suggest there is not a lot going on. We'll try to argue that the 'Gauquelin effect' is more humanly meaningful than other topics in modern psychology.

I used to attend the astrology-research conferences where the Gauquelins would turn up each year. They began in 1982 with people like Dr Frank McGillion, Patrick Curry, Beverley Steffert (psychology lecturer) and Simon Best. They took place at the Maudsley Hospital where Hans Eysenck was a professor. He had become interested in the subject through a chance or perhaps a rather fated meeting with MG

---

[6] Eysenck, *Correlation* 15(1) 1996: Review of *The Tenacious Mars-effect*, p.54.
[7] Hans Eysenck, Report of the 2nd World Congress of Astrology, Lucerne, Switzerland: *Correlation*, 1984, 4(1) p.4.

Foreword

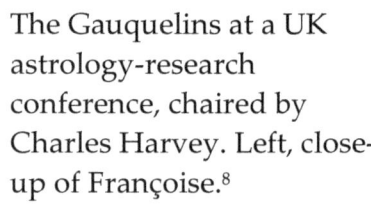

The Gauquelins at a UK astrology-research conference, chaired by Charles Harvey. Left, close-up of Françoise.[8]

---

[8] Photo by kind permission of Geoffrey Dean

in Paris.⁹ 1982 was the year when Pluto went inside the orbit of Neptune. There was a great hope in those days, that some new science in-between biology, psychology, astrology and astronomy was about to be born. Geniuses like Theodore Landscheit would turn up: always obscure, he seemed to understand the pulse of the Sun. The ever-optimistic Charles Harvey, president of the UK's Astrological Association, brought people together, and welcomed Michel each year – even despite the latter's consistently scornful and sceptical attitude towards astrology. The arch-sceptic Geoffrey Dean would lurk in the background. In later years one had to be careful to invite either Michel or Françoise, as they would brawl in public if put together.

Charles was the only major figure in British astrology in my lifetime who did not approve of sun-sign columns, or to declare publicly that he was not keen on them, and this enabled an atmosphere of intellectual integrity to flourish. In the mid-1970s there was 'a level of scientific interest in astrology that is now gone and may never arise again' in the somewhat pessimistic words of Dean and Smit.[10] It was the challenge put forth by the Gauquelins, together with the deep thought of John Addey, that stimulated this air of expectation, a sense that something important was going to be established: the rest of us were mere ancillary acts.

The great debate raged in *at least twenty* European and American journals:

>Astro-Psychological Problems
>The British Journal of Social and Clinical Psychology
>Les Cahiers du RAMS (Paris)
>Correlation, the Journal of Research in Astrology (UK)
>The Humanist
>The Journal of Scientific Exploration
>Journal of the American Statistical Association
>Journal of Interdisciplinary Cycles Research

---

[9] Eysenck was being interviewed by a French popular psychology journal, while in Paris visiting his mother. Michel Gauquelin was conducting the interview, and so they got talking. Eysenck, *Rebel with a Cause, the Autobiography of Hans Eysenck,* 1990, p. 242.
[10] Geoffrey Dean and Rudolf Smit, *Astrology under Scrutiny* (AuS) 2013, p.2.

Foreword

Leonardo
NCGR Research Journal
New Behaviour
New Scientist
Personality and Individual Differences
Phenomena, the News Journal of Cosmic Influence Research (Canadian)
Psychology Today
Scepsis, (Dutch)
The Sceptical Inquirer
Science et Vie (French)
Zeitschrift fur Parapsychologie (Germany)
The Zetetic Scholar.

- and that's not counting the astrological ones! Some of the essential journals are today online, viz the *Journal of Scientific Exploration*, which carried a major series of eleven articles on the subject; plus the *Zetetic Scholar*, and *Correlation the Journal of Research in Astrology*, of which I was a co-founder and consulting editor since its first issue in 1982.

In 1991 Michel committed suicide causing the whole topic to implode. The very idea of scientifically investigating these things faded away, or maybe hung around like some bad dream. There followed some hard-hitting articles by the skeptics, who claimed that the whole thing had been a fraud. Readers will receive an impartial evaluation of these claims.

As a science historian, and someone who has been a Fellow of the Royal Astronomical Society for several decades, I may have a facility to guide you through the perplexing issues. If you are not averse to grappling with a bit of simple maths, and like to have firm facts and figures as a basis for your belief, then this work could be what you're looking for.

A slight familiarity with some astrological concepts will help, so will a bit of astronomy, and maybe some maths for expected frequencies. No deep acquaintance with the 'astrological' archetypes is required – just put on Holst's *The Planets*, that should suffice! The ideal reader would get the difference between, say, declination and celestial latitude, and maybe at a push even recall the difference between a chi-squared and t-test of significance! We here embark on an interdisciplinary endeavour. The main thing to remember is that we are concerned with the *psychology of genius*, and that this endeavour is *non-specialist*.

This study is not concerned with the stars or the zodiac or even the Sun, but only with what is called the diurnal circle which is in effect the rotation of the Earth: it concerns those 'planets' that we *can see moving in the night sky*, and that includes the Moon. That's all! But, it may help - and this will sound rather odd – if you imagine the earth not rotating, but rather, that those visible planets move around the heavens in 24 hours, as they all rise, traverse the sky and then set. That framework is then divided into 12, as has always been done by astrologers. So it is the angle that planets make with the horizon that matters, in their sojourn across the sky.

Historically, the issue has revolved unduly around one person. 'In science nothing belongs to you unless you give it way' remarked the US science philosopher Robert K. Merton. May a new generation arise, which will enjoy looking at the distributions and correlations on the screen and will forget about the laborious arithmetic computations that were, in the last century, necessary. What a contrast between the great debates that used to go on and the oblivion into which the topic has today sunk: I'm never sure whether this is a victory of the sceptics or just the effect of Michel's suicide.

Michel wrote far too many books, all now forgotten. If he had just written one, *together with his wife,* identifying and defining the main databases they had used and their conclusions, then I suggest the 'Gauquelin edifice' would still be intact today. She had the degree in statistics, a top one from the prestigious Sorbonne university, while he had a diploma in psychology from the University of Paris. He worked for a psychology journal.

Françoise ceased producing her lively and controversial quarterly journal APP, *Astro-Psychological Problems,* in 1994, which she would typed out, staple together and and mail out to a hundred or so people, then she sunk into a deep silence for a Jupiter-cycle until her passing in 2007.[11] During that silent period, she in 2002 caused the Gauquelin databases to go up onto the web, on the late Patrice Guignard's CURA

---

[11] Also, her APP lasted for a Jupiter-cycle from March 1983 until March 1995.

Foreword

site. History on these matters is hard to come by. ('U' in 'CURA' stands for University, which does not exist, though maybe it did for some short while, or at least aspired to. It is or was I suggest the *only astrology site in the world* which you might want to call, intellectual). There is not a lot by way of biography of the Gauquelins, of their epic life-adventure, as they challenged the world[12.] She seems to have obtained the data in digital form from America, from the Californian Astro-computing Services of Neil Michelsen, where all their data had originally been digitised. Over the years various errors were corrected on the site and since 2009 these fundamental data-sets have become fully operational.[13]

Back in 2005, I was looking forward to a time when psychology students would browse online Gauquelin databases:

> In the 21st century, these databases need to become available in an interactive manner, so that psychology and astrology students can have fun playing with them. How do the graphs look using the different planetary days,[14] or plotted by either 12 or 36 diurnal divisions, and including or excluding this or that data sample? The computer would be able to plot the chance-expected frequency for any data-set, and would show groups of data by eminence-graded steps, using defined sources to assess eminence. Can it really be, that three published sceptics' databases, show, when pooled together, a clear and positive eminence-graded effect? Students will want to check this out for themselves using such a program, before believing it. They will surely want to inspect how the shocking reverse-shape diurnal curve looks on[15] MG's unpublished group of less-famous sportsmen [if

---

[12] But, for a fine 46-page account of them see *Astrology Under Scrutiny* by Dean & Smit, 2013. In 1969 Michel was awarded a medal 'for his psychological writings' from the Congress of Health in Ferrara, Italy. Between the ages of 20 and 39 he was constantly rated by the French tennis federation, 'as befits the discoverer of the Mars effect' (Ibid, p.94). Published in Holland, this bulky opus claims (rather strangely) to be the final edition of the Dutch journal, *Astrologie in Onderzoek.*

[13] In 2014 I had these professional groups reposted onto the CURA site page in a format that was easier to upload, as .dat files.

[14] Plotting these data-sets by the Sun would give their so-called 'nycthemeral distribution' whereby births are distributed unevenly through the course of the day.

[15] See Chapter 5, or www.newalchemypress.com/gauquelin/research3.php (my view here differs greatly from that in my earlier *How Ertel Rescued the Gauquelin Effect,* Correlation 2005, Vol 23 (1) online.

indeed it exists]; as well as how physicians over various periods of France's Académie de Médecine membership have displayed Saturn in their key sectors.

This book- with the aid of a couple of websites - aims to do that. My website newalchemypress.gauquelin went up in 2016, then a few years later Thierry Grafff's opengauquelin.org database site went up. That site has been developing slowly as a one-man effort and therefore this book had to wait several years until that French website was sufficiently ready. Let me suggest that 2023 is 'ground zero' for the Gauquelin work, being the year when hitherto lost or muddled databases have become sufficiently clear that at least some definite conclusions can be reached, obviating earlier results.

The Grafff website is seeking to check through and make available all of the main databases that have been collated and used by persons testing the Gauquelin work. That is a huge task, really too much for one person. Students of future psychology courses will surely wish to use this online data-base. Many of the results used in this book can be seen in my website newalchemypress.com/gauquelin/. In these labours I have been collaborating with Thierry Grafff.

Sceptics

There were three 'Sceptic' groups which volunteered to check the claims of the Gauquelins. Each of these obtained positive results but then declined to publish them, and instead covered them up and obfuscated them. For all three of these we now at last have the actual data (Chapter 4), thanks to sleuthing by Thierry Grafff. Thereby we become able to evaluate the warring claims.

In 1975, Luc de Marré resigned in distress from the Belgian Comité Para, the Euro-sceptic group. He gave his reason in a letter to the US sceptic Professor Paul Kurtz, saying: "It looks as if the committee's majority, conducted by its president, were seeking, under pseudoscientific pretexts, to hide a fact that they themselves have verified ... the relation existing between Mars and the champions."[16] Not many years later, Kurtz' group schemed to do exactly the same thing!

---

[16] Quoted by Ertel, JSE, 2000, 14(3) p.445: letter of 8.11.75.

Foreword

That doesn't sound much like the scientific method. It sounds more like a poem by Lewis Carroll -

> But I was thinking of a plan
> To dye one's whiskers green,
> And always use so large a fan
> That they could not be seen

(quoting the White Rabbit). Halfway through the third of these investigations Michel ended his life. Some blame this on his second wife who had just left him, but that may load an undue amount of blame upon her. Rather, we should view the tragedy as indicating the depth of MG's commitment to his great Mars-struggle, whereby he could not just detach himself and go off and play tennis. Ever did he yearn for some academic or public acknowledgement, but it was not forthcoming.

The story of what the Gauquelins did has been told and re-told by various authors[17], eg by Dean & Smit in an extensive critical review in their *Astrology Under Scrutiny*. (2013)[18] We are here returning to a topic which hardly anyone believes in any more, and salute the greatest astrology-research project ever undertaken.

Here is a photo of the British group of investigators, which used to meet say bi-monthly in the 1980s. I reckon that group make quite a lot of things happen.[19]

I've had a couple of articles in the US *ISAR* astrology journal: 'Is Mars passionate?' and 'The Gauquelin Mars-Effect: Did it Replicate?'[20] Both are now up online at newalchemypress.com/Gauquelin/research, pages 9 and 14 respectively.

---

[17] Eg, Eysenck & Nias 1972, *Astrology Science or Superstition?* John Anthony West *The Case for Astrology* 1991.

[18] They re-told the story in their *Tests of Astrology*, 2016. Useful links here are www.astrology-and-science.com/U-link2.htm and www.astrology-and-science.com/G-hist2.htm

[19] NB Jonathan Cainer on the far-right was not part of this group, he was just there for one meeting. Next to him is Graham Douglas, and beside him is Mike Startup: who later turned into a sceptic and was thereby able to pursue a successful academic career as a psychology lecturer, the only one in the group to do so. AIR used to meet at Patrick Curry's place in Hammersmith. Simon Best next to him was the first editor of *Correlation* which began in 1981.

[20] *ISAR* Journal, Dec 2017 Vol 46 and April 2020, Vol. 49.

Figure: the group AIR 'Astrologers in Research' taken in 1983 by Geoffrey Dean

1

LOOKING AT THE DATA

We're approaching a time when university psychology departments will be able to offer a module, showing how the different temperaments associated with the planets have helped people to excel in their professions. With one click,[21] computer programs can now upload each of the professional groups which were gathered by Michele and Françoise Gauquelin – ie, timed birthdata of eminent professionals, which it took them so many years to obtain. One can choose to look at one of them, say painters or journalists, then choose a planet, then choose a 12, 18 or 36-fold division[22] of the diurnal circle to plot the frequency-distribution.

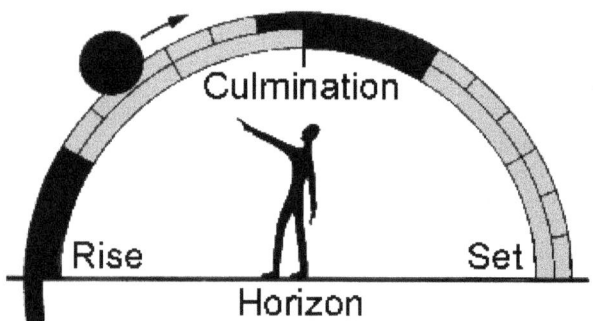

Figure 1: showing twelve-fold and 36-fold division of the 'day'[23]

---

[21] Download as Excel files from opengauquelin.org/history . Searching for 'Gauqelin' and 'CURA' will takes one to cura.free.fr/gauq/17archg.html. Scroll down to '.dat' files for the professional groups. Select a file, copy and paste into a notepad, save as a 'text' file then one can upload it with Jigsaw (Designed by Esoteric Technologies in Australia, this program is presently sold by Astrolabe).

[22] For his first books *L'Influence des Astres* (1955) he used both 12- and 18-fold sectors; then *Les Hommes et les Astres* (1960) exclusively used a twelvefold definition. Suitbert Ertel came to describe this twelve-sector approach as 'the narrow (classical) definition' in contrast with the 'extended definition' using 36-sectors (Ertel, *JSE* 'The Mars Effect is Genuine' 2000, 14,3, p.422).

[23] Used with kind permission of Geoffrey Dean.

The French site CURA loaded up the ten[24] professional groups analysed by the Gauquelins, its numbers being generally the same as specified in Michele's 1974 and 1980 textbooks.[25] Readers may prefer the more modern opengauquelin.org site for this data.

The 36-fold division of the diurnal circle may be more interesting for inspecting the data, especially if one has a decent number, say over a thousand. Over the last couple of decades of their creative life-work, the Gauquelins generally preferred to use this division, where they scored eight out of 36 sectors as shown in the diagram, rather than two out of twelve (so, 2/9 rather than 1/6). We will here conclude that this was a mistake, a historical blunder, because it generally gives a lower significance level.

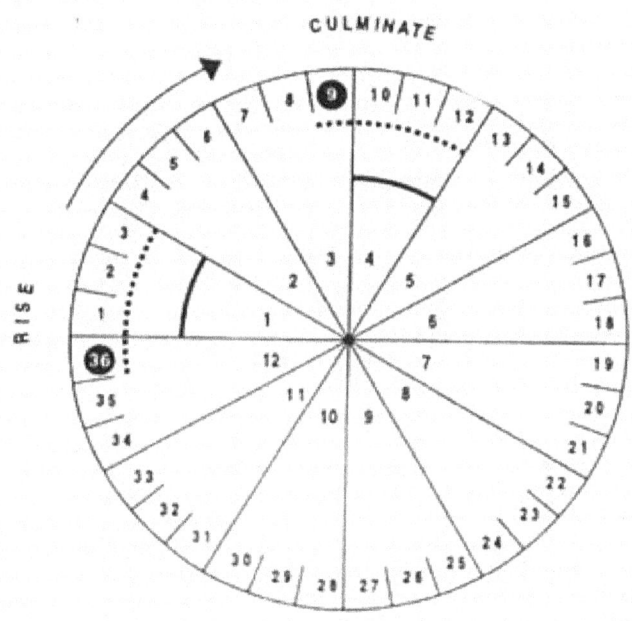

Figure 2: The 36-fold and 12-fold divisions of the circle showing the 'key sectors'

---

[24] MG's first book reported a weak Saturn effect for French priests; but this did not replicate in a second group (Les *Hommes et Les Astres* 1960) so he dismissed it. Ignoring this, gives us the ten professions found by the Gauquelins to have an 'astral' or planetary correlate, see Table 1.

[25] His 1974 *La Cosmopsychologie*, p.51 and his 1980 *Spheres of Destiny* p.16 give the same total numbers, as for the data-sets he published in 1970. For numerical analysis of these data sets see Michel and Françoise Gauquelin, *Profession-Heredity Results of series A&B, Series C Vol.1*, 1972.

Looking at The Data

A lot of the confusion in the great debates which raged just before and after MG's suicide in 1991, may have come from these different divisions of the diurnal circle.

We will here prefer MG's original twelve-fold division of the diurnal circle, with its two Key Sectors: one-sixth of each planetary 'day' is thus tested. Those divisions do not differ significantly from what is called the Placidus house system, which is the most popular one amongst astrologers, used since the 17th century. The framework we're using is traditional and straightforward. If there is an excess, we search for it using that twelvefold system. We here follow 'KISS' – Keep It Simple, Stupid.

LOCAL HORIZON

The Gauquelins divided up the diurnal circle by splitting the planetary 'day' into two unequal halves, above and below the horizon, then divided each of these halves into equal divisions of time. Thus his sectors 1-6 will tend to have a similar expected frequency as likewise will sectors 7-12; the above and below horizon sectors will not generally score at an equal frequency, or will only do so when averaged out over a period of time.

MG's two 'Key Sectors' happen each day after rising and after culminating, positions regarded by astrologers as special for a couple of millennia.[26] Even the US sceptic Paul Kurtz acknowledged this:

> ...in the traditional astrology of Ptolemy, the two most important points in the house divisions are the Ascendant ("oroscopos") and the Midheaven or *medium Coeli* – which are the initial boundaries of the Gauquelins' sectors 1 and 4.[27]

---

[26] André Barbault points this out in *L'Astrologie Certifiée* 2006, English trans. 2014, *The Value of Astrology*, p.92. See Claudius Ptolemy, *Tetrabiblos*: "...they [the planets] are most powerful when they are in mid-heaven or approaching it, and second when they are exactly on the horizon or in the succedent place; their power is less when they are in the orient [i.e near the Descendant], and less when they culminate beneath the Earth.(Book 1, Ch.24, Loeb Trans., 1940) "Also when the planets ... are at the angles, they give to him who is born thus marvellous power and a worldwide empire... If they are not at the angles ... he will live a lacklustre life and won't be paid well for what he does," Book 4, Ch. 3. See Appendix 1.

[27] Kurtz *et. al.*, 'Is the Mars Effect Genuine? *JSE*, 1997, 11,1 p19.

The main 'Gauquelin effect' concerns above-horizon phenomena, that is how he generally defined it[28] – as if one could forget about planets below the horizon.[29]

To find the Gauquelin sector for a birthtime, one requires the instant when a planet intersected with the horizon either rising or setting before the event, and then afterwards when it does so again. The interval of time between these two is divided by six, and then one scores whether or not the birth instant falls into a 'Key sector.' This computation uses the 'topocentric' co-ordinate of altitude, in that it takes the two instants of zero altitude.

Of the three celestial co-ordinate systems, we are not here concerned with the ecliptic system (latitude and longitude) as used by astrologers,[30] nor do we use the tropical co-ordinate system (right ascension and declination) as used by astronomers. We only use the topocentric (altitude and azimuth) reference-system, as used by surveyors. The last is what we might call the 'I am here' reference-system, experienced from where one stands on the Earth. It concerns an 'ideal' local horizon – not the actual one! - and the instant of zero altitude as thew planet reaches that spot. Thereby the time of rising is required to within, say, a minute.

HOW IT BEGAN

MG's first book *L'Influence des Astres* published in 1955 contained strongly fourfold-structure diagrams like those shown here. He collected birthdata from members of the prestigious *Academiciens de Medicine,* his very first project and that gave him the square-looking 'Mars effect'. It is the most simply-defined of the Gauquelin eminent professional groups, comprising all members of

---

[28] MG's article 'Is there a Mars Effect?' (JSE 1980, 2,1) advocated use of the 36-sector divisions: "…Investigators who have been examining my findings more recently generally work with the "enlarged key sector" definition" (p.38) and gave no hint of using below-horizon sectors.

[29] These come into use for the character-traits, Chapters 9-12.

[30] Except right at the end, chapter 10, but that is non-Gauquelin work, merely using their data.

Looking at The Data

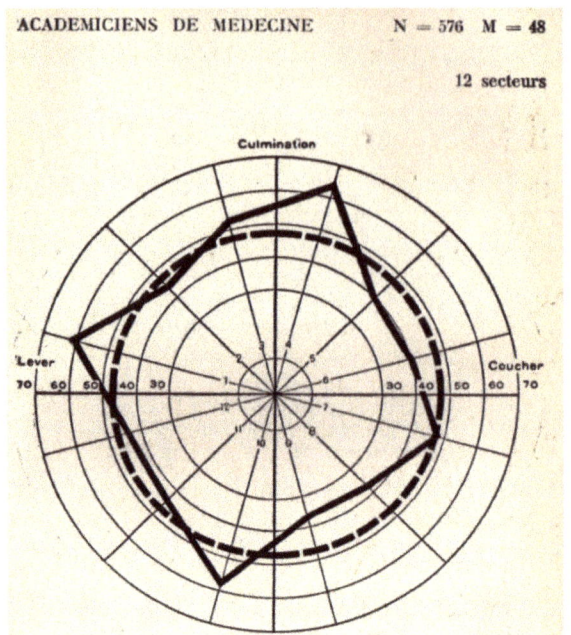

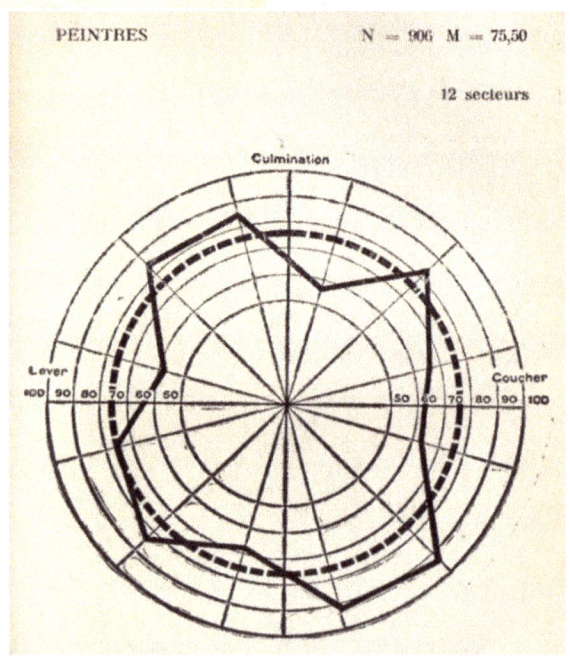

Figure 3: Diurnal Mars for 576 members of the Paris Academy of Medicine; and diurnal Saturn for 906 eminent painters (*L'Influence des Astres*, pp.113, 183), using 12 sectors.[31] 'M=48' in Figure 1 alludes to the average value per sector, drawn as the dotted circular line.

---

[31] These early graphs may confuse, because as well as the twelve sectors, they also have the horizontal and vertical axes drawn in (Asc-Desc and MC-IC).

the Paris Academy of Medicine for whom MG could find reliable birthdata. The excess of Saturn in the Key sectors of these top medics he found to be 37% above the chance-expected level.[32] (the next chapter will explain how this is found) Next, he collected nine hundred notable painters and found a very different and distinctive distribution of Saturn (see Figure). MG viewed this as a 'negative' Saturn-influence, in that it was in *deficit* over his 'key sectors'. It appeared from these early distributions as if a *fourfold pattern* was being expressed.

If we were to develop such a fourfold hypothesis, of four sectors that are to be scored – which is actually quite essential, as this book will attempt to show – then one would need to have 16-fold rather than twelvefold divisions of the diurnal circle. Thereby one would have four scores of the minimal, in-between values to compare with the four maxima. This approach would have the advantage of not requiring control values which can be quite difficult to ascertain.

Figure 4: Jupiter distribution in European scientists, by John Addey[33]

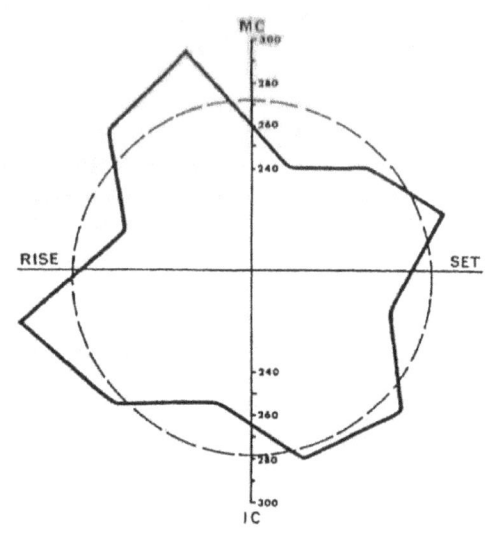

Here shown is another fourfold pattern showing Jupiter expressed in the birth-distribution of eminent European scientists. It's what the Gauquelins called a 'negative' effect, i.e. rotated one-eighth away from the 'key sector' positions. As John Addey who

---

[32] MG was able to collect a second group of 508 physicians (See Ch. 4, *Written in the Stars*). These were 'more or less well-known practitioners;' however, 'Most certainly, the members of the Académie de Médecine are, as a whole, more famous than the 'notable doctors.' This less-eminent group had only 6% excess of Saturn in the Key sectors: an early lesson to Michel on how his 'eminence effect' worked.

[33] Graph from John Addey *The New Study of Astrology* 1996 (posthumous), p.45, depicting 1940 European scientists, using data from MG, *Les Hommes et les Astres*, p.73. NB the scale on which the data is plotted is *not* from zero at the centre, but more like 200, which gives the impression that the effect is much larger than it is.

produced this graph expressed the matter – contrasting the characters of Jupiter and Saturn:

> Thus, Jupiter and Saturn (whom we might call *L'Allegro* and *Il Penseroso*, the lively man and the thoughtful man) show significant and opposite distributions in the charts of scientists, Saturn being often, Jupiter seldom, in sectors 1 or 4."[34]

We develop this all-important introvert-extravert theme in Chapter 13.

THE TEN PROFESSIONS

Going back to the late 1950s, the newly-married Gauquelins cheerfully visited the registry-offices of Europe in order to build up their formidable database of eminent-professional timed birthdata. Having the company of Françoise, who was Swiss by birth, greatly enabled Michel to collect birthdata from other European nations. Her degree in statistics, as well as her command of various European languages, helped to open the registry-office doors, while other would-be investigators found them to remain firmly closed. They would tell the registry offices that their work was ssociological or cosmo-biological, not mentioning the dreaded 'A-' word. These professional groups were finally defined in the data-sets published in six bulky volumes over 1970-71.[35]

A detailed analysis of these results was published by the two of them in 1972, with the rather uninspiring title, 'Series C, Volume 1, Profession-Heredity Results of Series A & B' and that has here been used: they were repeated in the Gauquelin books of 1975 and 1980, summarised together on one page[36], then given digital form on the CURA site.[37] They are the definitive totals for his main professional groups.

Table 1 shows ten professional groups gathered by MG together with the main planetary influences he discerned. Regrettably he

---

[34] Addey, *The New Study of Astrology* 1996 p.48.
[35] See Gauquelin Data Publications at end.
[36] See MG, *Connaitre Les Autres, La Cosmopsychologie*,1975, p.51 and his *Spheres of Destiny* 1980 p.16 (ref 3). The respective Key-sector values in Tables 1 & 2 are given on both those pages.
[37] After FG typed them in digitally in 2001-2, they were corrected by Guignard in 2009.

tended to group 'scientists and physicians' together and likewise writers and journalists, making thereby eight discrete groups.[38] Over 1980-84 all of the Gauquelins' hand-computed data was corrected by the US *Astro-Computing Services* in California, which process resulted in suspiciously *lower* significance levels than MG had found![39] The Teable shows that by comparing with results using a modern astrology-research program given on the right-hand columns,[40] showing more or less the same values as were then ascertained by ACS.[41]

The computer-derived results to the right are generally less significant than those hand-computed by the Gauquelins, but not much. it is a remarkable testimony to the integrity of MG's hand-computations in Paris – on a scale nowadays almost unimaginable – that they should be so well confirmed by a computer, in California. There were only two notable (and shocking) differences: total Mars for sports champions dropped by 17, while Saturn for scientists drops by 19.

Had MG been cheating, he would have tended to select his top military birthdata for having Mars in the Key Sectors, and that would never have produced a higher percent excess of Jupiter than Mars in the military group - as is here found, unexpectedly. The presence of more than one significant planetary effect in quite a few of these professional groups argues against the cheating hypothesis. Dr Geoffrey Dean has expressed the view that: 'Gauquelin planetary effects have tiny effect sizes,' comparing these allegedly 'tiny'effects to background traffic noise: 'In effect we tend to be faced with detecting whispers above the roar of city traffic.' [42] *Au contraire* I suggest that the size of the effect as shown in the above Table is of considerable magnitude, being generally around a twenty to thirty

---

[38] Textbooks by Dean *et. al.* give the same totals per profession as here, except that the above huge scientist group is split into two: *Tests of Astrology* 2016 p76 gives 1094 scientists and 2552 physicians, the same as in his *Astrology Under Scrutiny* 2014.
[39] MG, *Correlation*, 1984 3.1, 'Profess^n & Heredity Experiments: computer re-analysis.'
[40] Thus the top row gives 452 sports champions having Mars in thr Key Sectors, while the Jigsaw program (by 'Esoteric Technologies' Australia) only counted 435.
[41] Done by Tom Shanks, at Astro-Computing Services in San Diego; who alas no longer have archives of this matter (see ref. 61).
[42] Geoffrey Dean,'The Gauquelin Work 2' on http://www.astrology-and-science.com/G-arti2.htm

Looking at The Data

Profesn	Totals	Planet	Gaug K.S.	Exp.	% Xs	Jigsaw K.S.	CCRS Exp.	% Xs
Sports	2088	MA	452	358	26%	435	358	22%
Scientist	3643	SA	704	598	18%	685	605	13%
"		MA	697	626	14%	703	635	11%
Military	3046	JU	625	509	23%	614	519	18%
"		MA	604	523	16%	593	519	11%
Musicns	1248	VE	225	217	4%	223	213	5%
"	"	MA	188	214	-12%	192	212	-10%
Painters	1472	SA	203	253	-20%	198	240	-18%
"		MA	207	259	-20%	207	253	-18%
Writers	1352	MO	292	225	30%	288	224	29%
Politicns	1002	MO	189	167	13%	189	167	13%
"		JU	204	167	22%	202	169	19%
Actors	1409	JU	283	235	20%	273	238	14%

Table 1: Computer vs manual Computation: observed and expected values given by MG in his 1980 *Spheres of Destiny* in professional groups, these being the same as uploaded by CURA (physicians are grouped together with scientists). The values are compared to those found by the Jigsaw program. MG's earlier values differing by 3-4% have been highlighted. 'Control' values obtained by the US CCRS program are also shown[43,] which are sometimes similar to MG's control groups.

percent excess.[44] As the Table shows, the link of the Moon with poets and imaginative fiction-writers was his largest effect (as likewise the graph on page 33 shows this) - and yet Michel would never speak about it!

---

[43] Mark Pottenger kindly sent me this data, put into his CCRS Horoscope Program in 1990-92, see his 'Diurnal Sector Calculations,' APP, 1988, 6,2.
[44] See graph on page 33.

THE PLACIDUS ENIGMA

To get a picture of the Placidus house system, it helps to visualise the Mediaeval hours. These used to flow slowly in the summer time, because the Sun stays longer above the horizon, whereas in wintertime they would speed by quickly. Taking the duration of daylight, when the sun is above the horizon, and dividing by twelve, gives the Mediaeval hours. They are all equal. Night-time hours are then shorter, because in summertime the Sun stays below the horizon for a shorter time. Now imagine those hours mapped onto the diurnal circle, two hours at a time.[45]

Thus, if one has a chart (horoscope) for a moment of time, it will have a degree of the zodiac on the ascendant. That is alluded to as the 12th house cusp. Two 'hours' later, that degree will have moved to the 11th house cusp. Another two 'hours' later, it will be on the 10th house cusp. But, you will ask, why are we counting backwards? An answer to that is going to be obscure… and will go back into the mists of history! Suffice to say that the Gauquelins reversed this 'astrological' system of counting so that the Placidus sectors 12, 11 and 10 became their sectors 1, 2 and 3, etc.[46]

Here's a crisp definition of the first Gauquelin sector (12th Placidus house) which you might find helpful: 'The Sun is in the 12th house if in its journey from rising to culminating it is in the first 1/3 of this journey' - from US astrologer David Cochrane. That's because it spends an equal amount of time in each of the six above-horizon houses.

That way of dividing the circle in the sky uses the ecliptic, the plane in which Earth goes round the Sun. Any part of the ecliptic – where the planets are - rises above the horizon and then 'culminates', it reaches some highest point. We do not need to define this point, or even to wonder where it is, because we're simply using a sixfold

---

[45] If you want a formal definition, Placidus is 'time-based, in that every cusp marks the position that the degree on the ascendant would move to at a subsequent 'planetary hour.'' (Deborah Houlding, *The Houses, Temples of the Sky* 2006, p.103).

[46] Françoise Gauquelin, 'The Greek Error or Return to Babylon' APP September 1985 concerned which way round the houses should be counted': see Appendix 1.

Looking at The Data

division of time, where the planets have a more or less identical period as the Sun, as they move across the vault of heaven every day.

Michel's early books used these Placidus sectors. He then made a gear-change halfway through his career. Françoise tells the story of how, after she met Michel, she began to compute the actual rise and set times for his data and thereby ascertained what we now call the Gauquelin-sectors.[47] Mark Pottenger described how it was not until 1980 that these sectors could be properly ascertained, using the newly-available computer programs, because it was too much hard work to do them manually.[48]

Why did the Gauquelins want to make this change?[49] Was there some evidence that the new sectors worked better than Placidus? Did Michel ever tell us, that he had some results using his 3-D astronomical method, and that they came out better than using the old, Placidus system? Not really.

Using the program 'Jigsaw' it is easy to score the two systems and we don't find much difference between them. The groups score much the same except that:

- The group of writers score for Moon 4% better with the G-sectors than they do with Placidus.
- The group of sports champions score for Mars 2% better with Placidus than G-sectors.

We saw how, when the Gauquelins returned from the US in 1984, a general *reduction* in significance-levels was reported. The computer had supposedly removed human 'bias' in the calculations, and so they now had more accurate results, approved by the big new California computer. That should have been the point at which this new non-Placidus recomputation was evaluated.

The switch was no doubt important for their 'we're not astrologers' posture. For an astrologer, everything happens on the ecliptic, that is

---

[47] 'In Gauquelin's work the culminating point is identical to the MC but the rising point is not identical to the Ascendant.' Dean, RA p389.
[48] His comment was: "Rise and set based sectors [i.e., G-sectors] really only started to be used when the Gauquelins started having their computations done at ACS. This is what finally convinced me that it is OK for people to use Placidus houses as an approximation of Gauquelin sectors if they don't have a program available that does the true diurnal sectors." (M.P., 'Gauquelin sector calculations', ccrsdordona.org)
[49] Dean discussed this inconclusively, back in 1976: R.A., p.390.

22

where the action is. The ecliptic is so to speak the sensitive membrane onto which all planetary positions are projected, and where all aspects, rising and setting etc., have always been deemed to happen – *never* have the actual rising times of heavenly bodies been used. Whereas astronomers would never dream of taking such a view: they rather use 'real' times viz. the rising of a planet against an 'ideal,' flat horizon.

The Gauquelins brewed up a new, twelve-fold division of the heavens that no-one had ever heard of before, half-way between astrology and astronomy. They used the Mediaeval-hour concept as used in the Placidus system – which is by far the most popular house division system – and applied this using the physical or actual risings of the planets in 3-D space. They then counted the twelve sectors in a reverse sequence to the astrological tradition. None of the old tables could be used, and special programs had to be written to find these. Further, their twelvefold division was liable to splinter into 18-fold or 36-fold divisions. One can see why sceptics were liable to complain, and mutter, *ce n'est pas la science.*

Various sceptic groups were being approached, for a replication or test of the Gauquelin phenomenon. Their scepticism was enhanced by the perceived moving of goalposts, whereby (a) the Gauquelins were changing over to using a 3-D astronomy system, so that handy astrology programs or tables could no longer be used, and (b) they were preferring to use a 36-fold division of the heavens instead of 12 as earlier and that meant scoring two-ninths of the diurnal circle instead of one-sixth. In neither case was it evident that results would be thereby improved. There was even a further problem, that (c) they were claiming that the entire effect faded away around 1950 or 1960, for reasons that were far from evident to the sceptics.

Virtually the only Gauquelin-effect anyone has heard of these days is that of Mars for sportsmen, and the score for that that went *down* when the new co-ordinate system was used. So, what was the point? Let's look at some figures.

<u>Worked Example</u>

For Mars in the two Key Sectors, for the group of 2088 sports champions,

> Using the Placidus sectors 9 & 12: score 444, expect 360 => a 23% excess, highly significant at $\chi^2 = 20.6$

Using the G-sectors gives a score of 435, expect 360 => 32% excess, significant at $\chi^2 = 16$

Taking the more complicated eight-out-of-36 diurnal sectors, scores 553, expect 475 => 16% excess, $\chi^2 = 12$.

At each step, the significance goes down! I've here ventured to take the same expected score for the Placidus and G-sectors. The switchover to the astronomical or 3-D system was Françoise's contribution, but did it work? Was there a case for MG discarding two thousand years of tradition and brewing up new diurnal sectors that no-one had ever heard of before?

Michel explained the reduced-significance results (Table 1) by surmising that his new results were somewhat lower in significance due to inadvertent bias in the hand calculations when interpolating from tables

That could be so, if he had tended to select the Key Sectors in borderline cases. He reckoned there was 'little difference' in whether or not one used the Placidus sectors,[50] and asked the vital question, "So were my former results better because I worked with a Placidus division of the sectors?" He gave the obscure reply:

> Our Placidus material was perfectly accurate but was calculated only for geographical latitudes at intervals of 4 degrees and sidereal times at intervals of 12 minutes. Consequently, frequent interpolations by hand were necessary…[51]

Those approximations should have made his earlier results *less* accurate, owing to his having to interpolate from tables, while using the old Placidus method. The logic here is rather faulty.

Let's quote from an interview that Michel gave, to the lively Canadian journal *Phenomena, The Bulletin of Astrological News and Information* which was edited and published by Malcolm Dean, during the heyday of the great controversy:

> Phenomena: One question people ask about your study is about the arc you used to judge a planet's elevation in the

---

[50] For G-sectors being close to the Placidus house divisions, see MG, *Written in the Stars*, 1980, p.201.
[51] MG, *Correlation* 1984 4(1) 'Profession and Heredity Experiments: Computer Re-analysis' pp. 8-24, 11.

sky. Why did you choose an arc similar to the Placidean houses, yet not use the traditional ecliptic or zodiac?

Gauquelin: The Placidean system is the best one for statisticians, because it follows exactly the diurnal movement of the planet. Campanus or Regiomontanus are completely monstrous for statisticians. The planet has to behave like a drunk. Also, I divided the sky into 36 sectors.

(Interview with Michel Gauquelin, *Phenomena*, 1977 1.9 p12)

Notice that he didn't answer the question! He just said that the Placidean system was 'the best one for statisticians.' In that case, why did he stop using it?

MG did not I suggest give any very convincing account, as to why we should believe that the marked drop in significance he reported in 1984 was due to his by-hand errors, rather than moving over to the new reference-framework. Vainly we leaf through the volumes of Françoise's journal APP, seeking for some judgement by her on this matter. It was her idea, after all.

Further data-sets were published 1980-84, where the percent excess found by the Gauquelins, of planets in key sectors, was generally a lot lower than in the earlier samples, sometimes only half as much. As professor Hans Eysenck commented: 'These fresh samples display the same planetary effects .. that were found previously' but they were 'generally weaker' possibly due to a 'lower level of excellence in the new groups.'[52] This he saw as confirming the Gauquelin thesis.

In his later years MG's interest turned to other matters - to alleged correlations with geomagnetism, to character-traits using adjectives and to parent-child 'heredity' effects. The Gauquelin researches just went off in too many directions at once, not all of them valid, in a way that confused everyone. The professional groups were published in nine volumes by the Gauquelins, within which they discerned their four planetary types. I've listed those volumes which I could ascertain at the end of this book, but no-one has all of them.

Back in the 1980s when the great debates were ongoing, computer programs that could do the maths started to arrive. In 1980, both the Gauquelins and John Addey went all the way to California because

---

[52] MG's 'New Birthdata' series of 1984 http://cura.free.fr/gauq/17archg.html#MCD was reviewed by H.J.Eysenck in *Correlation* 4.2 1984.

Looking at The Data

there was there a computer that could do the calculations, at the ACS, Astro-Computing Service of Neil Michelsen in San Diego. In the mid-1980s a home computer program started to appear in Europe, maybe around 1984, that could analyse the data. Ah, remember the old 'CCRS' program written by Mark Pottenger in California? It was slow and clunky. But even then Professor Ertel wrote in 1987, 'The planetary sectors … were made accessible to the author on his visit to the Gauquelin laboratory,' in other words he had to obtain his data from the Gauquelins, obtaining from them the planetary, house-positions.[53]

We have still not quite reached a point where different programs will give the same answer. They give similar answers, maybe good enough. There today exist three main commercial programs, namely Pegasus in the US (David Cochrane), Jigsaw nowadays distributed by Astrocalc and the Fast Research program of Alfee Lavoie.

---

[53] Ertel, Corr 1987 7,1, p.7.

2

HOW BIG WAS THE EFFECT?

We've seen how the circle of the day divides into twelve intervals of time, six above the horizon and six below of which two are reckoned to 'count,' i.e. they are the 'key sectors,' above the horizon. They comprise 16.6% of the total (one sixth), that figure being what MG used in his first couple of books to obtain his chance-expected value.

But that is too low. It's too low because of an asymmetry of the sectors at the rising and culminating positions. Had MG taken four sectors, around the four cardinal points, then such a simple fraction of the whole would probably have been OK. This asymmetry came to be called, the 'Mars-dawn effect' and went as follows:

Women go into labour more at night-time than daytime

That means that births peak in the early-morning[1]

This is when the Sun is rising

Other planets orbit around the Sun, so they are more likely to be near to it in the heavens, than far away from it.

Therefore, Venus, Mars and Jupiter have an excessive frequency around dawn – which needs to be carefully evaluated as part of any 'Gauquelin-effect' judgement. Whereas this does not apply to Saturn or the Moon, because their diurnal frequencies are unlinked to the Sun's position.

Mercury and the Sun do not feature in the Gauquelin data, they refuse to show up at all, and in their distribution the diurnal variation of births (the so-called 'nycthemeral curve') is entirely dominant.

---

[1] Quoting Françoise, 'It is a current observation that mothers-to-be go more easily into labour during night than during day hours; consequently they give more often birth in the early morning hours than later in the day.' APP 1985 3,1p.21.

How big was the effect?

Planets beyond Saturn don't fare too well either, as their very slow motion around the zodiac can generate huge inequalities.[2]

Once the size of the professional groups are agreed upon - as on the French CURA website - then only one correct answer can exist for the score in the Key Sectors for a given planet. These may not yet have been exactly found, as different computer-programs still diverge somewhat.[3]

For that to be the case, we need to agree upon the celestial framework to be used – whether the old, traditional 'Placidus' house division, or the special 'Gauquelin sectors' which were more astronomical and modern-sounding. A lot of confusion was generated by MG switching over between these two halfway through his career and it is far from clear which of these was being used in the various debates which went on. In what follows we operate with the 'Gauquelin sectors.'

Control groups will always have slightly different values, depending upon the assumptions built into them: such modelling becomes more tricky the closer a planet is to the Sun. The longer a period over which the birth-data extends, the more uniform and easy-to-compute the control data will be. The most satisfactory solution here seems to have been the 'astro-demographic' expected frequencies found by Mark Pottenger of ACS in California, using his CCRS program (an early, Californian, DOS-based astro-research program). The graph below shows his expected frequencies for one professional group, that of 'scientists' converted to percent deviations from their mean. The mean value here marked as 100% on the graph is one-twelfth of the total.[4]

Expected values in the first G-sector (rise position) are generally

---

[2] For the near-impossible difficulties with the diurnal distribution of Neptune, see NK, 'Neptune & Alcoholics', *Correlation*, 2015, 30.1, pp.53-7.
[3] Thus for the group of Writers (n=1,352) Key Sector scores for the Moon were found as: 289 from the 'Sirius' program, 290 from 'Jigsaw', 292 by MG (both in Ch 1, Table 1) and 293 from 'CCRS': Facebook page '007'.
[4] For all of Pottenger's data as used in these graphs, which he obtained around 1990, go to https://newalchemypress.com/gauquelin/ page 2, 'Expected and Observed Planetary Frequencies.'

higher than in the opposite 6th (set position), owing to the excess of births around and just before dawn.[5] The dip in births at noon is here affecting the expected frequencies. On average the difference is found to be something like

Sector 1 / Sector 6:   VE +25%,   MA +10%,   JU +3%,   SA +1%

In his first two books MG used the same expected frequency for all twelve sectors (shown by the uniform-radius circles in Chapter 1, Figures 3 & 4): that was good enough for Saturn, which is far enough away to have almost no link with the Sun in its diurnal frequency, and also for the Moon which likewise has no such link, but not for other planets. From 1984 onwards, the expected frequency problem was essentially solved.

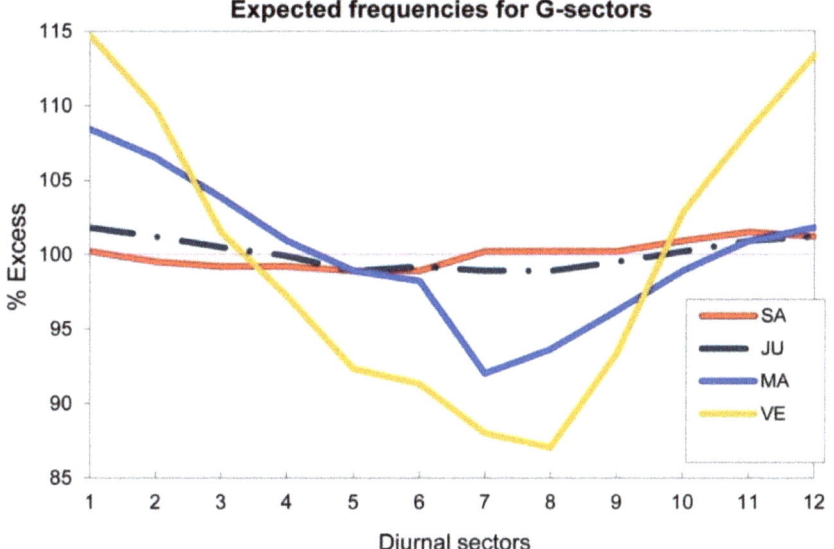

Figure 1: Expected frequencies through the twelve G-sectors of four planets, where 100% expresses the one-twelfth expected value and sectors 1 and 4 are 'key sectors.' Jupiter frequencies are represented by the dotted line.

Clearly, the Venus-line is highly skewed, showing how a planet nearer to the Sun than the others responds more to the diurnal

---

[5] Pottenger, 'Diurnal Sector Calculations' APP 1988, 6,2.

How big was the effect?

pattern of births, the so-called 'nycthemeral' curve: this will become important later on (Chapter 11) in relation to Venus.

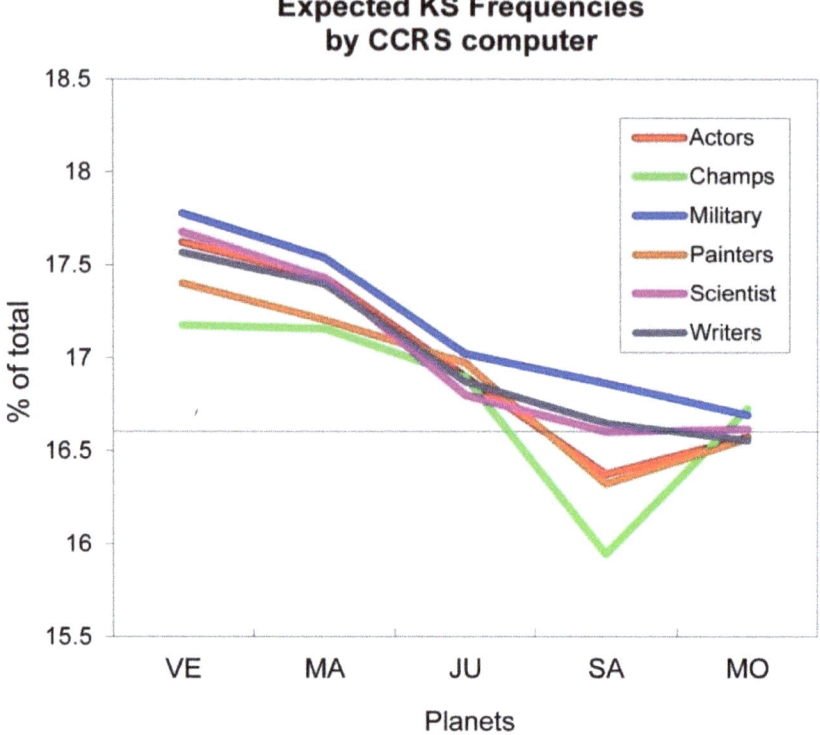

Figure 2: Expected frequencies as calculated by Mark Pottenger, with the two Key Sectors added together for six professional groups. Scores are as % of each group's total.

Here are the different professional groups, and this time the mean value (straight line) is one-sixth or two-twelfths of the total, expressed as a percentage. It is a mystery why Mr Pottenger obtained such a range of frequencies for Saturn. We see how around 17% of charts have the planet Jupiter in one of the two Key Sectors. Mars is scoring around 17.5% - a figure that became quite a storm-centre for intercontinental debates. The Moon is down at 16.6% as it should be, having no linkage with the Sun in its diurnal motion. This is *geocentric astronomy* we are here looking at.

Next we average those six lines together, to give an overall frequency. I constructed some control groups by combining all of the data from the G-professional groups and shuffling them around, altering the year and date,[6] but not the hour. Five control groups were thereby generated and their mean values here plotted. These results appear as being close to the Pottenger data, especially for Mars (Figure 3). Quite why Saturn's expected frequency should fall below the one-sixth threshold remains obscure: but, whatever the reason, my expected frequencies are lower than Pottenger's.

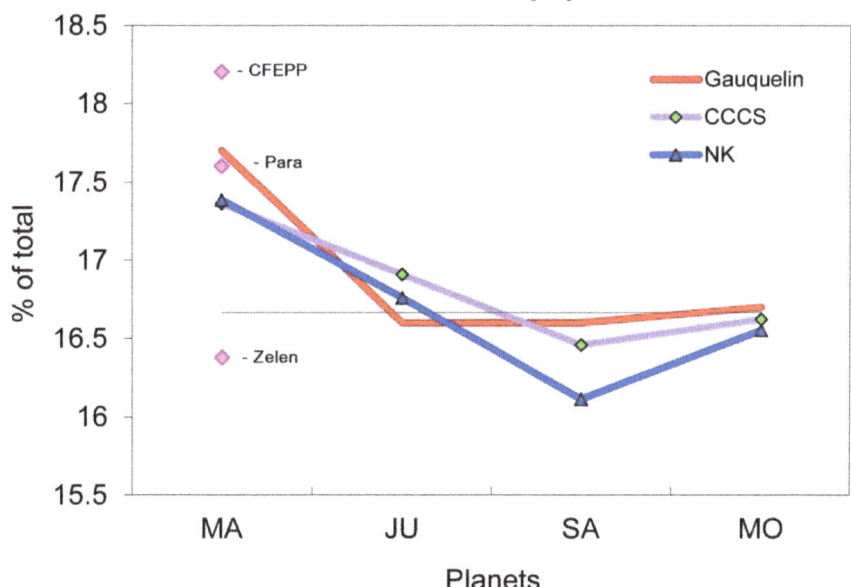

Figure 3: Collapsing the six values of the previous graph into one 'CCRS' line, and comparing with my and MG's chance-expected values, with data as before expressed as KS score as a % of the whole. Three different published values obtained by the skeptics groups (Chapter 6) are added for comparison.

We see in this graph that the Moon is very exactly on the chance-expected level, and that is because all of its inequalities will recur over 18-19 years, and it will go through that several times in any Gauquelin profession data-set, so they average out; whereas, Saturn takes thirty years to go round the zodiac and will therefore tend to show imbalances in any of these data-sets; that is why discussions of how to

---

[6] Also while shuffling, day and month were kept together, to avoid spurious dates eg a 30th of February.

How big was the effect?

generate a control-group can become quite complicated - and also why we can't really use the outer planets Uranus and Neptune, for their diurnal frequencies.

When he returned from the US in 1984, MG published an article based on the computerising of his data that was done in Calfornia.[7] The expected frequencies he then used are here included for comparison: he may have used the same source as Pottenger because we see here that they are similar.

In 1976 the Belgian Sceptics (the so-called 'Para' group) published their estimated value of this parameter for Mars, of 17.6%, then a year later the so-called 'Zelen test' of the US CSICOP sceptics published their strangely low 16.4% value. In 1996 the French skeptics published their 'nothing-to-see-here-move-along-now' report with a laughably high control-expected frequency of 18.2% for Mars.[8] These three have been included in Figure 3 for comparison. The wide scatter in these sceptics expected-values shows the difficulty experienced in fathoming this astronomical-demographic puzzle. We are here looking retrospectively at these endeavours, and can now attain a more accurate and reliable value than they did.

As a general statement, there cannot exist a single control-expected value, rather we are are here looking at a diffuse, fuzzy cloud of expected frequency.

Dennis Rawlins, the US astronomer and co-founder of the sceptical group CSICOP, in 1976 estimated this key parameter for Mars as 17.17%,[9] but neglected to explain how he reached that unduly-precise value. In the big debates that went on, a value of 17.2% was widely used.[10]

This value is not a constant, but varies with the shape of the 'Nycthemeral curve.' The 'Mars-dawn' linkage will tend to give a higher score in the first sector compared to the fourth, maybe five or ten percent more. Therefore the bigger peak will normally be in the

---

[7] MG, *Correlation* 1984 4(1) 8-24, p.11.
[8] Benski et.al, p.47.
[9] Rawlins, SI Winter 1979/80 p.26.
[10] In *The Zetetic Scholar*, 1982,9,p.65, Mr J. Good commented, of the Mars expected frequency: 'This percentage 17.17 was independently calculated astronomically both by Gauquelin and by Rawlins.'

first of the two Key Sectors (rising) compared to the second (culminating).

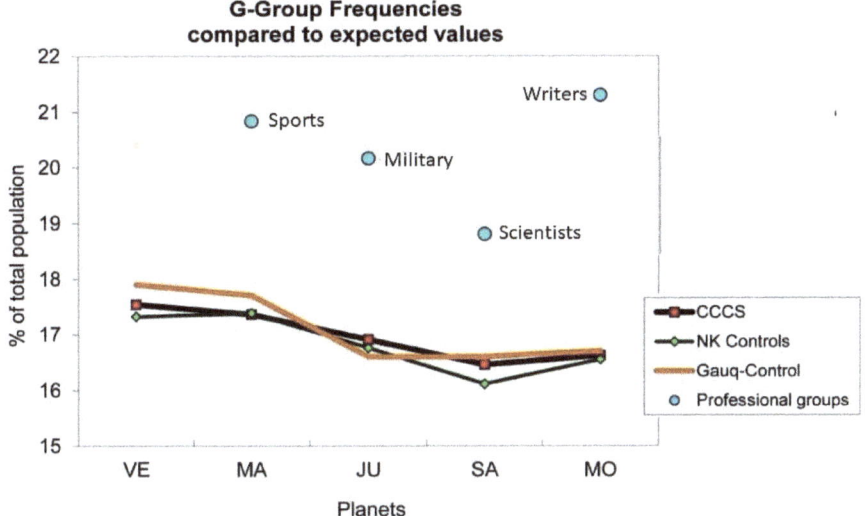

Figure 4: comparing the G-professional group scores as % score, over four professions, with the expected frequencies

Figure 4 shows 'actual' frequency values of the professional groups, again as a percentage of the total score. For Mars the group of sports champions has been used, for Jupiter, the military, for Saturn, scientists and for the Moon, writers. They hover around twenty percent, with the lowest value being Saturn in 'Scientists and Physicians' at 18.8% and the highest the Moon in 'Writers' at 21.3%.

They are here compared with expected values. It is fashionable to describe the Gauquelin effect as 'small' (Wiki) or 'tiny' (Dean), whereas the effects we see here are substantial. That of the Moon on writers is the largest but that intriguing topic was something Michel never ever spoke about. Suitbert Ertel did, he separated factual and historical writers from imaginative writers and poets, the two groups showing as one would expect different Saturn-effects (Chapter 9).

Two different kinds of percentages are required for the present work: Key Sector scores are expressed as a percentage of the total group (Figure 2, 3 and 4 of this chapter, eg); and then the percentage

How big was the effect?

excess within the Key Sectors[11] as in Table of Chapter 1. Both were used in the great debates.

Our argument will endeavor to resolve the great question: did Michel cheat – or, if not, was human fate really responding to the heavens above?

TWELVE OR THIRTY-SIX?

Two ways of dividing the circle were used in the debates of yesteryear, of 12 and 36 sectors, as we saw in Figures 1 and 2 of Chapter 1. For the first, key sectors comprised one-sixth, and for the second, two-ninths, of the whole. The latter became alluded to as the so-called 'enlarged' Key sectors. Here is Michel explaining why he adopted the 'enlarged' Key sectors:

> The two significant zones of the sky ... begin about 10° before the rise or the upper culmination...Since the significant zones somewhat exceed the sector 1 and 4 (in the 12 sector mapping) I now speak of enlarged key sectors or plus zones.[12]

Both Suitbert Ertel and Arno Müller (two German psychology professors, who we'll come to later on) used this extended definition for their work. The skeptics were not happy about such a 'moving of the goalposts':

> It is simply not permitted to change key sector definitions and then perform significance tests on already existing samples.[13]

Too right!

But, did they work better? To answer this,, chi-squared significance levels were computed for the major Gauquelin professional groups using the two different key-sector definitions.[14] A higher chi-square value means it is more significant.

---

[11] Roughly, this will be 100 x (n-N/6) / N/6 %, or for 36 key sectors, 100 x (n – 2N/9) / 2N/9 %, where n is key dector score and N is total population.
[12] MG Is there a Mars-Effect? JSE 1988 p.38.
[13] C.E. Koppeschaar, 'The Mars Effect Unriddled', Proc. Of 3rd Euroskeptics Congress 1991, p.170.
[14] The chi-squared significance test is performed by $(O - E)^2/E$ where O is observed score, E is expected score.

Professⁿ	Totals	Planet	χ^2	(+36)
Sports	2087	MA	22	17
Mility	3046	JU	22	20
"	"	MA	14	7
Sci.	3643	SA	11	14
"		MA	15	11
Painter	1472	SA	9	9
"		MA	8	7
Writer	1352	MO	19	11
Politn	1002	JU	9	4

Table 2: Chi-squared values using MG 1970 data, comparing the significance levels for planetary Key Sector excess[15] in six professional groups. The χ^2 values are shown using 12 and then 36-sector divisions. Compare Table 1, Chapter 1.

It is clear that the 'enlarged' key sectors perform worse.

It may help to examine these 'enlarged' key sectors, by combining the main professional groups. Saturn positions for all the scientists, Jupiter positions for military, actors and politicians, plus lunar positions for 1352 writers were added together, which gave a grand total of 11,283 sets of eminent-person birthdata. Data for Mars was excluded because of its skewed distribution.

The graph (Figure 5) adds up all this data and plots them by a 72-fold division (6 x 12 = 72), achieved using the US Pegasus astro-software. What the Gauquelins called Sector 1, the traditional '12th house,' here corresponds to sectors 1-6; while their other Key Sector, No. 4, was much the same as the '9th house' and corresponds to sectors 19-24.

The diagram shows a large excess for planets above the horizon, not hitherto noticed. The key planets were above the horizon 9% more of the time than they were below it. That accords with tradition, whereby persons who stand out upon the stage of life, who are seen in the spotlight, tend to have their key planet above the horizon. The above

---

[15] There is a logarithmic relation of chi-square to probability value, and to make that conversion one should 'divide the significance level by the number of possible positive outcomes from classical astrological rules' as Hans Eysenck explained (APP, 1983, 1,2, p.16; quoted in APP 1984, 2,2 p.8). For sports champions one could take the view that, from tradition, it had to be Mars and there was no other option.

How big was the effect?

/ below horizon difference here is not astronomical – it's astrological! The dots represent individual sector-values, plus a trendline (a three-point moving average) was put through them. Finally, a best-fit sinewave shows the above / below horizon effect.[16]

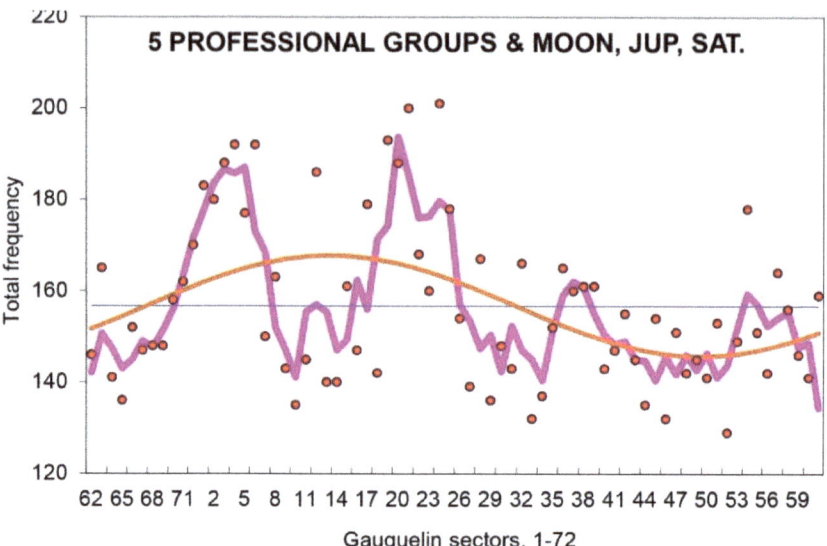

Figure 5: Combining five different professional groups, adding the scores of the respective planet, with a 72-fold division of the diurnal circles: Saturn for scientists, Moon for writers, Jupiter for military, actors and politicians, but none for Mars. David Cochrane's 'Pegasus' program was here used.

By subtracting out that primary waveform, we can inspect the 'Key Sector' concept more clearly. That gives us the Figure 6 where I have highlighted the two Key Sectors, which are Placidus houses – or, if you prefer, Gauquelin sectors 1 and 4. And what about the 'enlarged' Key-Sectors? By inspection one sees that the two data-points just prior to the Key Sectors are hardly above the mean value. The large excess is *within* the two 'Key sectors'. Applying the significance test to compare the two 'Key Sector' definitions gives:

> Chi-squared for two Key Sectors, 1/6 of the total (score 2222, expect 1880) = 62.2
>
> Chi-squared for two enlarged K.S., 2/9 of the total (score 2875, expect 2507) = 54.

---

[16] That best-fit sinewave has an amplitude that is 7% of the mean.

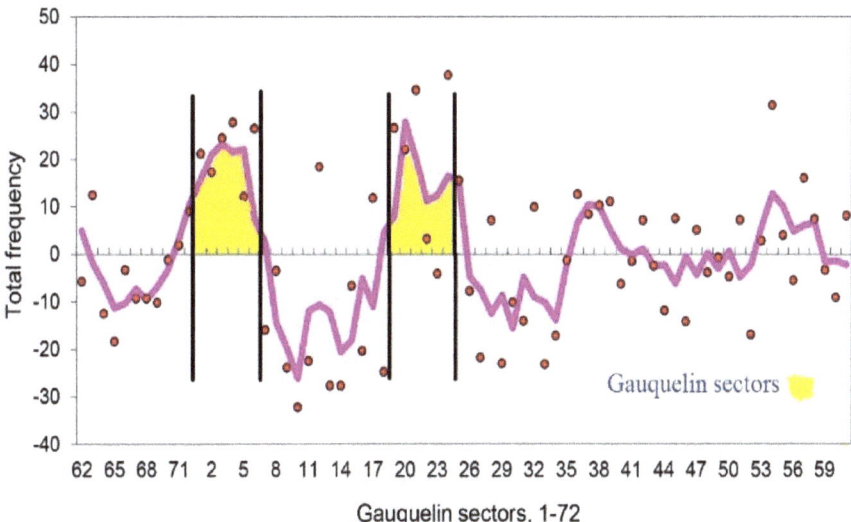

Figure 6: As for fig 5, after subtracting out the diurnal waveform

The 'enlarged' definition is massively *less* significant! We therefore conclude that the 'enlarged key sectors' concept was mistaken. It was, one could say, a collectively shared misperception, during several decades of the 20th century.

The graph shows a remarkable confirmation of the $1/12^{th}$ divisions of the heavens as practiced by astrologers for two millennia, as being optimal. The 'twin peaks' here shown are not subject to explanation by any 'social effects' (Dean) nor by some environmental factor for which the sceptics have searched.

Summary In this chapter we have seen firm evidence for the traditional 'houses' i.e that the twelvefold division of the sky using them worked better than any other. We heve acquired a basic notion of what the evidence for the Gauquelin thesis looks like and that was possible after ascertaining the chance-expected frequencies. We remain somewhat undecided as to whether the primary effect is fourfold within the diurnal circle, or whether it mainly works in the two above-horizon sectors.

3.

SO BRIEF A HOPE

The whole Gauquelin enterprise has faded away, with neither of the Gauquelins even having a Wikipedia page. We here retrace some historical steps, to follow what had looked so promising, then ended up as a perceived disaster. A wonderful new science was nearly but not quite born and then somehow aborted. Some major steps were -

1955 – MG's first book, *L'Influence des Astres, Etude critique et Experimentale*

1960 – The second book, *Les Hommes et Les Astres* – his collaboration with Francoise

1970-72 – the data-volumes are published, eg *Les Hommes de Science*, for each profession.

1980 – The ACS computer in San Diego recalibrates all of the data.

1988 – *Written in the Stars*, with a Foreword by Hans Eysenck

2003 – the data-volumes appear in digital form on the CURA website.

Michel's first book featured French data-sources for the major professions (except for writers). It gave all of the data and explained where it had come from, which was very commendable and meant that anyone could re-check its astonishing claims. In that sense it was the one properly scientific text that he produced.

Francoise paid for the publication of that book, a part of the deal of their coming together, a kind of wedding-dowry, as man and wife. She had a degree in statistics from the University of Paris, and from then on she dedicated her life to assisting Michel in his quest – for which we are grateful. Together they journeyed round the registry-offices of Europe and thereby they produced a sequel volume, *Les Hommes et Les*

Astres, which did successfully replicate the basic astral hypothesis within various professions, in Germany, Switzerland, Holland and Belgium. It gave details of where the data had come from, but did not give the data – so, no-one could check it.

Francoise was distressed to find that her name was not on the cover as a co-author.[17] She as the statistician had truly dedicated her life to working full-time on the matter, and it was she who had the command of several European languages. Without her they would not have managed entry into the European registry-offices, there would have been no book. Had she been co-author, one feels that more care would have been taken to hang onto and define the precious data.

Unduly high probabilities were cited, by grouping all of the data together for each profession. For example, the Jupiter excess in 'Men of War' was cited as five million to one. Nobody gets significance as high as that for a psychology test!

In 1970 the formal data-volumes started to appear, and this was the only time MG allowed Francoise's name to appear as co-author. These did not contain the same numbers as had earlier been alluded to, they were in general somewhat larger, nor did those volumes comment on where the data had come from. Each line of data was given a number, so that the enterprise now had an air of finality. Some years later, MG averred that that those 1970-72 volumes 'were directly compiled from material previously published,' viz the 1955 and 1960 books.[18] Was that so?

The G - groups	1960 Total	1970 Total
Sports Champ	1485	2088
Sci & Physicians	3305	3647
Military	3142	3047
Politicians	993	1003
Actors	1270	1409
Paint & Music	1345+703=2048	1473+1249=2722
Writers& Journos	826+824 = 1650	1352+674 = 2026

---

[17] She used to visit Mike O'Neil when she came to London. I was there on one occasion and she told us her story.
[18] MG, Corr 1984 4,1,8-24, p.23 note 1

Table: Totals for seven professional groups, as published in 1960 *Les Hommes et les Astres*, compared to the 1970-72 data-volumes for these same groups.

That is a shocking list. They don't match up and one would have preferred to have some explanation as to where each line of data had come from.[19]

There were two major points at which the professional-group data was published: firstly in 1955, and then in 1970-72. For a statistical test, one would take the latter data and subtract out the original 1955 data: then, we would be dealing with a replication, where a significance test is legitimate. To quote a sceptic of the Gauquelin endeavour:

> A significance test can be applied as long as predictions are made before sampling.[20]

A significance text should only be performed on a replication, after a hypothesis has been formulated in advance. One may question whether his first book should have cited significance levels, as it recorded his original discoveries and so was the first time that the phenomenon had appeared. Michel tells us that he first noticed the effect with the group of French physicians there given.

In 1980 all of the Gauquelin data was input into the big computer at Astro-Computing Services in California, and thereby freed from the manual computational errors. At last, it was error-free! And yet in 1988 one of his last books *Written in the Stars* merely repeated the results he had published in 1960. Why did he not prefer to use the 1970 data, which had been published, and had by then all been re-checked by the big California computer? The large Mars-error in his sports champion data published back in 1955 remained uncorrected! The couple separated in 1983, so this happened when he no longer had Francoise to check through his numbers.

Before home computers had arrived, both of the Gauquelins and John Addey spent a year or so at ACS Astro-Computing Services in

---

[19] All of the Para Comité sports-champ data published in 1968 (n=535, chapter 4) went into the 2088 total published by the Gauquelins in 1970. One finds no discussion of this bizarre fact, only stated in a US sceptics journal: Abell & MG, *The Humanist*, 'A Test of the G Mars-Effect', Sept/Oct '76, alluded to in the *JSE* 1997,11,1 by Kurtz *et al.* p20 fn.
[20] Carl Koppeschaar, 'The Mars Effect Unriddled' 1991 *Eurosceptics Conference* 162-184, p.170.

California, in 1980, managed by Neil Michelsen who had a degree in mathematics. All of the Gauquelin data was logged in, and various analyses performed, with techno-experts like Tom Shanks and Mark Pottenger involved. All of the top people were there, for a year! One might have hoped for some monthly bulletin to appear, some in-house journal? Ah, if only that centre had published the data and its analysis thereof – indeed, if only they could merely have kept the data - then there would have been some independent and widely-respected validation of the enterprise: *but they didn't* and all trace of that remarkable gathering of talent and all of the programming just faded away, and we're left in the usual situation where MG becomes our only source for whatever had happened.

It is a little-discussed fact, that the historic enterprise of gathering reliable birthdata from registry offices of five or six European nations, of eminent persons, for a theory which might have had such a far-reaching significance, as was published in the 1960 *Les Hommes et Les Astres* – that this data should remain unavailable. It is presumably contained in the published data-volumes. In each of the data-volumes, sequential numbers were given to each unit of birthdata, giving them an air of finality. One might have hoped that each of the data-volumes would contain an essay explaining the sources, or at a minimum they should have explained how the data there presented was related to the earlier-published volumes: that from French registry-offices (*L'Influence des Astres*) and that from other European nations (*L'Hommes et les Astres*) – as well as, where the new, extra data had come from (or, where the missing hundred eminent military went to).

If only this had been done, such that the birthdata they gave in 1970 corresponded to the data-analysis presented in 1960, with its account of the various data-sources: then, their work would surely have been indestructible, it could have withstood all of the sceptics' barbs. There would not be the core of vague confusion, for anyone trying to replicate the work, whereby the entire phenomenon keeps pointing back to Michel himself, because only he can explain the data.

THE MARS-EFFECT

In his first book *L'Influence des Astres* (1955) MG published his first results of the diurnal distribution of Mars for 570 French sports champions and the data-set is here reconstructed.[21] It used an 18-fold division of the circle. My modern reconstruction of his result does vaguely resemble what he reported six decades earlier. Comparing the score:

FRENCH CHAMPS	Tot. No.	Key Sector. scores	Exp. Score	% Xs	Chi-squ.	Prob[y]
MG 1955	570	68 + 68	97.8	39%	32	1: 70,000[22]
NK 2018	561	64 + 67	96.2	36%	13	1:500

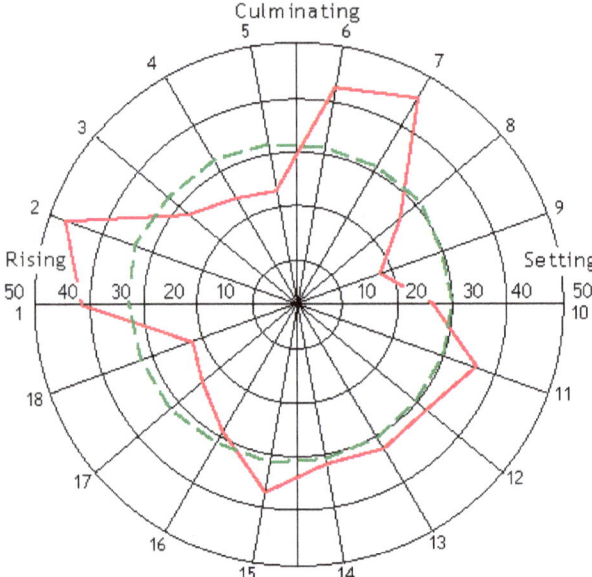

Figure 1: the Mars-day distribution at the births of 570 French sports-champions, as published by Gauquelin in 1955.[23]

Figure 2: reconstruction by the author using 561 of the 1955 list of champions, giving not the same result

---

[21] *L'Influence*, Page 143. The data given in his 1955 book is available from opengauquelin.org. Before that, I had to tick off the 570 data-sets in the 1970 volume 'Sports champions, Birth and planetary data' by the Gauquelins. Each line of data has its 'Gauquelin number' so these could be selected out from the CURA data set for sports champions (where NB names are *not* given), using those numbers. We're happy to forget all of that, now that the original data-sets are online.

[22] MG, *Les Hommes et les Astres* 1960 p.83. I'd say his χ^2 here was 14 not 32.

[23] See letter by MG: astrologicalreviewletters.org/2013/07/is-there-really-mars-effect.html : 1988, *Above and Below: Jnl of Astrol. Studies* Vol. 11 4-7.

In 1970-1972 the two Gauquelins published their complete volume of sports data, their 2088 top sportsmen, claiming that 452 of these had Mars in a Key Sector, a 26% excess.[24]

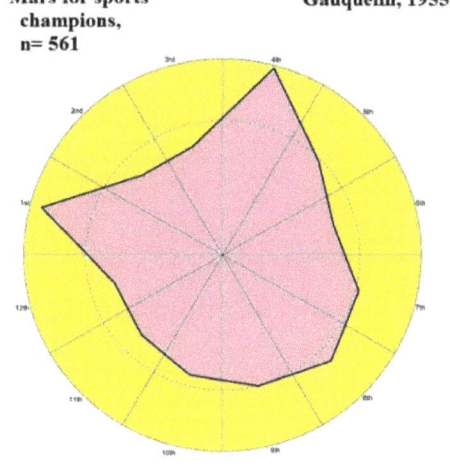

In 1982 while the great debate was raging in some twenty different journals on both sides of the Atlantic, the professional statistician Mr John Good summarised the matter as:

> The basic observation of Gauquelin was that of 2,088 European sports champions, of whom 452 were born when Mars was in Gauquelin's sectors 1 or 4…

This is the one person who published an article in a proper statistics journal about the matter. He here summarised the crux of the matter in terms of one figure – and it was wrong! Or at least, it is badly mistaken. This – the one mjor calculation-error in the Gauquelins' career - was far from being widely publicized. It was revealed only in an obscure table in MG's 1984 *Correlation* article, 'Profession and Heredity Experiments, computer re-analysis.'[25] Twelve years after the erroneous figure was first published, we gather that no-one has remedied the mistake. The correct and much lower figure had been obtained but Michel had not yet published it. It is looking like a story ready to fall apart rather quickly. Much of the Great Debate had been going on for years before this huge error was corrected.

Francoise's journal *Astro-Psychological Problems* lasted for twelve years 1982-94, during which period this great correction was made. None of its contributors ever commented on how, by under-estimating his chance-expected level and overestimating his actual

---

[24] Their 1970 'Sports Champions' data volume, plus computed results given in their 1972 'Profession-Heredity results of series A & B,' p.80.

[25] His total Mars-score for 2088 champions thus dropped from 452 to 435 from this correction: *Corr.* 4(1) 8-24: Table 1, p.11: from 26% down to a 19% excess.

score, MG had obtained the unduly high significance estimate. Should a significance test have been applied on the data, since these are only supposed to be applied when a prediction has been made and formulated in advance? One would have liked to hear some discussion on the matter.

Five years later, *Les Hommes et Les Astres* published an additional set of data, garnered from European registry offices: the couple had acquired 915 new birth-data of Euro-champions: cyclists, footballers, boxers and pilots, from Belgium, Holland and Germany. Michel's much-cited graph for what was then his total of 1,485 sports champions is here shown, with its dramatic peaks at rising and culmination.

This polar-coordinate graph is *not* measured from centre-zero, as was the previous one. It starts counting at fifty, which has the effect of enhancing what is seen to be the effect (some take the view that this is a form of cheating, whereby an effect is made to look much bigger than it is). The net effect was actually *smaller* than found in his first, French-only survey:

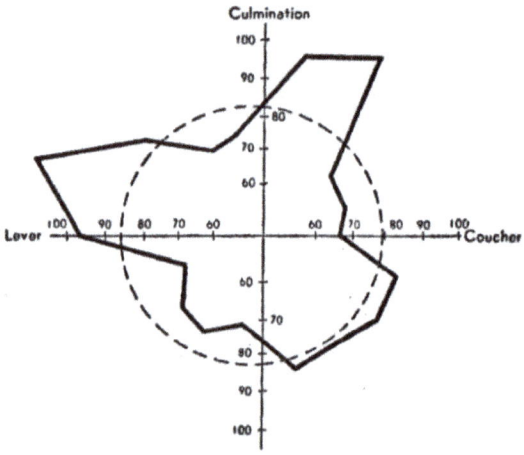

Fig. 7. 1 485 CHAMPIONS DE SPORT : MARS

Mars for Champions	No. of champs	K.S. scores	Exp. Score	% Xs	X²	Prob[y]
Gauq. 1960	915	99 + 92	156	22%	8	1: 700[26]
M & FG. 1970	2088	227+208	365.4	19%	13	1: 5m

Table Mars- sports champ data sets. The 1960 results are as alleged in the book, which cannot be checked

---

[26] *Hommes et les Astres*, P.86

For the new group of 915 Euro-sports champions, Michel recorded Mars Key-sector scores that were 22% in excess. But, the data remained unpublished. For this total sports-group, he was claiming a significance level of one in 5 million.[27]

A decade later, the Gauquelins published their 'final' total of 2,088 sports champions and, without explaining where the extra six hundred had come from, stated:

> The birth data published in this series corresponds roughly to the results given in 1960.[28]

We are shocked. The phrase 'corresponds roughly' is far from being an adequate account of the extra six hundred added.[29] The 1970 data-set score is given in the above Table for comparison, also its 18-fold polar-co-ordinate graph is here shown. The two graphs look so different, partly as explained because their scaling differs, but also because the former has a 29% excess in the Key sectors while the latter has merely 19%. How was such a large difference possible?

Years later, Gauquelin explained in a US journal where the remaining 2088 – 1485 = 603 sports chjampions had come from.[30] By simple subtraction, that group had merely a 3% excess of Mars in the Key sectors. In other words, the Gauquelins in 1970 would have been far better off sticking with the sports data they had published a decade earlier. All their final set had virtually no Mars-excess and - wherever it had come from – it greatly diluted the effect.

While perusing their 1970 *Men of Science* data-volume, one is struck by the way it goes off in various different directions: an alleged 'heredity' effect has parent-child data given in great detail, and then alleged effects of solar activity and geomagnetism upon it are discussed – all of which probably did not exist, but assuredly would have been better put aside so the authors could have focussed on what was here the essential matter: what was the provenance of this data, where had it come from? Also, it starts counting the data using a 36-

---

[27] MG, *Spheres of Destiny*, 1980, p.16: that was for the 2,088 total.
[28] M&F G., *Men of Science* Series A, Vol. 2, 1970, p.VI.
[29] For evaluation of this obscure question, see Ertel, JSE 1988 2,1, pp.58-61.
[30] 330 new names from the Belgian Comité Para (Chapter 4) plus 276 'aviators and rugby players' added to give 2088: Kurtz *et. al. JSE* 1997,11,1, p.20.

fold division of the circle - no wonder the sceptics felt that the goalposts were being shifted.

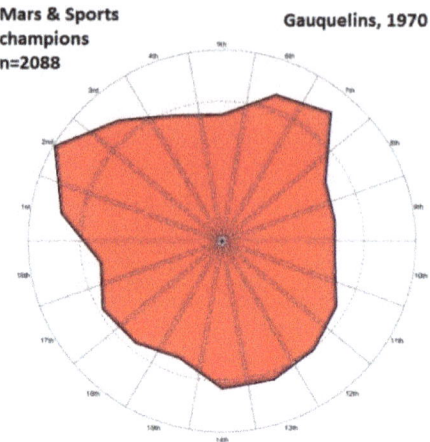

Figure: the 1970 published Sports-champion Mars data, with 18-fold division, showing a 19% excess in the two Key Sectors.

Of the Mars-sports champion data, John Addey commented: 'This must be the most discussed, scrutinised, checked and double-checked piece of astrological research ever.'[31] If so, how strange that its data-sources should have remained so fuzzy and unclear, paving the way for the later attacks by the skeptics.

Mars-Effect in Gauquelin sports data

1955: +39% claimed (I obtained 27%)   for 570 champions

1960: +22% claimed, for 915 champions, uncheckable because no data available.

1970: +3%   for the 603 added

It is a strange sequence. The sceptics should have used it! The last data-set (+3% for 1970) comes from assuming that (a) all the data from the 1960 volume really existed, as we surely must, and (b) that all of it went into the 1970 publication – which reflected their ethical commitment, that they would keep all their data.

We've here shown the two most famous Gauquelin graphs, that have been widely quoted and imprinted into our consciousness as 'the

---

[31] John Addey, 'The True Principles of Astrology...' *Correlation* 1981 1,1, 26-35, 27.

Mars effect.' They resemble the stories of the big fish that got away - while the actual Mars-graphs are by comparison quite dull.

In one of his last books, *Written in the Stars* (1988) MG repeated his 1960 graphs and analyses. Why, we cannot help wondering, did he not use the larger numbers he had published in the big data-volumes? Why did he instead go back to an earlier text? And - more to the point - why did none of us ask him about this while he was still alive?

A sceptical view here would have to be, that the 1970 published volumes were all of the data which the Gauquelins had collected, and for the 1960 publication MG had somehow filtered that data to improve the effect. Was Francoise not wanted as co-author because some data-selection was going on? That would to be sure take us into an Ertel-type 'furtive' MG, which we'd all prefer not to believe in.

One is here reminded of the sceptic view of astronomer George Abell: 'Gauquelin's findings represent an anomalous result that remains unconfirmed to the degree necessary to be accepted as scientific fact.' (1979)[32] [33] MG used to irritate people by the inflated significance-levels he claimed, citing them as millions to one – whereas, to obtain a valid significance level, the original test data (1955) ought surely to be subtracted out from the final total of 2,088 (1970). Because the hypothesis was formulated on the basis of that first test, therefore it cannot be included. The above figures then yield a chi-squared value of 7,[34] which is around 1 in 100, hardly adequate to validate a hypothesis of celestial influence.

Painters: In other groups the mismatch is not so bad, eg his 1960 opus had a total of 1345 eminent European painters, compared to the 1473 painters of the 1970 data-volume. – and we still we have no idea where the extra came from. This may not matter too much because he found no positive result for the group, but it leaves the data in a position where no academic or scientific institution is going to want to look twice at such confusion.

---

[32] Quoted in Eysenck & Nias, *Astrology, Science or Superstition?* p.208.
[33] Abell, The Mars Effect, *Psychology Today* 1982, 16(7) 8-13. NB, see reply by Barry Lynes, who called Abell's article 'laughable': 16(10), p.6. Abell repeated these words "The Gauquelins have no way of proving they did not cheat" in *Newsweek* 20 Aug 1982.
[34] For 1518 total, 309 in KS => expect 266.

so brief a hope

Actors and Jupiter: In his first book MG reported a strong 25% excess of Jupiter, for a group of five hundred French actors. Then birthdata for another nine hundred European actors were gathered, with Francoise helping him. The excess here was *less than half* of that – merely +10% - and it was *not* significant.

Did Francoise experience some degree of suspicion, as she noticed that when she participated in gathering the data, the effects came out as being a lot weaker than that gathered by Michel? If so, she said nothing.

ACTORS	Total	JU in KS	Excess
1955 MG	500	105	25%
1970 CURA	1409	273	15%
Difference	909	168	10%

Saturn and Science MG would bracket Science and Medicine together, probably because they both scored positive for Saturn. He here claimed a significance level of 1 in 300,000! Comparing those two groups, His medical group showed a stronger effect than the scientists. His first batch of French physicians data showed a 35% excess, of Saturn in the Key sectors. Here is his graph, showing the amazing effect. But … do we believe it? Once Francoise arrives on the scene, they gather some more data, and the net excess strangely plummets.

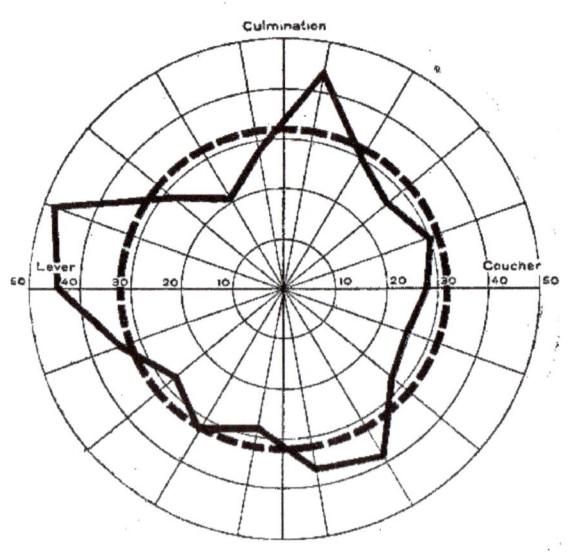

Figure: 1955 Saturn for French physicians, 35% excess in Key sectors.

Was it significant? To find out, we, as before, subtract the group used first (from which the hypothesis was formulated) from the rest. The chi-square value drops massively when thousands more are gathered, as once again, the effect fails to replicate. We can separate the French data and the rest, and compare the data upon the CURA website (equivalent to that published in 1970) with the results in in his second book *Les Hommes et Les Astres* of 1960 (reprinted in his 1988 opus, *Written in the Stars*), as follows.

The several totals of eminent physicians' birthdata

Medicine	French	'Foreign'	Totals
MG 1960	1084	1231	2315
CURA data	1321	1231	2552

His group of 'foreign' data has stayed the same, which means the data is accessible. We can therefore check his scores for those non-French {Scientists + Medics}, though he only gives the two added together:

'Foreign' Sci + Med	Total No.	Saturn in KS	Mars in KS
MG 1960	1941	372 => 19%	385 => 16%
CURA	1941	358 => 10.5%	365 => 7%

We thereby get about half of his effect – as we earlier saw for the Mars & sports champion data. The 1970 totals combining French and 'foreign,' are:

1970	Tot.	Saturn in KS	Mars in KS
Medics	2552	243+243=> 14%	262+247 => 14%
Sci+Med	3643	685 => 12%	697 => 9%

The Saturn-score for the total {science + medicine} here is the same as was ascertained at the ACS computer in California in 1980 (n=685), but the Mars-score (697) is six points lower[35] – a computer could surely not have made such an error?

---

[35] The ACS data was reported by MG in 1984: *Correlation*. 4,1,pp8-14, 11.

so brief a hope

This has been a rather shocking chapter, in which we tended to find that the famous Gauquelin data hardly reached statistical significance. We return later to this unresolved question. Let's look at a couple of bar-charts, which demonstrate the polar opposite effects of Jupiter and Saturn, using the usual twelve sectors. They tend to suggest something rather fourfold is going on, though one sees that the two Key Sectors have the highest score. We will develop this theme in due course. For any future data-set, the optimal prediction here will tend to involve the difference between Saturn and Jupiter scores in the two Key sectors.

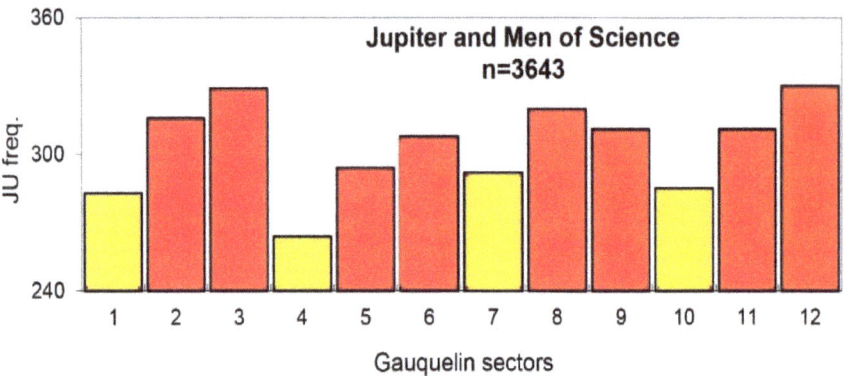

Notice how these tables echo the question we asked earlier, as to whether we're dealing with a fourfold effect or should one just focus upon the two above-horizon key sectors? That decision needs to be made and made clearly prior to the design of a statistical test.

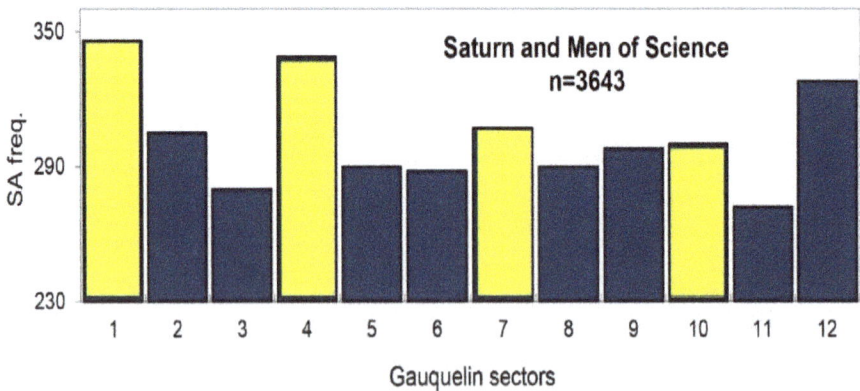

Figures: Jupiter and Saturn contrasted in the four Key sectors, for MG's group of Scientists and Physicians (3643 of them, up on the CURA website)

4

SCEPTICS HIT BACK

Isn't it a little strange that after thousands of years of debate and argument, when we finally have solid scientific evidence, on the nature of planetary influences, that so little attention, and such bizarre attention, is being given to the whole event?[36]

-Malcolm Dean, editor of Phenomena the Canadian Bulletin of Astrological News & Information' 1978

Faced with unfaultable evidence of a connection between the position of planet Mars at birth and success in sports, skeptical Professors Paul Kurtz, George Abell and Marvin Zelen repeatedly offered fallacious statistics to deny astrology's only ray of hope. Focusing only on a small section of the Mars data, deleting the favorable results for females, dividing the sub-sample into tiny bits and applying the wrong statistical tests, the trio still could not get rid of the Mars effect. They ultimately argued that it was based on faulty data, due either to incompetence or cheating by Michel Gauquelin of France, who produced the original finding.

- Prof. Kammann[37]

We here follow a set of closely-linked events in the mid-1970s. The great *Humanist* attack upon astrology echoed around the world's media, followed a year later by a report from the Belgian Skeptics so-called 'para committee.' The US Sceptics Society was then founded, with a report of their Mars-test. Thus, reports of independent testing

---

[36] *Phenomena* 1978 2.2, Editorial.
[37] Psychology professor Richard Kammann: 'The True Disbelievers, Mars Effect Drives sceptics to Irrationality', *Zetetic Scholar* 10, December 1982, pp. 50-65. (discord.org/~lippard/kammann.html) The article was first submitted to *The Humanist*, *Psychology Today* and *The Skeptical Enquirer* but they declined to publish it.

of the Gauquelin Mars-effect happened close to each other – followed in both cases by cover-ups.

The following date-sequence may help in keeping track of events described in this chapter:

1962, January		Para Committee president discusses an experiment with MG
1968, October		Para Committee announces Results
1975, January		Zelen proposal re Para Committee results, in *The Humanist*
	Sept.	*The Humanist* attack on astrology
1976, May		The US Sceptics group CSICOP is created. Para Committee result published in Nouvelles Brèves.
1977, June		Paul Kurtz visits MG in Paris, testifies that his 'Laboratoire' seems OK.
	July	Kurtz, Zelen, Abell and MG plan US test.
	Nov.	Zelen Test results in KZA *Humanist* report
1978, June		Rawlins computes US sportsmen data-sets
1979, June		Randi: Rawlins a 'problem child,' Fate mag.
	Winter	SI publishes the CSICOP 'replication' with significantly negative result.
1980	Decem.	CSICOP drops Dennis Rawlins from Council.
1981, March		*Science et Vie* article by French skeptics
	July	Patrick Curry writes his account of events
	October	Rawlins publishes his exposé "sTarbaby" in *Fate* magazine.

THE BELGIAN TEST

The Belgian Sceptics obtained a startling positive result - then declined to publish it! As the British psychology professors Hans Eysenck and David Nias observed:

> The Belgian Committee Para, which set out to disprove Gauquelin's findings in fact supported them. This is very unusual in science. It means that our knowledge of the

Committee's findings derives mainly from Gauquelin's quotations and discussions of them; and while we have little doubt that these are accurate (because otherwise the Committee would certainly have issued a disclaimer) it would still have been preferable to have the Committee's own report available for consultation.[38]

The Belgian 'Committee for Investigation of alleged Paranormal Phenomena' was called for short the 'Comité Para.' As its name somewhat implies, it was opposed to anything that it called 'paranormal.' This Belgian Para Committee claimed to be on the side of 'science' and viewed MG's claims as paranormal. MG disputed this and reckoned his work was 'normal' science because it was repeatable.

The Gauquelins needed someone else to collect birthdata and put their theory to the test. There would be little point in them just gathering further data and publishing it. Michel harangued the Belgian sceptics for some years until finally they agreed, if new data could be found. A problem here was that the Gauquelins had already scoured the registry offices of Europe and selected eminent people, in the different professions. It came to be agreed, that a test could be performed provided new data could be obtained.[39] As Michel reasoned, 'Sporting glory is swift but ephemeral,'[40] and therefore it should not be hard to find hundreds of new sportsmen. Or, in the words of Ertel and Irving:

> ...why sports champions were singled out to be the subject of nearly twenty years of debate between the Gauquelins and three different sceptic committees? The answer is that there is a greater turnover in the sports group than in most of the others. People who excel in sports generally do so when young and usually fade quickly, only to be replaced by others. For that reason, this group offered the greatest promise for fresh data to which others could apply the

---

[38] Eysenck and Nias, *Astrology Science or Superstition?* 1982, p.201.
[39] It was never very clear to what extent the Belgian Para data was 'fresh:' in 1977 Kurtz and Nienhuys averred that 205 were in MG's 1955 book while 330 were new (JSE 11(1), p.20.)
[40] MG *The Truth about Astrology*, p.101.

Gauquelins' procedures in order to try and reproduce their results.[41]

And so in 1967 MG conveyed a simple message to the President of the Para Committee:

> In order for the new experiment to verify our earlier work, the group studied must present a surplus of the position of Mars after the rise and culmination.[42]

It took the Committee a year to collect 535 champions, and then perhaps surprisingly they sent their results to MG. Here is what it found:

1968: Belgian Committee Para result

535 sports champions had Mars in Key Sectors 119 times, Expect 94 => 26% excess of Mars in KS, Chi-Square 7, p < 0.008 or one in a hundred.

They had confirmed his 'Mars-Effect'! Clearly, this could not be published.

The Para Committee had used a sound method of finding their expected frequencies by using 'time-shift' controls, which meant moving the times of birth on from one champion to the next, and they generated nine such samples.[43] This startling result did not appear in their Belgian sceptics journal report[44] and not until years later in 1982 did the world hear about it, when Gauquelin spilled the beans in the *Zetetic Scholar* (Vo. 10, p.70), using a manuscript text they had earlier sent him. The editor sent his text to the Para committee for comment and they did not object. One has to agree with Dean and Smit that this rather Kafkaesque concealing of the method 'was a classic example of pathological science.'[45]

The standard deviation of their time-shift controls was ten, meaning that the observed score was two standard deviations away from the expected score, which is a decently significant result, at around a 95% confidence limit. One should endeavour (I suggest) to

---

[41] *Tenacious Mars Effect*, KI-7.
[42] MG *The Truth About Astrology*, p.102.
[43] Dean & Smit, AuS, p.109
[44] *Nouvelles Breves* 1976, 43, pp 327-343.
[45] Dean & Smit, Ibid, p.110.

keep a significance test fairly simple. Their expected-frequency was a bit high (94/535=17.6%,) and we might prefer to put it at more like, say, 92 (The figure on page 31 shows their error).

The Para Committee later tried to claim that the expected frequency they came up with was in some way doubtful. Horrible verbiage was produced around this test, like a squid ejecting black ink to make its getaway. The Committee's report droned on with mathematical-sounding hocus-pocus:

> MG has certainly underestimated the complexity of astronomical questions which he thought to represent accurately in elementary formulae. The astronomers and statisticians of the Para Committee, after a conscientious examination, have declared these formulae to be inadequate. This conclusion will reassure all those whom MG's propositions have alarmed.'[46]

But there were no formulae, apart from the simple chi-square test, because the distributions were empirical. The Committee found itself unable to admit what it had found. Years of silence went by, until finally in 1976 they published in French a 17-page report - accusing MG of imaginary demographic errors.[47]

There was a general problem which the skeptics faced, in that using demographic effects one might *attempt* to account for a peak observed at a planet's rising position, but no way could that be done for two daily positions, at both rise and culmination – that required a different paradigm, so to speak.

The Para data-set is available, and thereby I obtained a higher score, 121 rather than 119[48,49]. The chance-expected frequency is

---

[46] Paul Couderc, *l'Astrologie* 1978 'Le Cas M.G.', English translation in MG, *the Truth About Astrology* p.104.
[47] Comité Para (1976). 'Considerations critiques sur une recherche faite par M. M.Gauquelin dans le domaine des influences planetaires'. *Nouvelles Brèves*, 43,327 (obtainable on demand from the Comité Para).
[48] Also for the 121 figure see Ertel, *Tenacious,* p. 20.
[49] The US sceptics averred the true score was here only 118, as 'both Gauquelin's and CFEPP's investigations showed that the birth data of the boxing champion Hippolyte Annex was wrong' (Kurtz & Nienhuys, JSE 1997, 11(1) p.37). But, the data given for this fellow by CFEPP of 3 am 14.7.33 in Penezas, France, was the same as given in the Gauquelins' sports-champion data-book.

probably best set somewhat lower, so one may give a 'corrected' Belgian result as:

<u>Corrected Belgian Committee Para result, for 535 sports champions</u>

Mars in KS for 121, Expect 92 => 32% excess of Mars in KS,

Chi-Square 9, p < 0.002 or one in five hundred.

That effect was, as one of their committee members noted, *stronger* than MG had obtained for sports champions.[50]

One can further divide their data-set into two halves, by separating earlier and later birthdata, say around the year 1920, which roughly divides it into half. The earlier data is highly significant, with a fifty percent excess,[51] while the later is insignificant. Much the same effect later turned up with the French skeptics data-set. Why this should happen may be a mystery, but that is does so argues for an internal consistency in the phenomenon.

Michel managed to generate a debate in the US journal *The Humanist* in that year 1976, which spilled over into *Leonardo*, and then the journal *Phenomena* chipped in. The US astronomer George Abell contributed to *The Humanist* debate. The US Sceptics had published their attack upon astrology the year before, and thereby found themselves being drawn in. Tests of the Gauquelin Mars-claim made by groups of sceptics in Belgium, the US and France were sequential, in that each followed on from the previous one. Each time we see Michel issuing the challenge, and then generating debate afterwards, thereby drawing matters on to the next stage.

We now go back a year or two, to that historic attack, which brought about the foundation of the US Sceptics.

THE CLASH

In September 1975 'Objections to Astrology' was published in *The Humanist*, and it had a worldwide impact. That famous manifesto,

---

[50] One Para committee member admitted this: '... the actual results of the 535-test were a confirmation (and even a small improvement!) of Mr. Gauquelin's previous results' - Piet Hein Hoebens, commenting on Patrick Curry's review in the *Zetetic Scholar*, 1982, 9, p.71.

[51] For pre-1920 CP (n=246), KS score 64 => Chi-Sq 11, highly significant.

signed by 180 Nobel-prize winning scientists, declared of astrology: 'there is no scientific foundation for its tenets.' Therefore, belief in it was contributing to 'the growth of irrationalism and obscurantism.' They had decided to 'challenge directly and forcibly the pretentious claims of astrological charlatans.' Bart Bok or Bartholemaeus Jan Bok to give him his proper name was the astronomer behind this initiative, and Paul Kurtz was the Editor of *The Humanist* which published it. "Objections" and its child CSICOP were both the creation of *The Humanist*'s then-editor Paul Kurtz. Let's quote from an interview with him by the Editor of *Phenomena, The Bulletin of Astrological News & Information,* Malcolm Dean:

> Phenomena: About two years ago now, you led a movement to publish a statement which was signed by nearly 200 scientists, philosophers...
>
> Kurtz: In 1975, it was mostly astronomers and astrophysicists.
>
> Phenomena: And this was entitled 'Objections to Astrology.' The press reaction was nothing short of incredible. You must have sent it to nearly every newspaper in North America and many in the world besides...
>
> Kurtz: ...*The Humanist* magazine sparked this new Committee for the Scientific Investigation of Claims of the Paranormal. I don't think you can investigate astrology out of context with, let us say, psychokinesis, UFO's, various monsters, and a whole range of exorcism, cults of the devil.'
>
> Phenomena: But surely astrologers argue that they are not necessarily connected with those other things?
>
> Kurtz: No, that's true, uh, though in our view, it seems to be a return to the mediaeval, pre-scientific work-view.[52]

Historically, it was surely the biggest attack upon astrology since Pico della Mirandola published his diatribe against the Royal Art in 1493. No wait, it was bigger ... [53]

---

[52] *Phenomena* (Toronto) March/April 1978 2.2 p.15.
[53] The September 1st launch-date saw an awesome stellar alignment, with Mars exactly opposite Neptune aligned with the fixed stars Antares and Aldebaran, two first-magnitude stars which exactly oppose each other in the heavens. As well as that, Mars and Neptune

Sceptics hit back

An article in that same issue of *The Humanist* by Lawrence Jerome cast a slur upon the Gauquelins' work (One gathers that scarcely any of the Nobel-prize winning scientists who put their name to *Objections* had perused this page). It averred: 'Moreover, statistics can be easily manipulated (consciously or unconsciously) to yield desired results; the statistical studies of the Gauquelins are a case in point.... an interesting case where totally fallacious results appear to be scientifically valid... as I have shown in a recent publication *(Leonardo* 1975, 8 p.270). Gauquelin has been improperly applying binomial probability statistics to his data...'[54] No binomial probability theory had been used by MG. After such calumny, *Humanist* editor Paul Kurtz soon had MG on the other end of the telephone, hinting at legal action unless he took steps to remedy the situation.

BIRTH OF THE SCEPTICS

In the aftermath of this great event, which was broadcast around the world, a meeting was held in Buffalo, N.Y., on April 30 and May 1, 1976, when 'The forces of antioccultism' as Dennis Rawlins described them met to found CSICOP, the 'Committee for Sceptical Investigation of Claims of the Paramormal'. Rawlins, a positional astronomy expert, made a 'Founders' Day speech' which 'contained enough good press copy and one-liners to get me selected for the nine-man ruling Council of CSICOP.' Its bold mission, he explained, was to battle pseudoscientific bunk. CSICOP promoted itself as a small and heroic band providing a steady buoy of rationality in a vast sea of public superstition.

For this group of godless atheistic materialists, gathered together to usher in the Brave New World of scientific rationality, psychology meant the rat-oriented conditioning of the behaviourist B.F.Skinner, and definitely not the archetypal soul-meanings that the Gauquelins

---

were *precisely* conjunct Jupiter and Mercury in the two natal charts of Kurtz and Bok - all within one degree. Can one imagine any better 'proof' of astrology? Astrologers eschew use of the fixed stars and so missed this ace card which Fate had dealt them. Mars-opposite-Neptune is an ideal symbol for an attack upon 'superstition' and the two stars Antares-Aldebaran have traditionally been associated with great conflicts. Mars transiting Bok's Jupiter-conjunct-Aldebaran had to be the ideal moment for lauching the big attack.

For an intelligent discussion of the event see Rob Hand, 'The Proper relationship of Astrology and Science,' 1989 online.

[54] Jerome, Astrology- Magic or Science? pp10-15 *The Humanist* Sept-Oct 1975.

were trying to rentroduce. Their heroes were American materialists such as Isaac Asimov and Carl Sagan. It was a follow-through to the massively successful 1973 *Humanist Manifesto* - 'No god will save us, we must save ourselves' - co-authored by the philosophy professor and editor of *The Humanist*, Paul Kurtz.

THE ZELEN TEST

Earlier in 1976, Kurtz approached Marvin Zelen the Harvard professor of Statistical Science. Gauquelin's reply to the Manifesto published by *The Humanist*[55] alluded to the Belgian Sceptics experiment. At this early stage of the debate, the skeptics were far from clear about how expected frequencies of Mars in Key Sectors were to be ascertained. In January of 1976 the statistician Marvin Zelen published an article about the Belgian result, suggesting how to clarify it.[56] He proposed that members of the US sceptics should select about three hundred cases of sports champions, and compare then with a much larger group of non-eminent sportsmen. That was soon done, and yielded the following result:

CSICOP Committee 1977 Result

303 sports champions had Mars in Key Sectors 66 times, expect 52 => 27% excess. Chi-square = 4, just about significant

For such a small number that was not bad. One would generally not recommend such a test with a sample of only three hundred. What here mattered however, was that both sides, the US Sceptics and the Gauquelins had agreed upon the selection.

That result emerged in the November/December 1977 issue of *The Humanist* as a test of the 'Mars Effect,' authored by the philosopher Paul Kurtz, statistician Marvin Zelen and astronomer George Abell, three founder-members of the newly-formed US Society of Sceptics. Soon it was called the KZA report. Their article falsely averred that a *negative result* had been found. Their deceptive logic started off by deleting the women from the group – nine female champions scoring three times in Key Sectors were removed, on the grounds that 'Our

---

[55] MG, *The Humanist*, 1976, September/October p.60.
[56] Zelen, *The Humanist*, Jan/Feb 1976, pp.32-33.

analysis shows no demonstrable effect for females.'[57] They then subdivided their group of champions into small lots, each of which was insignificant! Thereby they endeavoured to convince readers that 294 male sports champions scoring 63 Mars-in-Key-Sectors was insignificant. As John Anthony West rightly observed, 'the published report (*The Humanist,* Nov/Dec 1977) was couched in language designed to obscure and mislead.'[58]

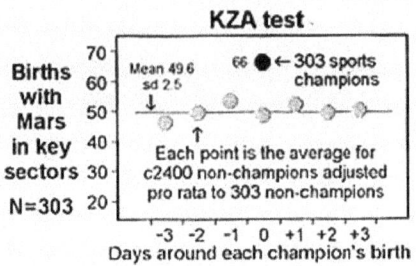

Figure: Dean & Smit depict the US Sceptics tests results (used with kind permission)

The number three hundred was selected and recommended by MG as being the bare-minimum size of a group for testing the effect – maybe, a bit too small – so clearly it could not bear further subdivision.

Their control-expected frequency came out as strangely low (see page 31). After Prof. Zelen had made his proposal, the two Gauquelins spent four months collecting sixteen thousand non-sports champions who were born within three days of the champion group.[59] In September they sent a copy of all the data to CSICOP. The computed Mars-KS scores are shown in the diagram. Overall, they generated an expected frequency of 16.4%[60] whereas they should, as Rawlins

---

[57] K-Z-A, 'The Mars Effect and the Zelen Test,' The Humanist, Nov / Dec 1977.
[58] JAWest, *The Case for Astrology* p.286.
[59] We are here short of details, but the Belgian Luc de Marré recalled how he assisted MG with the Zelen test, 'I spent days and days in the registries to gather hundreds of birth records' (*Zetetic Scholar*, 1982,9, p.72) which sounds reasonable, but hardly amounts to sixteen thousand. MG claimed that Owen Gingerich did spot-checks on 2000 of these non-champions and wrote him a letter of saying 'no discrepancy was found.' (SI 1983 KZA 7(3) 77-82.)
[60] Data given by M&F. Gauquelin, *The Humanist,* November 1977, p34; reviewed by Dean and Smit, AuS, 2013, p.110. In the diagram, 49.6/303 = 16.4. I'm disagreeing with Ken Irving that the expected value came out at 51.5 for n=303, or 17.0% (*Tenacious*, p.KI-18).

pointed out, have reached a value of 17.2%.[61] As we saw in Chapter Two, one-sixth of the total is 16.7%. Some years later, as the controversy rumbled on, the *improbability* of this *extra-low result* was reckoned at around one in three hundred.[62] One regrets that no-one checked at least some small fraction of this control-data to see if it was error-free. One regrets that the US Sceptics have kept no archival record of what they did. Throughout this debate, far too much has depended on just one or two people viz. the Gauquelins, and that is what (I suggest) has led to the discrediting of their marvellous discovery.

Rawlins, in his terse but lucid style, explained the 'Mars-dawn' effect as follows:

> 17.17- 2/12 = 0.5% is due to Gauquelin's careful accounting for the small astronomical-demographic influences inherent in the problem.[63]

Equally tersely, he indicated how the two Key Sectors had emerged from millennia of tradition:

> Traditionally (at least since Ptolemy's *Tetrabiblos*, 18 centuries ago), the two most significant points of astrologers' house divisions are the Ascendent ("*oroscopos*") and the Midheaven. The east bound of Gauquelin's sector 1 is the Ascendent, and the east bound of his sector 4 is the Midheaven.'[64]

We appreciate here the comment of a science historian, though inevitably a sceptic.

A follow-up was called for and the new Sceptics group decided to collect US champions. It tried to obtain champion sports data from US states, but most of them refused to provide such information, and only a paltry 128 lots of birth-data could be obtained. The Mars-excess there

---

[61] Rawlins, 'Report on US Test of the Gauquelins "Mars Effect"' SI, Winter 1979/80, pp.26-31, 26.
[62] J.Good, *The Zetetic Scholar*, 1982,9,p.65. Concerning the expected frequency: 'This percentage 17.17 was independently calculated astronomically both by Gauquelin and by Rawlins.'
[63] For readers foxed by Rawlins cryptic style: 2/12=1/6=16.66%, as the theoretically-expected KS frequency in the absence of any Mars-dawn effect, e.g. for the Moon.
[64] Rawlins SI Ibid, p.27.

was significant, however more were required. In the view of British psychologists Eysenck and Nias:

> Unfortunately, these extra cases included many sportsmen who were well below international class...The Gauquelins have pointed out that this test of their work was unfair because the required standards of sporting achievement were lowered too much in order to increase the sample.[65]

Dennis Rawlins, the only CSICOP founder-member who could do the astronomy, recalled that he received the first two of the three batches in July of 1978. A scandalous descending percent of KS scores through the three samples became evident. As the historian of this whole saga, Patrick Curry, commented:

> In this context, the dramatic drop in the Mars effect over the three sub-samples --from 19.5% to 12.5% to a significantly lower 7%-- may pose much less of a problem for Gauquelin (which prima facie it appears to do) than it adds to a host of reservations about Kurtz's sampling. (Similarly, almost amusingly, of the 83 names in the last "canvass," 54 are those of basketball players.)...

Rawlins in his graphic prose recalled how, in November he phoned through the initial results to CSICOP's chair and founder Professor Kurtz:

> At one point (after 120 names) I told him by phone (he preferred hearing the accumulated score instantly, without waiting the few days the mail took) that the key-sector score was now at 22 percent. [A too-high figure, see below] He groaned. l emphasized that the sample size was too small for the result to be statistically meaningful. He drew no comfort from this remark. l asked if he were sure that this was a clean sample. He was, so I assured him that the score was bound to revert to roughly 17 percent as the sample got larger -- unless astrological claims were true, which I certainly didn't believe.[66]

---

[65] ASS p199-200.
[66] Everything here is wrong. Rawlins has to be alluding to the first sample of 128, not 120, which reached 19.5% not 22%, and yes it was significant, just about. Nor was the score 'bound' to revert to the chance-expected level (assuming as Rawlins did that the

Nonetheless he continued speaking in a pained voice, as someone cursed with a demon that would not go away.

It seems rather strange that Rawlins could have given him or would have wanted to give him that assurance, of what did in the event happen.

Summarising,

<u>CSICOP Mars Test 1977</u>

	Total	KS	Mars
First sample -	128	25	19.5%
2nd sample -	197	24	12%
3rd sample -	83	6	7%
total:	408	55	13.5%

Expect 69.6 => Chi-square = 4, i.e. the *deficit* is just about significant.[67]

MG had earlier pointed out that basketball players as a group appeared not to show the Mars-effect. Overall, this replication obtained a significant *deficit*. Rawlins was convinced that Kurtz had not cheated, despite the fact that he was the only person on the committee responsible for the data-selection.[68] Kurtz's future career as America's top sceptic hinged upon his getting a negative result. Again we quote the historian of this drama, Patrick Curry:

> It seems fairly clear, therefore, that Kurtz and his assistants (F.Dolce and G Harnden) had sole control over the first, second and third selections, statements to the contrary notwithstanding.... The evidence is also, on balance, against there ever having been a prior agreement as to sources of data.

---

phenomenon did not exist) - that would only be the case for a much larger sample. The whole *sTarbaby* had a manic tone, whereas normally one would expect terse mathematical precision from Rawlins, in his studies of astronomical history. *Fate Magazine*, 1934.

[67] Patrick Curry: Rawlins as the CSICOP astronomer had found 'a Mars effect of 55 out of 408 or 13.5%.' ('Research on the Mars Effect' *The Zetetic Scholar*, 1983, p.39). The actual figures (opengauquelin.org) I compute be 72 out of 408 or 17.6% i.e. exactly chance level. That I believe is the largest error in the entire Gauquelin saga.

[68] D.R., 'Report on the US Test of the Gauquelins' "Mars Effect"' SI Winter 1979-80, p31: 'I more than anyone can vouch for the fact that Kurtz's selection was unbiased.'

In other words, Kurtz was under no constraints over selecting the data. Rawlins could do the astronomical calculations and had access to the astronomy programs.[69] It never dawned upon him that a simple astrology program would find Placidus houses which were probably just as good as the harder-to-find 'astronomical' divisions that Rawlins was able to ascertain (the 'Gauquelin-sectors').[70] Kurtz could get his 'sneak peek' quite cheaply, and no-one need ever know.[71]

Analyzing the new sample of 408 US Sportsmen, the Gauquelins found it to be largely comprised of medium-eminence champions but only 88 who were 'truly great.' They used US sports reference-sources the Lincoln Library of Sports Champions (used by KZA) and Olympic champions plus the the 1978 World Almanac and Book of Facts. Thereby they derived only the 88 from within in the CSICOP list, who gave quite a decent Mars in KS score.[72] The remaining CSICOP sportmen, they explained, differed from the famous champions by 'their incapacity to pull themselves up to the top rank in very important competitions.' They did not accept that *Who's Who?* (Who's Who in Boxing, etc) was a good enough source for defining champions: 'As we demonstrated, to be listed in a national *Who's Who* does not offer a sufficient standard for observing the Mars effect.'[73]

The debate spilled over into the *New Scientist*, where MG averred: 'The US test was done by Kurtz alone and in secrecy.'[74] MG was suspicious of the last of these three data-sets, which scored only 7% in KS, and he quoted Rawlins: 'No sooner was this task finished and the American test supposedly completed than Kurtz phoned me up and

---

[69] The finger of accusation here points at Paul Kurtz, not at astronomer Dennis Rawlins. Rawlins mistakenly assumed that Kurtz had no means of finding the Mars-sector scores, other than through the analysis which he (Rawlins) was providing.

[70] In the US data-sample, he noted: 'The sector 1 and 4 scores both represent sharp relative minima in relation to their adjacent sector-counts – the very opposite of the European findings.' (SI 1979 p.28) That was (I suggest) where Kurtz had removed the data.

[71] Kurtz defended himself against this accusation by averring that 'the records of that test are still available' but neglected to say where: JSE 1997,11,1,p.36. The archivist of CSICOP (at Amherst, NY) knows nothing of them.

[72] M&FG, 'Star U.S.Sportsmen Display the Mars Effect' *SI* winter 1979-80. p39.

[73] Ertel on CSICOP sample eminence: *SI,* Winter 1992, 16(2) 150-160.

[74] MG, *New Scientist* 7.1.82, p.40, letter 'Mars effect.'

said oops, we accidentally missed a lot of names...I returned to San Diego some weeks later. The last 72 names came in at summer's end.'[75]

After the fiddled data-selection, Kurtz needed to claim that the extremely low score found was 'not significant,' so he could walk away from it. A fiddled statistics test was necessary, as given in their 1979 report[76] – while in fact, as Ertel pointed out, their data was significantly negative![77] They had slyly taken the 1/6th value, or 16.6% as the chance-expected level, giving them a low chi-square value, however Rawlins had already gone into print saying that the value had to be higher than that owing to the 'Mars-Dawn' effect, and put it at 17.2%. That value will give a just-about-significant chi-square value, or at any rate one which cannot be described as insignificant.

In this 21st century the data is online at opengauquelin.org. The CSICOP group of 408 eminent US champions scores at chance level with Mars in Key Sectors 72 times, expect 71. Whereas, quoting US sceptic Paul Kurtz in 1997: "The American group was able to assemble a sample of 408 sports champions. The results were negative, with 55 (13.5%) of the sports champions born with Mars in the first and fourth sectors. With a null-hypothesis of 16.67% ..."[78] That is all far too low.

'DRINK THE KOOL-AID, DENNIS'

Years later, I became well-acquainted with Dennis Rawlins, as a brilliant but maverick US historian of ancient astronomy. I was then enjoying a safe perch in the History of Science department at UCL in London, and as such we would meet up at conferences now and then.[79] We would discuss the obscure topic of how Neptune was discovered. He once confided to me that he had his doubts about MG, but he did feel that Françoise 'had some integrity.'

---

[75] The last group has to be 83 not 72, Rawlins may have got muddled. All quotes are from his *sTarbaby* article.
[76] SI Winter 1979/80 p.25.
[77] Ertel, *Correlation* Winter 1999/2000,18(2): Debunking with Caution, p.17.
[78] Kurtz et. al., 'Is the Mars Effect Genuine? *JSE* 1997, 11,1, p.24.
[79] I published half a dozen academic papers on the discovery of Neptune, a theme I obtained from Rawlins, see dioi.org/kn/neptune/index.htm. Rawlins requested that my UCL academic history of science published articles be put onto his 'Dio' history of astronomy website, after I was ejected from my college UCL in 2008: dioi.org/kn/index.htm. He edited the journal *Dio*, which published an article of mine about the discovery of Neptune.

Sceptics hit back

He became entrapped by the situation, through being opposed to astrology, as an astronomer and founder-member of CSICOP. He could do the computations but wouldn't compromise himself by deception. The newly-formed US Sceptics Society ejected its only founder-member who had the required astronomy – and intellectual integrity.

He understood the 'Mars-dawn' effect, alluding to the degree of linkage of Mars diurnal frequencies with the solar day. We've earlier shown how this linkage is differentially linked to solar distance. It becomes acute for Mars and had to be resolved. As regards how difficult this problem then was, Figure 3 of Chapter Two shows an astonishing range over which the chance-expected Mars values were computed to be, by the three sceptic groups.

In the columns of *Leonardo* and *The Humanist*, a lively discussion on MG's Mars-Effect had been rumbling since 1973. We've seen how, in the year after *Objections*, the publication of some impressive positive results appeared, published by the Belgian Para Committee, and how the statistician Marvin Zelen proposed in *The Humanist* a test to try and settle this matter (Zelen 1976). Rawlins' comment upon the 1977 KZA *Humanist* article was:

> The KZA [Kurtz-Zelen-Abell] Control Test report appeared in November-December 1977 *Humanist*. It marked the beginning of the end of CSICOP's credibility - because it was at this point that the handling of the Gauquelin problem was transformed from mere bungling to deliberate cover-up.[80]

> In the KZA's November-December 1977 *Humanist* Control Test report, they tried to obscure the clear success Gauquelin had scored. The Control Test had entailed analyzing 16,756 nonchampions born near (in time and space) 303 champions (a subsample of the original 2088 champions). KZA had believed that they too would score at 22 percent in key sectors (I and 4) thus establishing that the champions' 22 percent hit-rate was "natural." Instead the nonchampions scored at exactly the chance - level (17

---

[80] Rawlins, 'sTarbaby', *Fate* magazine No. 34, October 1981, pp.67-98.

percent) that Gauquelin and I had predicted from our Mars/dawn-corrected expectation-curve analysis.

Quotes are from his *sTarbaby* article unless otherwise specified. Michel had challenged the skeptics, and as Rawlins recalled:

> In mid-April of 1978 Kurtz visited California and we saw quite a bit of each other. He couldn't stop talking about the Gauquelin business. In the middle of conversations on other matters he would grow silent and go back to discussing some possible "out." During this visit and subsequent phone conversations Kurtz tried out various schemes for getting off the hook. My favorite was the notion that Gauquelin fudged the nonchampions to force the score down to 17 percent.
>
> Hilarious.

Stress built up as Rawlins objected to the data-fiddling. 'I noticed that Randi was his usual friendly self when Kurtz wasn't around but when he was within earshot Randi made different noises. He repeatedly cracked loudly, "Drink the Kool-Aid, Dennis."' The dreadful Jonestown Kool-Aid mass suicide had just happened (November 1978). A year later Rawlins was booted off the council - or as Randi put it, he had been 'not re-elected.' In vain he objected, that no reasons had been given to him in writing for his ejection from the CSICOP Executive Council (December 15, 1979), or the SI editorial board (Spring 1980), or the Fellows (October 1980).

As a fervent skeptic, he just had not understood the necessity for cover-up.

Marcello Truzzi started a magazine *The Zetetic* and its first issue was dated Fall 1976. A couple of years later this morphed into the *Skeptical Inquirer*. He then fell out with CSICOP, because he wasn't a sufficiently tough sceptic, and started in 1978 another journal, *The Zetetic Scholar*. There was a major theoretical difference here, because the latter journal had an open-minded approach to borderland or 'psy-type' phenomena while the SI was simply a campaign to promote godless, materialistic atheism. It was part of a war against the human spirit in the name of science and rationalism, which is and has been massively successful.

Sceptics hit back

Rawlins had scruples about Truzzi being a card-carrying member of the Church of Satan, as well as being a personal friend of its founder Anton LaVey (author of *The Satanic Bible*). Truzzi averred that he had merely been doing 'field work' on the occult, which happened to include study of the Church of Satan. He was friends with Anton LaVey, but disagreed with "Anton LaVey's satanic philosophy." He claimed that his Church of Satan membership was 'just a joke': 'Dennis' wild statements alleging that I am a sort of Machiavellian Satanist border on the libellous,' Truzzi complained. But Rawlins didn't get why there should be "cult leaders and active promoters of the paranormal" on the Committee, and still less why they should remain on it after he had been booted off.

Astronomer George Abell (who has an asteroid named in his honour) turned out to be doing the math wrongly: "His computer analysis relied on an almanac provided by the U.S. Naval Observatory which listed Mars' celestial longitudes at a fixed interval, instead of using spherical trigonometry to convert Mars' positions to equatorial coordinates (as the Gauquelin experiment required)." This story was not about ecliptic longitudes.

> In 1975 and 1976 it was just a dumb, arrogant mistake by only three CSICOP Fellows. In 1977 it was their BS report, deliberate deception-cover-up. The next year, 1978, brought Kurtz's attempts first to bribe me and then (secretly) to eject me. The language of the original Control Test Challenge and subsequent testaments to its "definitive" nature had left no way around the fact that we had lost and Gauquelin had won.

You might suppose from the above that Rawlins was admitting that the Mars-effect really existed. However that was not and never would be his position. Astrology – and that included any version of 'neo-astrology' – eternally was and is the enemy of true astronomy, that was his Skeptic outlook. Thus,

> During all this Kurtz never took into account the depth of my reluctance to harm CSICOP, a movement I had cofounded with him. So to Kurtz's surprise and temporary relief I said nothing at the press conference and did not even raise my

hand to ask a question. Naively, I still had hopes for CSICOP -- shortly to be dashed forever.[81]

MG reported these events in the *New Scientist,* as follows:

> In 1968, the Belgian Committee for the Scientific Investigation of the Paranormal (Para Committee) to its surprise replicated the Mars effect on a new sample of 535 sports champions. Members of this committee selected the sample and did the computations. In its report the Para Committee unequivocally states, "The distribution of the actual frequencies of Mars is far from uniform; they display the same general pattern found by M.M. Gauquelin with samples of the other champions, the main characteristic being a clear predominance of Sector 1 (rising) above all the others. The Para Committee therefore gives its agreement on this point with the results of M.M. Gauquelin (Nouvelles Brèves, September 1976, p.331)." The two scientists who performed the test, the astronomer J. Dommanget and the statistician J. Dath, are both linked as scientific consultants of CSICOP.
>
> My computations for the Zelen test were checked on the request of CSICOP, by the astronomer Owen Gingerich, of Harvard University. The calculations of my own sample of athletes were checked by G.O.Abell, a CSICOP member and his collaborator Albert Lee in 1980. They not only verified the actual computation of Mars but also the calculation of the expected frequencies of Mars. They found all of them accurate. Moreover, Paul Kurtz himself visited my laboratory in 1977. He thoroughly controlled the objectivity of my original sample and the documents I received from the registry offices.[82]

That last remark was rather illegitimate - never had that been Kurtz's view. In a follow-up letter to the *New Scientist,* he denied that he had 'thoroughly controlled the objectivity of the selection of the original

---

[81] See Rawlins' brilliant and witty 'Astronomy vs Astrology: The Ancient Conflict' (*Queen's quarterly,* Winter 1984, 969-989), where astrology appears as 'Astronomy's dark-shadowy parasitic companion.'
[82] *New Scientist* 7.1.82, p.40, letter 'Mars effect;' follow-up letter from Kurtz 11.2.82.

sample,' while visiting Michel – all he had done was 'a few spot checks'. Kurtz always remained doubtful about how MG had selected his sports champions.

That letter may indicate to us the magnitude of MG's achievement. Owen Gingerich was America's best-known science historian, and had connections with the Harvard-Smithsonian Astrophysics department. He and Rawlins were (I suggest) America's best known astronomy historians, though Rawlins always remained outside Academe with his rebellious and independent temperament. With such prestigious people involved, one can only regret that nobody kept records. None of the sceptics have kept archive-records - and neither did the Gauquelins.

In 1982 CSICOP astronomer Abell wrote: 'To date, the only claims in favour of a Mars effect for athletes are based on data gathered by the Gauquelins themselves,'[83] an outrageous lie – he had to know of the Belgian Sceptics' report whose data had been gathered independently of MG.[84]

FINAL STATEMENT FROM BELGIUM

There appeared in 1982 a final comment from the Belgian Para group.[85] It appears as a psychotically unhinged comment, having an air of finality. First of all they claimed to have been the butt of 'personal antiscientific attacks' from MG – not very credible – then gave what was declared to be their final judgement:

> The controversy lies in the mathematical formula used by M. GAUQUELIN for computing the theoretical diagram and the one proposed by the Committee on the basis of a full analysis that has never been scientifically denied by anyone on any specific point. What make M. GAUQUELIN so reluctant since 1976 for any clear answer on such a simple point? Such an answer would certainly open the way for a new clear

---

[83] George Abell, *Psychology Today*, 16(7) 8-13. See *Tenacious*, p.A2-20. The CCICOP data (n=303) gathered by the US Sceptics was drawn from a pool of 'Gauquelin data' so would not here be included.

[84] More or less: 'The Belgian sample was mildly affected by Gauquelin who assisted the data collectors.' Ertel & Irving, JSE 2000 14,2 p.422.

[85] Committee PARA (1976b): 'The Committee Para replies to Gauquelin'. *The Humanist*, 36, 1,3 1.

dialogue! The Committee wishes to take this opportunity to state again that to its present knowledge, no other such full analysis (leading to a mathematical "model" of the problem) has been done by any other scientist.[86]

It's a nice pipedream, that some mathematical model would help to sort things out, but in fact the diurnal distribution of births is empirical, no formula will model it, still less the differential manner in which this bleeds through into the five different planetary-day frequencies - these just have to be randomly generated. The Belgian Comité Para were dreaming of some Wonderland, in which a beautiful formula 'would certainly open the way for a new clear dialogue!'

But remaining silent after a 'final' judgement isn't easy: years later in 1997 there appeared twenty pages of waffle on this topic, by Jean Dommanget, Chairman of Comité PARA. Its irrelevant math never hinted at the fact that a positive result had been obtained, just as predicted.[87]

NOT THE SCIENTIFIC METHOD

Why had the scientific method not worked, in any of this - not even remotely? We here remind ourselves of what it supposedly entails. It is only concerned with phenomena that are repeatable. Conditions have to be specified for when an effect can be observed, so that another laboratory can reproduce it. If that can't be done, then – *ce n'est pas la science*. Science concerns regular phenomena in the universe, i.e. it seeks for *laws*. A laboratory which reckons it has ascertained something will describe the conditions under which another lab can also detect it. If that other lab can do so, it will then be compelled to believe in the effect – unless its members can come up with some other explanation. Thus, science is about *public knowledge,* which can be shared.

To be repeatable, a scientific theory has to expose itself to 'the hazard of falsification' to use Sir Karl Popper's fine phrase. MG

---

[86] Committee PARA (1982). On the Mars effect: A last answer to M. Gauquelin. The Zetetic Scholar, 10,66
[87] 'The "Mars Effect" As Seen by the Committee PARA, *Journal of Scientific Exploration*, Vol. 11, No. 3, pp. 275-295.

wanted to do that, that was why he bothered to contact the sceptic groups. Scientific theories have to be testable, in a way that exposes them to being falsified. Otherwise they are not scientific theories but something else. In the history of science one finds the concept of *experimentum crucis* the crucial experiment, on which the success or failure of the theory will depend, and that distinguishes true from false. The proverbial bad guys were the ones who thought they knew the answer in advance - such as the fabled cardinals who refused to look down Galileo's telescope.

The scientific method involves scrutinising the evidence, and then deriving a testable theory *from* it. This has to be done *without* certainty – that's the hard bit - with an open mind, i.e. one capable of *doubt*. If one is certain of the answer beforehand, then one is not really putting a question to Mother Nature, by means of an experiment, or listening to the answer given. While testing a hypothesis, one is supposed to be prepared to change one's mind on the basis of new evidence. Generally speaking, the theory or hypothesis has to be in some degree mathematical.

The sceptics saw themselves as defending the citadel of Science and Rationalism, set up to combat Superstition (a Latin word meaning, that-which-stands-above). The test involved a planet in the sky, sectors of its diurnal arc, and excellence in a profession. A concept of 'supremely eminent' persons was at its core.

After these tests, did we hear anyone saying, 'O-Kay, I guess that settles it' or, 'Well we have to accept these results and admit that MG was right after all'? We surely did not. The nearest to that was probably the astronomer Abell's

> Gauquelin's findings represent an anomalous result that remains unconfirmed to the degree necessary to be accepted as scientific fact. (1979)[88]

It was hard to find anyone who professed themselves convinced by the new data, who had not been so before. The moral could be that drawn by John Anthony West, writing in 1991:

> The Gauquelin data, and the saga of the data, make up one of the more important scholarly episodes of the century. As

---

[88] Quoted in Eysenck & Nias, ASS p.208.

saga, told in detail, it reveals, perhaps better than any other single story, the true inquisitorial nature of the Church of Progress and the general level of disregard in which the search for truth is held by many eminent scientist and academics... without Gauquelin, there would be no point in insisting, as we do, that the fundamental premise of astrology now stands vindicated – according to the ground rules laid down by science itself.[89]

There was no forum in the world, where these experiments could be evaluated. *It could not be.*

What is the point, we may ask, of a sceptics group? They have a conference, and in the morning they look at a crashed-out UFO, or a picture of one, then they discuss say the Loch Ness monster, or maybe they discuss someone who has been having precognitive dreams, and so forth. Maybe the astronomers would discuss the Velikovsy theories (Venus crashed into the Earth ...). I never get what the point of this activity is supposed to be. People's religious beliefs are scoffed at of course, except for Judaism – don't go there, it might affect our funding. Nothing is learnt, nothing is discovered, but the axiom 'Science = materialist atheism' is promoted. What the Sceptics are allowed to be skeptical about has been and still is tightly controlled – but, let's not go into that.

Let's hear Françoise's opinion concerning one of the Sceptic-Society's conferences. This one, held at Ostende in 1994, was organized by Paul Kurtz:

> They offered non-stop detailed suggestions of how the Gauquelins might have artificially created groups of sports champions displaying non-existent Mars-effect.
>
> Actually creating *ex nihilo* as consistent results as the various Gauquelin professional effects would have been an incredibly complex feat. It was made all the more difficult by the fact that we had published all our sources, all the data extracted from them, the quite classical methods we had used for their analysis, and the results obtained. Therefore, although the CSICOP speakers had certainly carefully

---

[89] JA West, *The Case for Astrology*, p.233.

prepared their little demonstrations of how to cheat and trick in pseudo-science, their explanations were long, boring and completely unbelievable. Our procedure had been so much simpler than the contrived Machiavellian plots imagined by the CSICOP speakers that I had sometime a hard time repressing my hilarity.[90]

The sceptics had a commitment to a world-view that would have shocked any of the founders of modern science, prior to, say, the mid-19th century. "Science affirms that the human species is an emergence from natural evolutionary forces" declared the second Humanist Manifesto, written in 1973. Was this the future of America? 'With the de-Christianization of America has come the overthrow of the old moral order based on Judeo-Christian teachings and the establishment of the new moral order of the Humanist Manifesto' to quote a wise American.[91] There was a commitment to 'natural' or materialistic explanations. Michel was crushed by this juggernaut.

Scientia is the latin word meaning 'knowledge.' The equivalent Greek word is *gnosis*, knowledge: an 'agnostic' is someone who does not have that. *Gnosis* has come to mean more an inner knowledge, about the meaning of things, if perchance there is such, whereas *scientia* in our culture is a more external and material affair.

In Chapter Six we'll scrutinise the third and last of the sceptic groups with which MG was involved, and here again find the same phenomenon, of a decently positive result followed by a cover-up. Thereby we begin to appreciate the adjective on the Ertel & Irving book title: does there really exist a *Tenacious Mars-Effect*? In the meantime we look at Ertel's shocking intervention, which decisively altered the debate.

---

[90] Françoise Gauquelin, APP March 1995 (the last issue, NB), 'The Ostende Eurosceptics Conference,' p.4.
[91] 'Pat Buchanan, *The Death of the West*, 2002, p.189. For sceptic tomes by Dean, see Appendix 5.

5

ERTEL: DID MICHEL CHEAT?

Had they deceived us,
Or deceived themselves, the quiet-voiced elders?

T.S. Eliott, East Coker

'The case is already stronger than that for almost any area of research in psychology,' wrote the British psychologists Eysenck and Nias in 1982, concerning the Gauquelins' work, adding:

> Because Gauquelin has, all along, published full details of his research in a series of documents, it is possible to evaluate independently the design and methods used in the research. This we have done, and we have been unable to find anything seriously wrong. On the contrary, we have been impressed by the meticulous care...[1]

The 1980s were the great period of optimism in the Gauquelin work. Research journals sprung up, international conferences happened – at which the Gauquelins were normally the stars of the show - and academic psychology journals published positive-result reports on the subject.[2] The debate seethed on both sides of the Atlantic, in at least a couple of dozen different journals.

---

[1] Hans Eysenck & David Nias, *Astrology: Science or Superstition?* 1982 p.208. Eysenck had earlier made a similar affirmation in 'Planets, Stars & Personality', *New Behaviour*, 1975, p.246-9.

[2] There were four: Geoff Mayo, O. White and Hans Eysenck (1978) An empirical Study of the relation between astrological factors and personality *Jnl. Social Psychology*, 105, 229-236; Gauquelin, M& F. and Eysenck, S. B. G. (1979) 'Personality and position of the planets at birth: An empirical study *British Journal of Social and Clinical Psychology*, Vol:18: pp.71-75; Gauquelin, M& F. and Eysenck, S. B. G. (1981) 'Eysenck's personality analysis and position of the planets at birth: A replication on American subjects' *Personality and Individual Differences,* Vol 2(4) pp.346-350; Smithers and Cooper, 'Personality and Season of Birth', *Jnl. Soc. Psy.* 1987, 105, 237-241. They all concerned introversion-extraversion.

Nothing, it seemed, could stop the 'Mars Effect.' Michel had challenged the sceptics to replicate his results, they had done so and been caught trying to fiddle the data to cover-up their positive results.[3] As a champion tennis player Michel had slammed the ball back into their court! Hans Eysenck affirmed,

> Perhaps the time has come to state quite unequivocally that a new science is in the process of being born.[4]

So ... how did it all go wrong?

Later in 1988 the arch-skeptic Geoffrey Dean wrote an approving postscript to a review of the Gauquelin edifice, concluding optimistically, 'One looks forward to his autobiography.'[5] A new edition of West's *The Case for Astrology* appeared in 1991, portraying the Gauquelin findings as rock-solid, where those stubborn scientists who refused to acknowledge them were akin to the fabled cardinals who refused to peer down Galileo's telescope. What killed the great hope - why did Michel take his life?

ERTEL PAYS A VISIT

In the mid-1980s, Suitbert Ertel (1932-2017), a German psychology professor at Göttingen University psychology department came onto the scene. His learned-sounding articles brought an academic tone into the debate. His first English article concerned a procedure for grading champions by eminence: "Further grading of eminence. Planetary correlations with musicians, painters, writers."[6] It had the slightly obscure argument that Mars scoring negatively with musicians increased with their level of eminence. The next year saw "Planetary relations with female notabilities" *in Astro-Psychological Problems,* presented at the Third Eysenck Research Seminar in Astrology – the title of which indicates a degree of seriousness in approaching the subject which is today hard even to remember. That paper indicated some intriguing gender-difference in the data especially Mars - never alas followed up, which I think would help to

---

[3] See report by Patrick Curry, *Zetetic Scholar* 1982, 9: 'Research on the Mars Effect' (online).
[4] Eysenck and Nias, op. cit., p.209.
[5] Michel Gauquelin, *Written in the Stars,* Aquarian Press 1988, Dean postscript 191-5.
[6] Correlation 7(1), 1987.

generate more interest in the subject. Then a negative result that same year, with celestial aspects: "Relating planetary aspects to human birth: Improved method yields negative results."[7] Then, in a German journal, 'Gauquelin's planetary hypothesis. A bone of contention or a touchstone for reason?' (*Psychologische Rundschau* 1988, 39(4))

That was all rather impressive.

Figure: Suitbert Ertel, psychology professor at Göttingen university, 1971-1997; photo and painting.

His first article on the subject appeared in the prestigious German journal, *Zeitschrift fur Parapsychologie*, where Jung's Synchronicity article had first appeared. It was entitled '"Wisenchafftliche Qualitat und progressive Dynamik im Gauquelin Paradigms"[8] (which one might translate as, 'The quality of science-knowledge and dynamic progression of the Gauquelin paradigms'). Thirty pages long, it was immensely learned, with over eighty books and articles alluded to. It discussed different hypotheses such as temperament, heredity, geomagnetism, solar activity, trials by the sceptics and the suspicion of cheating. Ertel evidently had access to all the Gauquelin data-source volumes, which are now hard to find. The article looks like being the

---

[7] Correlation 8(1).
[8] S.E., *Zeitschrift fur Parapsychologie und Grenzgebiete der Psychologie* 1986, 28 104-35

fruit of years of careful study, but all he ever said about it in English was quite defensive: 'I myself needed the span from 1975 to 1985 to overcome my disgust on imagining that some jelly superstition might have been confirmed by exact statistics...'[9] - a scornful comment, indeed.

In that year he paid a visit the Gauquelin's 'laboratoire' in Rue Amyot, Paris:

> In 1986 I spent three days in Gauquelin's laboratory to document unpublished athletes data.'[10]

How pleased Michel must have felt, after all those years when he had yearned for academic recognition, as one who had no degrees after his name. At last, a German psychology professor had come to see him!

Soon after that he began work on an article which appeared in 1988, in the then little-known American *Journal of Scientific Exploration*. It alleged that he had performed an 'eminence-grading' of no less than 4,391 sports champions. This huge, enigmatic number of sports champions of known birth-data appears - more than twice as many as the Gauquelins ever claimed to have - that only he ever used.[11]

His first public address on the subject was given in the UK to the 5th International Astrological Research Conference in November 1986 and its transcript was published in *Correlation* of June 1987.[12] He followed that up the next year with a talk given to 6th annual meeting of the *Society for Scientific Exploration* in Austin, Texas, in May 1987 which was then published as 'Raising the Hurdle for the Athlete's Mars Effect' in the *Journal of Scientific Exploration,* 1988,2,1. It contained, politely expressed, the accusation of cheating.

That 1987 article alluded to the 1988 one as 'in press,' indicating that the later-published one was written first. So fairly soon after Ertel arrives on the scene, he is claiming to have (a) concluded MG was a cheat, (b) amassed his huge database that no-one else ever saw, and

---

[9] *The Tenacious Mars-Effect,* Ertel & Ken Irving 1996, p.v.
[10] Ibid, p.SE-17.
[11] But, MG endorsed this: 'he used birth data for all the sportsmen, both well-know and less well-known, which had been gathered ... both by me and by the American and Belgian Committees of Sceptics, totalling 4391 cases.' MG, *Written in the Stars,* 1988, p154.
[12] Ertel,, *Correlation,* 1987, 7(1) 'Further Grading of eminence: musicians, painters, writers,' pp.4-17.

(c) applied the eminence-grading procedure (first recommended by Eysenck in 1983) to that database with help of some psychology students, and (d) decided – which is what he is most known for – that this eminence-grading could resolve the problem which he had himself formulated, viz. that the Gauquelins had been cheating.

The 58-year old Michel seems not to have been especially concerned with Ertel copying out data during this visit, and he just let him get on with it. After returning home to Gottingen, Ertel averred that

> For one group of football players, Gauquelin gave this author permission to take the original index cards back to Gottingen University for manual transcription.

The Laboratoire of the Gauquelins in Rue Amyot, Paris, then comprised a room full of filing cabinets, containing cards. Each card had a name, birth data, source, and then the five planets with Placidus house-sectors. Michel proudly showed it to the present author back in the 1970s. It was understood that their work in compiling the data went through the sequence:

Finding the birth-data => putting it onto cards => publishing it.

Suitbert Ertel re-adjusted that perception for everyone by implying that, in their Laboratoire, they put the data onto cards – at which point it becomes evident whether the planets are in the Key Sectors or not – and then *decided* whether or not to publish them, and had in fact over a thousand athletes where such a *negative* judgement had been reached, in a corner somewhere. That was what he, Suitbert, had 'discovered' on his visit. The notion that the Gauquelins would agree to send such original cards to a German university, may strain our credulity.

Around the time of Ertel's visit, MG may have been preparing material for the *Written in the Stars* anthology which appeared in 1988. Its section, 'Not very well-known sportsmen' comprised a group of '717 less well-known sportsmen from the same period' as his champions: 'This group comprises 599 Italian footballers who played in first division championships but had never been selected to play in a national team,' etc, plus some other German sportsmen, for whom not enough data existed to decide whether or not they were champions.¹³ This group had no significant excess: Mars scored 124 times in key sectors instead of 121.2 times so there was no deficit in the score.¹⁴

Rather than showing some sort of furtive behaviour, in hiding away low-scoring data, this shows MG's integrity in publicising the fact that he had a group of lesser-eminence sportsmen. MG's definitions whereby he was able to distinguish between champions and mere professional athletes are fairly clear and support his argument that only the most eminent sportsmen, i.e. champions, showed his Mars-effect.

There remains an important sequence of seven articles in the *Journal of Scientific Exploration* by Ertel on the topic:

> 1988, 2,1 Raising the Hurdle for the Athletes' Mars Effect: Association Co-Varies With Eminence
>
> 1992, 6,3 The Gauquelin Effect Explained? Comments on Arno Mueller's Hypothesis of Planetary Correlations
>
> 1993, 7,2 Puzzling Eminence Effects Might Make Good Sense
>
> 1993, 7,3 Dutch Investigations of the Gauquelin Mars Effect
>
> 1997, 11,1 Is the "Mars Effect" Genuine? (with Ken Irving)
>
> 2000, 14,3 The Mars Effect Is Genuine: On Kurtz, Nienhuys, and Sandhu's Missing the Evidence (with Ken Irving)
>
> 2000, 14,3 Bulky Mars Effect Hard to Hide: Comment on Dommanget's Account of the Belgian Skeptics' Research

From the rather obscure title of that 1988 article, one would hardly gather that it featured a radical devaluation, if not indeed a de-legitimising of MG's previous work. Kudos will normally come to a tenured psychology professor for adopting a posture of scepticism towards the 'paranormal.' By this means he catapulted himself into a centre-stage position, in what was then an ongoing inter-continental debate.

Only once is Ertel known to have sought out primary-source birth-data, and that was for a replication of the French physicians' data

---

¹³ MG, *Written in the Stars*, 1988, p.113.
¹⁴ Compare this with the categories Ertel gave in JSE 1988, 2,1 pp.58-9.

where he collaborated with Arno Müller. So, where had all the new data come from? In this huge number he suddenly produced, there would be some of the Belgian sceptics data which he acquired as well as that which he found in MG's Laboratoire.

The implications of Ertel's 1988 article lay dormant for a few years, in fact until after Michel's suicide. The *Journal for Scientific Exploration* was then hardly known in Europe, and Ertel's obscure title 'Raising the hurdle...' helped to prevent anyone from noticing the dire accusation. The sceptics took up the theme within months of the tragic event: to quote the Dutch mathematician and sceptic Jan Nienhuys,

> I will repeat Koppeschaar's (1992) judgment: 'No conclusions should have been drawn after Ertel discovered selection bias in Gauquelin's data. That discovery should have been the end of the Gauquelin affair.[15]

Koppeschaar gave that presentation to a Eurosceptics conference in October of 1991.

We, in England, began to hear the awful accusations only after his suicide, and so wondered, was that why he had taken his life? Did it imply that the accusations were valid? And so it happened, that more or less all interest in astrology-research vanished from the world. Only in this century have faint glimmers started to re-emerge here and there.

The following judgement was made many years later, by the skeptic Paul Kurtz, president and co-founder of the US Humanist Society:

> Ertel discovered in Gauquelin's archives 1,503 champions whose birth times Gauquelin had requested but whose names and birth data he had not published. The Mars percentage among these was 14.77%, whereas among the total of 2,888 published champions it was 21.75%. The discovery of such a strong bias should have been reason to dismiss all of Gauquelin's data.[16]

Did that happen, or not? Yes the Key-sector Mars positions in the G-data did average 21.8% (see page 33 graph), compared to an expected

---

[15] Jan Nienhuys, Ertel's 'Mars Effect': Anatomy of a pseudo-science'
[16] Kurtz et al., 'Is the Mars-Effect Genuine? JSE, 1997 (11,1) p.31.

frequency of just over 17%. We surely agree with Kurtz, that if indeed 1503 lots of birthdata had been 'discovered' in the Laboratoire, unpublished, of low-eminence sport professionals (NB, not champions), and if it had such low scores, then that would be a reason to dismiss the enterprise. However, the 14.77% figure seems to have been plucked out of thin air, though Kurtz endeavours to confer credibility by giving it to two decimal places.

MG, who laboured all those years to construct some new science and who was one may concede rather egoistic and an outrageous male chauvinist in the way his wife was sidelined – now suddenly gets re-cast by Ertel as a total fraud at worst, or at best a bumbling incompetent who hardly knew what was going on in his own *Laboratoire*:

> Selection bias is more likely to enter if decisions to discard or not to discard individuals are made by someone who is aware of their Mars sectors at birth.[17]

This matter is in principle checkable, insofar as one can consult the data-sources given by the Gauquelins and re-find the data, which was done by Arno Müller as we'll see in Chapter Seven.

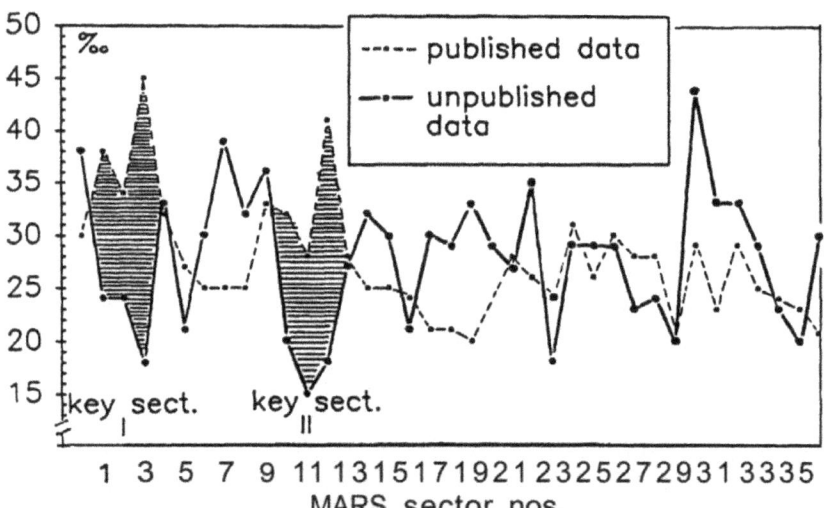

Fig. 5. Gauquelin bias effect: Mars sector frequencies ‰ for published Gauquelin athletes (N = 2888). dashed line; and for a subsample of unpublished athletes (N = 659). solid line. Marked negative deviations are apparent in key sector areas for unpublished data.

---

[17] Ertel, JSE 1988, 2,1,p.72.

Figure 1 – Ertel's shocking graph of published and unpublished sports data, showing Key Sector minima (1988).

In his 1988 article, Ertel explained how his grand total of 4,391 had come from adding 1503 'unpublished' to an alleged 'published Gauquelin athletes (n=2888)'. No-one had previously heard of this total – the figure usually given was 2,088. The graph, which did (I suggest) so much to delegitimise the life-work of MG, is here shown. A 36-fold division of the circle is here used, so Ertel's 'unpublished' group would have to be averaging merely 18 per sector, impossibly too small.[18] Not to quibble, but how come there are 37 points on this graph, 37 different values?

Suddenly, a new, furtive image of the Gauquelins made its appearance – or maybe just of Michel, as Françoise was by then separated from him. Shocking dips in the key sectors appeared using 'unpublished data', where peaks should be. Ertel would now and then scoff at the Gauquelins in this respect, in order to draw attention to his supposed resolution of the problem, eg in his book of 1996:

> Gauquelin had tended to discard his own mediocre sports people somewhat less strictly when they had Mars in the rising or culminating zone, the G% level of low achievers thus became inflated.[19]

Thereby the reputation of 'the world's most famous and formidable scientific researchers in astrology'[20] became pretty well extinguished, or at least it never recovered. Never could they pick themselves up off the floor again after that. They became yesterday's news. Their *virtu* passed over to Ertel, who now came onto centre-stage.

EMINENCE-GRADING

Ertel's eminence-grading procedure appeared in his very first articles, above-cited. The basic procedure had been proposed by Eysenck in 1983:

> It might be possible to arrive at some agreed conclusion by throwing together all the data collected by Gauquelin, the

---

[18] Tenths of % plotted, i.e. mean-expected value here is 100/36=2.8%.
[19] *The Tenacious Mars-Effect*, 1996, p. 19.
[20] Dean et al.,, *Astrology under Scrutiny*, 2014, p.89.

Belgian Para Committee, and the American group, and then getting an independent group of sportsmen and critics familiar with the various types of sports involved, to grade each sportsmen included as 'absolutely outstanding', outstanding' and less famous.'[21]

That could be problematic as champions of yesteryear might not be well remembered. Ertel had a better idea, of using various sports encyclopaedias. He found students to assist him and who are we to doubt that? One only wishes that one of them had left a record or a diary of this remarkable labour. Using an agreed-upon variety of sports encyclopaedias and reference-books, they counted how often the champs and athletes were cited in all of these, and thereby sort them into five categories – with the unpublished low-eminence cases being mainly in the first category. Had a dedicated team indeed done this for four thousand, three hundred champions from all over Europe? If so, they left no record.

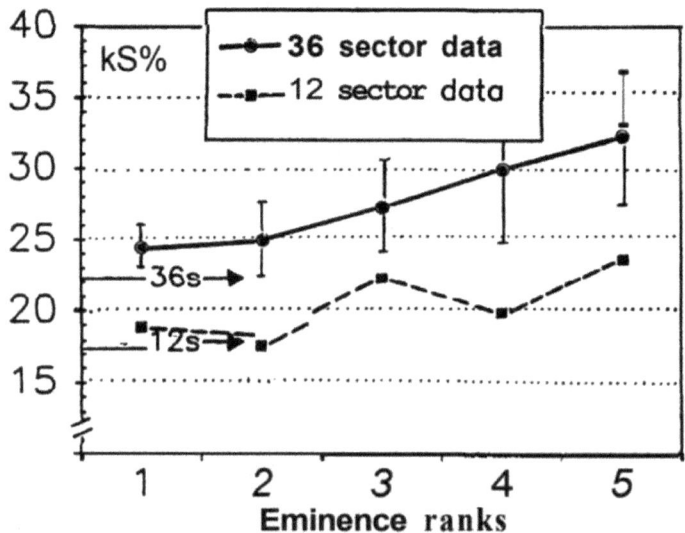

Graph: From Ertel 1988 JSE, showing sports data graded by eminence plotted by Mars in Key sectors, using both 12-fold and 36-fold divisions.[22]

---

[21] H J Eysenck. 'Methodological errors of Astrological claims', APP September 1983, p. 15.
[22] Ertel, JSE 1988 *op.cit.;* see also Ertel, 'Further Grading of Eminence' *Correlation* 1987,7, 4-17, Fig 1.

His grading procedure showed, he found, 'The regular increase of a Mars effect with fame determined objectively by using a great number of sources.'[23] Here is how Ertel expressed the matter in 1988:

> The present study incorporates the entire repertoire of birth data of athletes available to date (N = 4391) ... It is contended that this procedure is superior to Gauquelin's own; and that the predicted eminence function could hardly be expected to materialize in case his former results were due to biased data treatment.
>
> If Gauquelin had excluded those athletes whose birth hours did not match the kS [Key Sector] passages of Mars so as to obtain an eminence trend for KS%, the latter could hardly have emerged in the present instance. The reason is that all athletes whose data had originally been excluded from publication and/or analysis have now, too, become part of the study population."

It's not at once evident how his procedure would lend itself to statistical testing.

Year after year the Gauquelins kept coming to British conferences – Michel would talk about the Mars-effect to considerable tedium - but no-one ever asked them about this re-evaluation of what they had claimed to be doing. In retrospect, if only questions could have been asked then, surely this 'astro-psychological problem' could have been resolved.

CREATIVE NUMBERS?

The next year 1989 saw Ertel at a *Geo-Cosmic Relations* conference at Amsterdam, when I in the audience heard him hold forth about the huge total of 4,391 he had somehow acquired, and its grading by eminence-levels. Was not this real science, whereby he had obviated the arbitrary distinction between the top champions and other less-eminent persons? He used the 36-fold divisions, claiming that they worked better. He gave totals thus divided for the various professions, and we here compare them with those published by the Gauquelins:

---

[23] Ibid..

Ertel: did michel cheat?

Ertel's profession-Group totals, published in 1990[24]

	Sports	Actor	Mility	Mus	Paint	Writer	Pol	Sci+Phys
MG:	2088	1409	3046	1248	1472	1352	1002	3643
Ertel:	2440	1761	3942	977	1662	1669	1773	4712

Mysteriously, Ertel seems here to have acquired a lot more birthdata per professional group than ever did the Gauquelins. One can only regret that he did not share it with anyone or put it in an archive somewhere. No-one heard about him looking for birth-data (except for the above-mentioned study of physicians which he did together with Arno Müller). The Gauquelin professional-group totals remained fairly steady since Michel and Françoise published them in the 1970s, and are as given in eg his *Spheres of Destiny* (1980) or by Geoffrey Dean[25] and then in this 21st century on the CURA and opengauquelin websites.

There is usually some sort of back-story as regards how the Gauquelins totals were developed and where they came from, which may be hard to find (but N.B. there is one library where the main Gauquelin volumes are collected together, the Bibliothéque Nationale in Paris). To the military group, they added some aviators to give 3438, as shown on the CURA site. The total for musicians was reached by including 383 band leaders together with 866 eminent musicians, and one may prefer to separate these. Likewise the 1094 scientists and 2552 medical doctors were rather dubiously grouped together to give his big total of 3643. The Gauquelin's list of 1345 painters published in 1970 included 309 'famous' painters and 361 'obscure' painters, then finally their total for painters reached 1473. But, none of this will give us the totals that Ertel presented in 1990. We never hear where he got them from, on what program he analysed them, or who ever saw them.

The text of this presentation[26] alluded to the grand total of 4,391, however the data-analysis presented only showed 2,440 sports

---

[24] *Geo-Cosmic Relations, the Earth and its macro-environment* 1990 Ed Tomnassen et al., Ertel, *Gauquelin's Contentions Scrutinised*, pp.255-266, 265.
[25] Dean, *Tests of Astrology*, 2016, p.76 gives the same totals, but sensibly separates 1094 scientists and 2552 physicians, as likewise he did in his *Astrology Under Scrutiny* of 2014.
[26] Ertel, Ibid., 1990, pp.255-271.

champions. A year later – as he tells us in his only book, *The Tenacious Mars Effect* (which does not contain any data):

> <u>1991 Sept 23 Ertel to de Jager,</u> Ertel sends his sports champions data including Ertel's citation counts for eminence assessment. This diskette contains sports champions data with birth hours as you requested. The number is 2,440.

His data now appears on a disc, sent to the sceptic astronomer Cornelis de Jager, with the same total. That is clearly the published Gauquelin total of 2088 plus an extra 332 from the Belgian para committee.[27] He had access to the latter through his academic position.

These 322 from the Belgian Para committee had earlier featured in Ertel's group of 1502 'unpublished' sports data, described in his 1988 JSE article. We saw earlier in Chapter Three how this data was significant and positive: published in 1982 in the *Zetetic Scholar* by MG it showed a 26% excess of Mars in Key Sectors reported (though I, checking the data-set, found a somewhat higher effect, viz 32%). None of this will help us to appreciate how Ertel could claim to have found a large group of negative-scoring-for-Mars sportsmen birthdata.

In the last year of Suitbert Ertel's life, I was constructing a 'Gauquelin database,' at newalchemypress.com/gauquelin/. I wrote asking him - not having any of the dark suspicions here expressed - if he had any data-sets from his life's work on the subject, which I might post up? In particular, could he send the complete data set of 4,391 sports champions? He kindly did this and I posted it up.[28] I then failed to notice that *half of the birth-times were missing*. That was only pointed out to me after his passing. Readers may wish to check, by visiting the above site, going to Chapter 3 'The Ertel Enigma,' scrolling down to 'main data collection' and sorting it by the 'stund' column (hour). Precisely 2088 lots of complete birth-data are thereby obtained. That is

---

[27] The total used for the Belgian Para committee was 535, but Ertel explained how some of these overlapped with the Gauquelin data, so there were 332 new ones: Ertel 1988, JSE pp.59, 60.
[28] newalchemypress.com/gauquelin/research3.php: click on the top line to obtain an Excel spreadsheet; or, right-click and 'save as,' copy into a text file, save it, then re-open into a spreadsheet file.

the original Gauquelin-published list (more or less – about half a dozen were different) - all the others are untimed, i.e. worthless.

The data has no latitude and longitude co-ordinates anywhere, only names of towns, indicating that it was never used for calculation.[29]

I discussed the matter with Ken Irving who knew most of the people involved, being co-author of the book *The Tenacious Mars Effect* with Ertel. Concerning this Ertel database he stated: "I'm familiar with the data, as I have a copy. Birth times are missing on most if not all of the unpublished athletes, Michel's controls, because this is the way they were recorded in his card files." A shame he couldn't have said that in his book.

The account I had given in my 2005 essay 'How Ertel rescued the Gauquelin effect' (online) was so wrong! That article had fully believed Ertel and described what all of us then felt, concerning the implosion of credibility in Michel's work as having lead presumably to his suicide. After discussing the matter with Graham Douglas[30] it was agreed that (a) no-one had ever seen this Ertel data, or indeed any other Ertel data, and (b) one of us should write to his son, Christian, to ask if perchance he knew of any possible location for data used in his fathers' work? I did so and as a result some megabytes of his work are now with the UK Astrological Association's library. I believe this cache does not contain data, only graphs.

As a result I came to appreciate the fundamental contrast between Ertel and the Gauquelins: the latter had published *all* of their source-data, while Ertel had published *none* - what he worked with remains simply a mystery. No-one will say they saw it.

There is no evidence, apart from his say-so, that Ertel ever had more sports champion data than that published by the Gauquelins. He assumed a posture of detached objectivity and judgement while destroying the hard-won reputation of the Gauquelins. Michel yearned for support from a tenured university psychology professor, but would he not have been better off if he never met Ertel? We today

---

[29] This data-set has been reposted onto the OpenGauquelin site as '1988 Suitbert Ertel 4384 athletes – Complete group' with latitude and longitudes added.

[30] G.D is the only other member of our AIR group of the 1980s (Astrologers in Research) who still has a focus on the subject.

are left wondering, now that the great debates are over, what data really existed?

Here is the experience of one European researcher who contacted Ertel, two decades ago:

> J.R.: I should add that I had a peculiar experience with Suitbert Ertel over 20 years ago. I asked him to send me the birth data of couples from some volumes of Gauquelin's Heredity study that I did not have. Ertel was so kind to send me a disk with the digital birth data of all the volumes as well as the paper volumes that I did not possess. To my surprise I found that about one third of the digital birth times were wrong! It seemed as if somebody had just entered random birth times in the file. When I asked Ertel about this he replied that a secretary had entered these data and that apparently she had made errors.

One could compare the reply I received, when asking him why there was no longitude-latitude data on the 4,391 sports-champion data-set he had sent me: "I had asked my assistant to copy birth data from various Gauquelin's publications. I did not recalculate planetary positions so longitude and latitude of birth places were not needed." His data had been copied from Gauquelin publications, and didn't need the spatial co-ordinates because it was not to be used for calculation.

I checked the eminence-grading procedure, using the data he sent me.[31] His rankings 1 and 2 gave a score of 21.5% (of Mars in Key sectors) while rankings 3,4 and 5 scored 22.3%. That is a less than 1% difference. Did the *Journal for Scientific Exploration* really accept an article based on this? The grading groups are of very unequal size, with the most eminent (grade 5) ten times smaller than grade 1. The top two sectors are too small to derive from them any reliable % value, as Ertel did in his oft-reproduced graph (see page 109). If we instead use the 36-fold division, then rankings 1 and 2 give 26.2%, (expected 22.6%) while rankings 3, 4 and 5 score 27.7% - that is still only around 1% difference (with the last three groups comprising about one-

---

[31] After obtaining the data-set as described in footnote 10, sort by the column 'stund' (hour) to obtain the 2088, then sort by the column 'zitrang' the eminence-grading 1-5; then score for Mars-sectors, column 'MA12.'

quarter of the total). That is a very slender basis for going into print with a series of articles.³²

If we wish to compare the Mars-scores for differences in eminence-level amongst the sports champions, I suggest that we should keep the group sizes to an arbitrary minimum of four hundred, and that will give us the three groups as shown. Ertel used small size 4 & 5 groups, both scoring around a hundred, unduly small to meaningfully estimate a % excess in two Key Sectors. Over half of the group are 'non-eminent' using Ertel's definition, viz they did not score in the selected standard reference-books, and this is his category number one. That bottom group is still scoring above chance-level - thus we have no hint of the strange concept Ertel came out with, of a group of low-eminence sportsmen scoring negatively.

Eminence Level	Emin-ence 'rank'	No.in grp.	% of total	MA in K.S. score 12 sect	MA in K.S. score 36 sect.
No citns	1	1161	56%	247 => 21.3%	314 => 27.1
1 citn	2	437	21%	98 => 22.4%	125 => 28.7
2+ citns	3 +	490	24%	113 => 22.9%	139 => 28.4

<u>Table:</u> showing Mars-effect strength vs Ertel's eminence levels for the 2,088 champions

The tiny differences in Key Sector scores hardly resemble those plotted by Ertel on his often-reproduced graph. Maybe we can now appreciate why the Gauquelins did not want to use the eminence-grading procedure.

The timed birthdata which he sent me has over half, 56%, scoring at the bottom level of eminence with no citations, whereas the large group which he published in the JSE in 1988 had just 51% in this grade. If the very large group was formed by adding low-eminence sportsmen to the Gauquelin data – and that is what he told us – then it ought to have a larger proportion in the bottom grade, not less. Nothing is here adding up.

---

³² In 2023 the opengauquelin .org website posted a similar 'complete list' of Ertel's sports champions. It too contained merely 2088 timed data-sets, and also had the eminence grading 1-6: I found that grades 4, 5 & 6 (n= 364) had a 26% KS excess while grade 1 (n=1291) had a 14% excess.

Our position has to be defined by the axiom, 'Only that data exists, which can be shown to exist.' The word 'data' means, 'that which has been given' (Latin) - it has to have been given to be data! We have no wish to judge personalities, only to ascertain what data is reliable. But, having said that, M.G. emerges unscathed from our re-evaluation, and unjustly maligned, while Ertel's work is looking very doubtful. Science is public knowledge, it is about what can be shared and is a procedure for making statements that can be checked by others.

Supposing we try to believe that Ertel really had persuaded his students to grade over four thousand sports champions – for which he had birth-data - by looking each one up in several standard reference-books. We are told that 'Ertel collected typically 15 biographicaL reference sources for each profession',[33] which sounds like maybe sixty thousand lots of reference-checking - and with no record having been kept? Surely, a volume would then have been published - somewhat as Arno Müller self-published his *Astro-Forschungs Daten* summarising all the work - stating in which reference-work each sports champion was cited, plus preferably birth-data and source. There would only need to be one or two such volumes, maybe stored in the basement of a library in Göttingen somewhere, but the point is that anyone could in principle come along and check it – spending a week maybe checking just one letter of the alphabet. Thus the concept of verifiability would be present. That is what science is all about, and what is here so completely lacking.

We are here perplexed, at the notion that at least half of the Gauquelin sports champions did not feature in any of Ertel's designated reference-books. That is only one reason as to why we wish he had left somewhere a record, of the sportsmen in his database plus the reference-books in which they featured.

The present defence or vindication of MG has alas involved casting some degree of doubt upon the methodology of Professor Suitbert Ertel (which I had not at all expected). He worked in a liminal zone where his university psychology department would not want to know much about what he did because it was 'astrology' while the small band of astro-researchers would tend to assume he had really done everything he said he had done, because he was at a university. He

---

[33] Dean et al.,, *Astrology Under Scrutiny*, 2013, p.105.

published prolifically on the subject, more than anyone else except the Gauquelins. It was the main thing he did or that he was known for in his life. But the approach of the present work involves ascertaining what reliable data is actually available. The fringe and possibly 'paranormal' nature of the topic means that we simply cannot take anyone's word.

It was only after his passing that I came to doubt his claims, for example that he had a team of psychology students who would assist with his eminence-grading. The nearest we have to someone who worked with him, is the German psychologist Arno Müller, and it is only because of his careful, methodical reporting that we do at least have the Ertel-Müller report on the physicians data that is reliable, almost the one totally valid replication of MG's work (See next chapter). But I remain extremely suspicious of what happened in 1986 when Ertel suddenly came upon the scene, suddenly started giving talks and publishing papers, suddenly accused Michel of fraud based on what he Ertel had seen in MG's laboratoire, and suddenly had a far larger group of sports champions than anyone else had ever seen …. which he did not however show anyone. How is it possible that we did not ask him about this, in our yearly conferences? I can only give a personal answer to this, that the meaning and impact of the accusation of fraud only developed *after* MG's suicide, and none of us even saw the then little-known *Journal of Scientific Exploration* with his 1988 article in it, before that.

While the great debates were raging over his integrity, sadly compounded by his suicide, Françoise remained silent. Only in the very last issue of her journal APP did she allow herself this comment:

> I knew how sincerely MG had striven, during all his life, to carry out his research projects with impeccable objectivity… The separation of our personal life and research projects had allowed me also to witness how exaggeratedly sure of himself MG had become…I was quite upset when, after MG's demise, Suitbert Ertel started writing articles presenting my ex-husband more and more definitely as an unreliable cheater, and simultaneously me too because I had been his collaborator. I was not sure that MG had been completely objective up to the very end of his collaboration with SE. But I was sure that he had maintained a high

standard of scientific honesty during our thirty years of collaboration.[34]

There is an implication here that her husband had been unwise in collaborating with Ertel. As well as implying they had cheated, he also expressed scepticism towards both their character-trait method and their 'heredity effect.' In one of these he was correct as we shall see - but not the other! Ertel basically dismissed their life-work except only for what could be shown using his eminence-gradation procedure!

---

[34] APP September 1994 p.27.

6

FRENCH SCEPTICS SEE THE MARS EFFECT

OR, HOW TO DRIVE A GOOD MAN TO SUICIDE

And that the field of battle should be Mars – what a symbol for astrology![1]

Michel Gauquelin, 1983

By the year 1996 the French group of sceptics could not any longer delay publishing their *The "Mars Effect" A French test of over 1000 Sports Champions*, a project they had begun working on since 1982. Its opening words were:

> The CFEPP has concluded a study based on more than a thousand athletes in order to assess Michel Gauquelin's "neo-astrological" theory. This study does not support Gauquelin's theory and it shows no evidence of any influence whatsoever of Mars on the birth of athletes.

A conclusion normally appears at the end of a study, not in the first paragraph. In case one had any doubt, Jan Nienhuys, editor of *Scepter* the magazine for Dutch skeptics, from the Department of Mathematics and Computing Science, Eindhoven University of Technology, added a final section in this booklet which concluded:

> But the whole point of this laborious exercise was to find out what remains of the Mars Effect when one starts entirely from scratch, without the help of Gauquelin, and the answer is: nothing. The CFEPP is therefore correct in its conclusion that the French test of over a thousand champions shows no evidence for the Mars effect (Ibid, p145).

---

[1] MG, *The Truth about Astrology* 1983, p.114.

This impartial survey was published by Prometheus Books, an aggressively materialistic US Sceptics imprint founded by the philosophy Professor Paul Kurtz (1925-2012), the 'father of secular humanism.' In an Intro by him, readers were briefed on how Suitbert Ertel and Michel Gauquelin had gone wrong - in case we needed more guidance.

It may hardly seem worthwhile bothering with the subject after so firm a rejection by such grave authorities. However, we here add some cautious remarks.

Soon after the group of French skeptics (*Comité Francais pour l'Etude des Phénomènes Paranormaux* or CFEPP) was founded in 1979, its secretary wrote an article for *Science et Vie* in 1981, gloating over how the so-called 'Mars effect' had been demolished by the US Sceptics: 'sportsmen no more have Mars than Neptune at the ascendent.'[2] It impugned MG's integrity, averring that he had 'skill in fitting up graphs,' and that the Belgian sceptics trial had shown nothing. MG was allowed no reply.

But Michel happened to know the editor of *Science et Vie*, being a regular contributor. He managed a deal whereby French skeptics would perform their own test. MG drew up what he called 'an extremely precise six-page statement' for the experiment – an unduly dogmatic text, as we'll see - and sent it to CFEPP.

---

[2] Michel Rouzé, Effet Mars: la néo-astrologie en échec' *Science et Vie*, (March 1981 pp.39-45.

AN IMPOSSIBLE PROTOCOL

That Protocol for the experiment was published in *Science et Vie* of October, 1982. MG there laid down exactly what the French skeptics had to do, to test for his Mars effect. It opened with the dogmatic statement:

> Since planetary effects are observable only for births that are entirely natural, the champions chosen must be born before 1950, when the practice of inducing labour (and cesarians) began to be more common.

The scientific method, we remind ourselves, is not about following somebody else's instructions. The above view could be a conclusion which the French skeptics might want to drew from their data - but it was wrong for them to be given it, as if it were some sort of instruction. If they eventually found a Mars-effect in their data, then they could be invited to ascertain whether or not it faded away at any point in time, eg around 1950.

The Gauquelins took the view that the effect had faded away in the mid-20th century because artificial induction of birth was then becoming common, whereas on the sceptics' view, it faded away as more exact and reliable timing of birth became available.[3] It was hardly MG's brief to direct the skeptics as to which of these interpretations, if either, they should endorse.

The next paragraph affirmed that the champions selected 'must be of supreme eminence,' which is fair enough and is very much the crux of the matter. However that was followed by some contentious and irrelevant theorizing by MG:

> The Mars effect observed among these champions would, in fact, be only the residue of a true correlation between, not the planet and the profession, but rather between the planet and the principal personality traits. These latter traits would be manifested more clearly among athletes who succeed the most.

---

[3] The latter view has been advocated by Geoffrey Dean, see eg 5.1.02, 'Is the Mars Effect a Social Effect?'

What business did he have, to thrust his opinion onto a committee of sceptics, trying to present it as if it were some kind of fact? Not many people were ever convinced by MG's character-traits 'explanation', and it had no business being in an experimental protocol. What this paragraph really needed, was some hint as regards how 'supreme eminence' could be recognized and located – for example, using reference-source citations. Later that decade, the German psychologist Suitbert Ertel would resolve this issue by his eminence-grading procedure, of scoring the number of citations in major international sports-reference-books.

The next paragraph averred that the criteria defining the group of 'great champions' was to be established 'by a commission of sports specialists, notably journalists.' Why would journalists know what the criteria should be for defining 'great champions'? Would they even be interested? The CFEPP report describes how sports journalists were approached but declined to be involved. CFEPP thereby started off with an abortive attempt to define supreme eminence in the world of sport. Over a thousand birthdates of such eminent persons had to be gathered, using sports annuals and a sports dictionary.

It was next specified that the control-expected frequencies had to be gathered by collating birthtimes of non-eminent sportsmen, ten times more than for the actual group – ten thousand non eminent birthtimes had to be gathered! That would take years of work, and what was the point? Why not just shuffle the birthdates around in the group one has, by altering years, months etc? Impossibly difficult conditions were laid down, whereby longitudes and dates of birth for this control group had to be similar to the champions,[4] i.e. they had to live nearby.

Then 'Once the definitive list is established, no champion may be eliminated before the experiment for any reason whatsoever.' But, the process of gathering such a group ought to be subject to error-correction, if and when the birth-data turns out to be unreliable. The process of finding the champions may be final and irrevocable, especially once they have been 'scored' i.e. the Mars-position

---

[4] In the event and despite this Protocol, the control group was obtained (allegedly) by such a shuffling procedure.

ascertained: however the corrections and improvement of the birthdata should be a continuous, ongoing process.

An exact outline of the chi-square test that 'will be used' then follows, and again this was rather impertinent: it should have been up to the French Sceptics to determine what statistical test they deemed appropriate in the circumstances. The chi-squared test has the disadvantage of requiring an exact value for the 'expected' frequency (of the sum of the two Key Sectors) whereas that is more in the nature of a cloud of probability, for which estimates will normally lie between 17%-17.5% of the total.

The Protocol concludes by saying, 'the CFEPP will inform M. Gauquelin about the successive stages of the experiment as they are completed... the CFEPP will gladly welcome any observations from M. Gauquelin and will endeavour to take them into account' – why would they want to do that? They should notify him, as well as everyone else, once it was complete. If this was supposed to be an independent test then it should not need his guidance at every step, as the Protocol implied. This is an impertinent condition whereby MG is being allowed to interfere whenever he wishes. It then adds, 'It goes without saying that M. Gauquelin will be free to use, as he sees fit, the data that will be communicated to him.' (Appendix 1, Benski Report, pp.43-45) One is startled that anyone could have wanted to comply with such a document.

We never hear anything from its Seven Silent Authors. Only for the first of them, a M. Claude Benski, do we gather, from a letter by MG of February 1991, that he visited Paris for the purpose of checking data in MG's archives, where it had seemed to diverge from the data CFEPP had obtained from registry offices.[5] Why would he have wanted to do that? Surely the CFEPP report was supposed to be independent, using data verified independently of MG's archive? The explanations we later heard about the project, in various debating-forums, came from one man, Jan Nienhuys.

Once this Protocol was published, the enterprise was I suggest doomed. Its conditions were the antithesis of the scientific method, prohibiting independent initiative by the Authors of this study. Sadly

---

[5] Claude Benski et. al., *The "Mars Effect," A French Test of over 1000 Sports Champions*, 1996, p.91.

stillborn, the project hung suspended for years in paralysis, only appearing in print once the Gauquelins were gone. Much of the thirty pages of the Report which appeared in 1996 comprised letters from MG. There was some discussion of French time-zones.

WHAT SIZE WAS THE GROUP?

As to how many sports champions with reliable birth-data were eventually selected by CFEPP, one might expect that this would be a fairly straightforward question, but alas it remained shrouded in mystery. Of two letters from MG reproduced in the Benski report, the first stated:

> As agreed, you will find a check list of dates, times, and places worked out for your list of 1430 athletes. The resulting check list is probably not complete – certain verification will be made in Paris – but it is already substantial. (6.12.90)

This indicates that for a list of 1430 champions list they had dates, times and places. A couple of weeks later, a CFEPP 'Technical Report' 'Vérification de l'effect de Mars' appeared which described the method but gave no data analysis, and it had an Appendix where 'birth dates/times/hours/ places of 1439 sportsmen listed in in the *Dictionnaire des Sports* or *L'Athlege* or in both sources'[6] were given. Next year MG wrote again:

> You will read that ultimately I propose only very minimal change to your initial list of 1439 sports champions…As soon as the list is completed and corrected, and is considered as definitive by the CFEPP, please make a copy for me. (7.2.91)

The Appendix 4 of the Benski report entitled, 'List of the 1439 French athletes retained by the CFEPP' did not give that list as such, but did have several pages of extra birthdata of sports champions, including 73 'cases for which Neither the CFEPP nor MG has been able to obtain information.' One might here infer, that out of this list of 1439, 73 had no reliable birth-data.

After that, we are startled to read in the account of the experiment: 'birth records were complete – and therefore usable – for 1066

---

[6] Ertel & Irving, *The Tenacious Mars-Effect* 1996, p.A3-3, 'Chronology' for 20.6.90. NB I haven't seen this.

champions,' a list which was given in Appendix 3. What, we may wonder, happened to the 1439-1066 = 373 of these cases? The two Gauquelin letters give us no clue. Was their birth-data not sufficiently eminent?

Or, were they too eminent?

Psychology professor Ertel grappled with this enigma (and this was prior to the publication of the CFEPP report, which had been hanging around for years): 'The original sample size was 1439, the workable sample size after obtaining birth times from the offices was 1076. The total of misses is N=363. For 130 of 363 missing CFEPP data complete information is provided in Gauquelin's published lists. Why is this data of 363 athletes missing?' He reckoned there was an 'association between high eminence and missing data,' plus a bias 'towards disfavouring the eminence demand.' His eminence-grading method showed that 'The CFEPP had included N=397 mediocre athletes.' Nonetheless, in conclusion, 'The CFEPP's preference for low eminence athletes apparently did not remove the Mars effect'[7]

There is a mystery about the 'Seven Silent Authors' of this book, who never speak, comment, or get heard.[8] They performed the chi-squared test with the aid of 'the Systat software system.' (p26) They needed a software package to perform a chi-square test??

At the end of the Benski Report, the Dutch skeptic Jan Nienhuys added a forty-page 'commentary' - longer than the CFEPP Report. One might have supposed that seven authors were sufficient to say whatever needed to be said, especially after spending some fourteen years on the project. Presumably being a colleague of Paul Kurtz the publisher Nienhuys was invited to add this. This commentary accepts that final CFEPP total. Kurtz' Intro explained:

> After receiving the French study, *Prometheus Books* asked Jan Willem Nienhuys to review it. He spoke to the principal French investigators, visited France, and sifted through all of the original data to see if there were any discrepancies.

---

[7] Ibid, 1996, SE- 35-37.
[8] 'Like the other two skeptic groups, they [the CFEPP] behaved less like scientists and more like a secret society with an agenda.' AuS, p.113.

He found that the French research committee had inadvertently made a few errors, which he corrected. However, Nienhuys observes that these did not change the results, nor the conclusion of their study.

This French survey reached a much too-high 'control-expected' value. From permutations of the original group, they generated a control group of 85,820, from which they somehow found a Mars KS score of 18.2% of the total (see page 32). That is a valid way of making a control group, but such a too-high value could not have been reached by any such method. Nienhuys here felt at liberty to comment upon the incompetence of the authors:

> Even after the book was published, I found some errors. The most intractable error was CFEPP's miscalculation of the base rate (they had 18.20 percent instead of 17.70 percent). A suboptimal placement of a single instruction in their backup randomization program had slowed the speed of convergence.[9]

We are here concerned not merely with 'some errors' but with a blunder which invalidated the book's conclusion. If he is trying to tell us that the randomization program they were using had a fault whereby it mysteriously generated too many Mars-in-key-sector birthcharts –and that is what he is trying to tell us – then we would have liked some more details.

The book ends with Nienhuys scoffing: 'Ertels' *post hoc* analyses are rather like tea-leaf readings and he had not understood the scientific value of the CFEPP's experiments at all.' We happily admit that a Mars-debate should boil over with anger, but the question of how the eminent or sub-eminent cases were selected still remains.

Three years after the book was published, we again heard from Nienhuys who this time had a different group total.[10,11] Again he harps

---

[9] Jan Nienhuys, http://skepsis.nl/mars.html SI, 'The Mars Effect in Retrospect' 1997 21(6), November/December 1997, p. 24-29
[10] *Correlation* 1999.[10]
[11] Jan Nienhuys, 'The Mars Effect in Retrospect,' *Skeptical Inquirer,* 1997 21(6) alludes to "1,120 CFEPP champions"; also *Correlation* 1999 18(2) Nanninga and Nienhuys, 'There is no Mars-Effect!' pp.47-40.

French Sceptics see the Mars effect

on about the ineptitude of the Seven Silent Authors of the CFEPP report:

> The French skeptics tried to obtain the birth data of 1439 champions. In 1990 they supplied Gauquelin with a preliminary report showing all 1439 names, 1071 of whom had full data (i.e. year, month, day and time of birth). Ertel got hold of this report. Unfortunately, personal problems (e.g. serious illness) and lack of manpower prevented the CFEPP from completing their study. [NK: If there were seven authors, how could this be?] Nienhuys was asked for help. [NK: Was he??] He checked all data, correcting several errors and inaccuracies. Halfway during this process the CFEPP announced a result about 1066 champions. Finally, Nienhuys established that the CFEPP had received 1120 usable answers to their request (in 4 cases no answer was received at all).

As usual, no-one's voice except Nienhuys gets heard. The Seven Silent Authors are rebuked for prematurely announcing 'halfway during' the study a list of merely, 1066 - instead of the proper total of 1120 which Nienhuys is fortunately able to provide. One would hardly guess from this that the CFEPP took fourteen years to prepare their Report.

At the dawn of the new millenium one more version of events appeared, in a book published by Kurtz.[12] Its version of events differed from the published volume, presumably fed to him by Nienhuys. Altogether 1439 champions were selected, and these resulted eventually (after corrections by Jan William Nienhuys) in 1,120 reliable data received. It claimed 'Among the 1,120 champions, 207 (18.48%) were born in the 1st and 4th sector, which does not differ significantly from the values obtained from the control group.' (p.93) The CFEPP report never mentioned these figures.[13]

A BEAUTIFUL MARS-EFFECT

Meanwhile, back in the real world, the heavens had come up with quite a decent Mars-effect. Scoring Mars in Key Sectors for the total

---

[12] Paul Kurtz, *Skepticism and Humanism, the new Paradigm*, 2001
[13] The one thorough critique of the Benski report is by Ken Irving: *Correlation* 1996, 15.1, 54-60.

group of 1120 champions gives 122+85 = 207. But, taking just the original KS number one, i.e. Mars rising, there is here a 24% excess.[14] Twenty-four percent, and they called it a negative result? How did those Seven Silent Authors keep a straight face while averring they had a negative result, with a quarter in excess of Mars-rising at the birth of great sports champions? It's not rocket science.

The CFEPP data divides in a startling manner over time. We first separate out the births before and after 1930[15]:

1830-1930 (n=592) gives 125 in KS, Expect 101, 23% excess $\chi^2 = 6$

1930-1949 (n=782) gives 114 in KS, Expect 134, 15% deficit $\chi^2 = 3$

There was a quite significant result using their data up to 1930, then an almost significant result the other way i.e. a deficit, for later data.

<u>The CFEPP Mars-Effect</u>

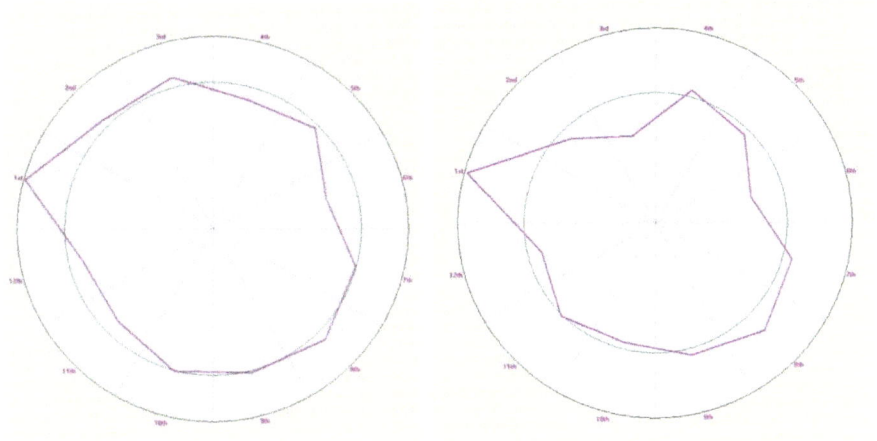

All sports champions (n=1120)   Only pre-1930 data (n=592)

We see a massive excess in the first sector, which scored 73 expect 50.7 - a 44% excess![16] Should they not have commented upon this non-uniformity (to say the least) in their data? That's a forty percent excess of Mars rising, in the French skeptics data! That includes all of their

---

[14] Scored 122, Expect 98 => 24%.
[15] I'm grateful to Graham Douglas for suggesting this.
[16] Chance-expected values were ascertained using Mark Pottenger's 'CCCS' US astrology-research program, see Chapter 3. It generated an expected-frequency estimate here of 51.9 for first sector, compared to observed 73.

data up to 1930. One begins to appreciate why they took twelve years to announce their result, and why they kept silent.

Let's further subdivide the data, going only up to 1920, as shown in the left-hand diagram.[17] We now see an overall 36% excess in the two Key Sectors (n=362, 84 expect 62, chi-square =8) which is significant at 0.005 or one in two hundred.

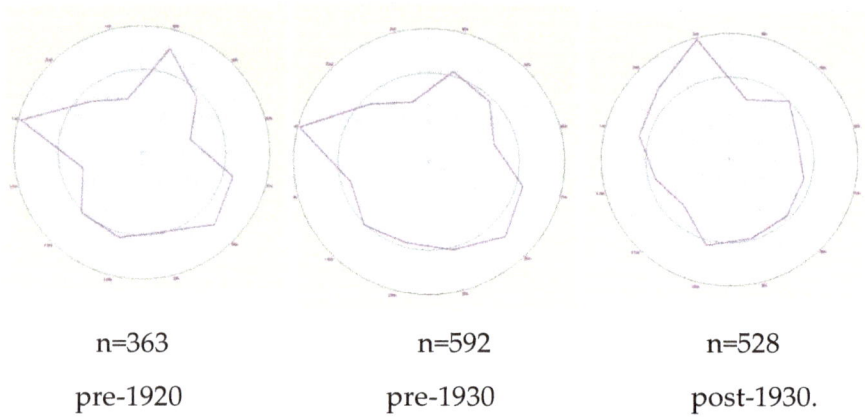

| n=363 | n=592 | n=528 |
| pre-1920 | pre-1930 | post-1930. |

We are now looking at a classic Gauquelin effect: it could not be better and that is the data up to 1920. It serves to remind us, that quite a small group can give a viable effect. The middle graph goes a decade later and we see the peak after MC has faded away. Then later In contrast, the more recent data 1930-1949 (n=528) gives 82, expect 90 - its in deficit. Is his suspicious? It's certainly odd and we could have done with some comment from the CFEPP authors on this subject: how come that, in the data after 1930, both peaks have vanished?

There is a comparison here with the Belgian Comité Para report, published two decades earlier, whose 535 champions were born over 1872 – 1945. We saw how dividing them at 1920 showed a huge differential, with an even larger excess in the group born before that date than we find here in the French group – fifty percent, compared to 36% here. The scientific method involves comparing different sets of data and attempting to generalise.

---

[17] I am grateful to Graham Douglas for pointing out this difference, for the CFEPP data: see his 2015 CURA article 'The Gauquelin Effect is Born at Conception,' section 'The Skeptics' 'debunking' of the Gauquelin Effect.'

Could different levels of eminence account for this? The older pre-1920 champions were remembered because they really were distinguished, so that half a century later books still have their names and birthdata. The contemporary sports scene in contrast has much larger numbers, as crowds of people are given the laurels of victory, who will however soon recede into oblivion.

Suitbert Ertel was the first psychologist to measure eminence, solving acrimonious disputes by use of selected reference books. He had students who counted how often the champs appeared in each. Here, two reference-books were used: Bernard Le Roy's *Dictionnaire Bibliographique des Sports*, 1973, and *l'Athlege* of 1961. Nearly all of the CFEPP champions were listed in one or the other. The sub-group which featured in both these reference-books would tend to be more eminent than those which featured in only one.

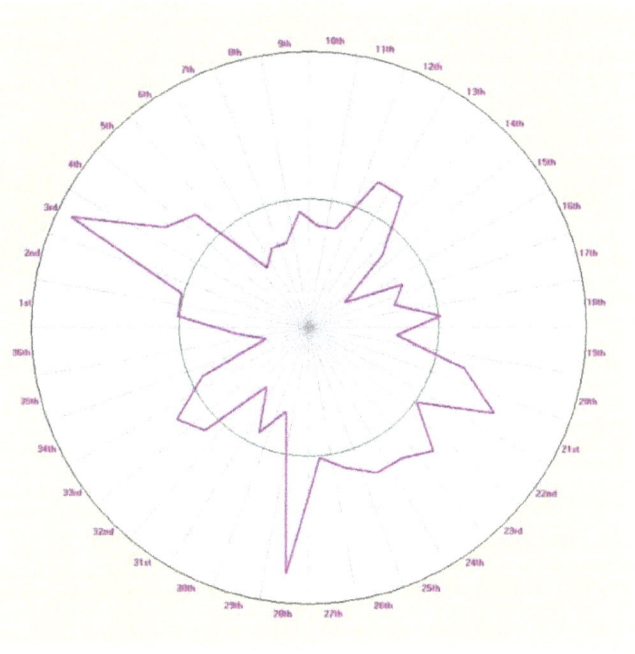

Selecting the sports champions who featured in both, I obtained the image shown, using a 36-fold division. A strong peak appears in the 3rd sector with a secondary peak in the 12th. We again notice a bit of a fourfold structure here, with other peaks in the 21st sector (opposite to 3rd) and 28th (opposite to 10th). The phenomenon does sometimes tend to show this fourfold structure, even though the statistical testing only scores the first two which are above the horizon. As a general comment it is of interest to examine data using the 36-fold division, although statistical tests are better limited to the simple two-out-of-twelve divisions.

THE MIDNIGHT HOUR

One might expect a scientific investigation to allude to the biggest effect present in its data, and, even hear discussion of its astronomical-demographic implications. Unmentioned in the Benski Report was the 'midnight avoidance' phenomenon, whereby parents consistently avoid recording the midnight hour on the birth certificate. As is shown in the bar-chart, the zero hour is very low, while in contrast there are extra high values on the hours before and after. Without conjecturing why this could be happening - whether from superstitious fear or a desire to avoid uncertainty over the date – we should be concerned with, whether it could have affected the outcome? That is far from being easy to answer.

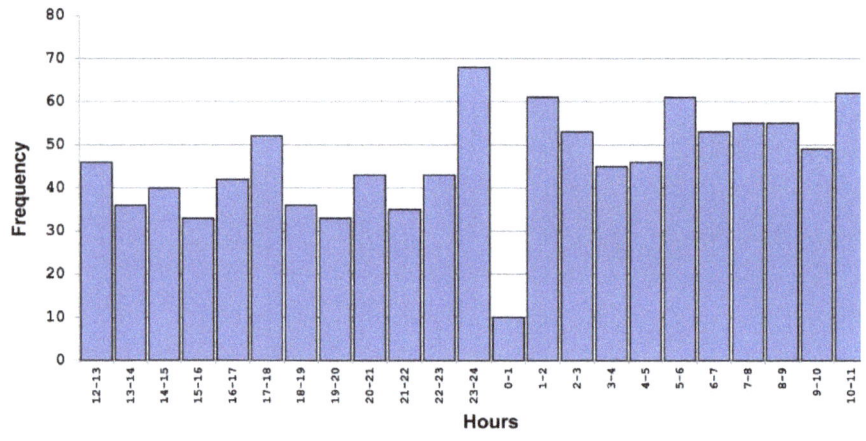

Figure: French sceptic's birth-data plotted over 24 hours of the day, showing the 'midnight minimum' of 0-1 am.

The Sun at the midnight hour stands at the I.C. position, the *Immum Coeli*, the bottom of the chart, while one of the two Key Sectors has Mars at the top of the chart. That signifies a relationship of opposition, Sun-opposite-Mars and also is the time when Mars goes retrograde in the sky. That happens every 2.2 years, as it weaves its loop in the night sky. It will spend a very different amount of time there, from the rest of its orbit. If one were to delete data for one or two of the hours around midnight, then that would greatly affect the relative Mars-score in the second of the Key Sectors and push the expected frequencies way out of kilter.

The 'midnight-avoidance' phenomenon means that the data recorded around that hour has to be unreliable, or less so than the rest of the data, and one would appreciate hearing some discussion about this matter. In constructing a control group, one takes care to ensure that the midnight-hour deficit effect remains intact, not erased by random shuffling.

The French study may not have been intentionally dishonest, but it does appear as curiously concerned *not* to look at what the data was showing. Its authors hung on for so many years not publishing, until both Gauquelins were finished - as if they did not wish to hear the excoriating reply they would without a doubt have received had either of those two been around. After Françoise's journal faded out in 1995,[18] she lived on but her health was poor and she no longer corresponded. But, here she is commenting in 1994, in the very last issue of her Journal, on a report Ertel gave at the then-yearly London Astro-Research conference:

> Prof Ertel announced that his control of the Gauquelin Mars effect with the citation count method had once more proven the Mars effect to be genuinely linked... Ertel had tested this time sportsmen collected by the particularly hostile CFEPP. This group of French 'rationalists' has secretly manipulated the agreed-upon sample of sportsmen, eliminating a number of very eminent subjects and adding instead non-eminent subjects, ie cases predicted not to display any Mars-effect in the preliminary protocols signed by CFEPP leaders and Michel Gauquelin. When the non-significant results of this sample were announced and commented in a well-known French magazine, CFEPP, with their unequalled cynicism, refused to let Michel know how their sample had been put together.

But, Ertel was able to access the data, with his university position and degrees:

---

[18] See CURA website, for its contents. The other French astro-research journal RAMS, *Recherche Astrologue Methodes de Science* did however survive a few years longer.

Armed with the citation count method, Ertel demonstrated that the CFEPP sample included the lowest ranking sportsmen ever analysed, then concluded with subtle humour, that of course the CFEPP sample was not statically significant... In this way they revealed their secret belief, that the Mars effect would appear if they didn't cheat! (*APP* Volume 11, Spring '95, p.4)

THE THREE SCEPTIC TRIALS

There have been three published replications by sceptical groups, wishing to test MG's 'Mars effect' with athletes, Belgian (1976), American (1977) and French (1996), each reporting a negative result. The first two have been discussed in the previous chapter. Ertel somehow managed to obtain the data for each of these, giving him a total of 1664[19] sports champions of reliably-known birthdata.. He applied his eminence-grading protocol and thereby obtained a graph[20] that has been described as 'too good to be true'[21] (Figure 5). Here four 'key-sectors' are used including below-the-horizon zones, giving as can be seen a much higher expected frequency. As well as the two 'primary sectors' there are 'secondary sectors' that are below horizon (Mars' setting and lower culmination). Ertel here referenced the Dutch sceptic Jan Nienhuys.[22] His graph comparing the combined sceptics data (n=1664) with that for the Gauquelin data (n=4384) plotted around a 36-sector Mars-day appears in this JSE article.

The US sceptics had clearly cheated in their 'replication' using the US sports champions, as shown by the way the three successive sets of data-gathering they had performed obtained steeply-declining key-

---

[19] He obtained this total from summing the Belgian Para Committee's 535 champions, the French CFEPP's 1066 champions and the US sceptics' 408 champions (the first two had a considerable overlap).
[20] Ertel, S. 'Het weerbarstige Marseffect' *Skepter*, 1996, 45; reprinted in, 'Debunking with caution - Cleaning up Mars-Effect Research,' *Correlation*, 2000, 18, 9-41. For another version see *The Tenacious Mars Effect*, Ertel and Ken Irving, Urania 1996, p.15.
[21] 'Die Graphik von Prof Ertel (Abb 3) ist ebenfalls viel schon:' Jan Nienhuys, 'Ertel's Mars-Effect: anatomie einer Pseudowissenchaft'. *Skeptiker*, 1997, 10, 92-98, p.96.
[22] Nienhuys in Benski (ref. 14), pp.125: 'primary' key sectors above horizon vs. 'secondary' sectors below; as in eg MG's *Spheres of Destiny* 1981. Ertel presents this as the third and last definition of planetary KS, the first two being: two out of 12 and 8 out of 26, both using the two positions of rise and culmination: JSE, 2000 14(3): 'The Mars Effect is Genuine: On Kurtz, Nienhuys, and Sandhu's Missing the Evidence.'

sector scores of 19%, 12% and finally a mere 7% (Chapter 4): their mean of 13% for their 408 champions' key-sector scores being in deficit at a

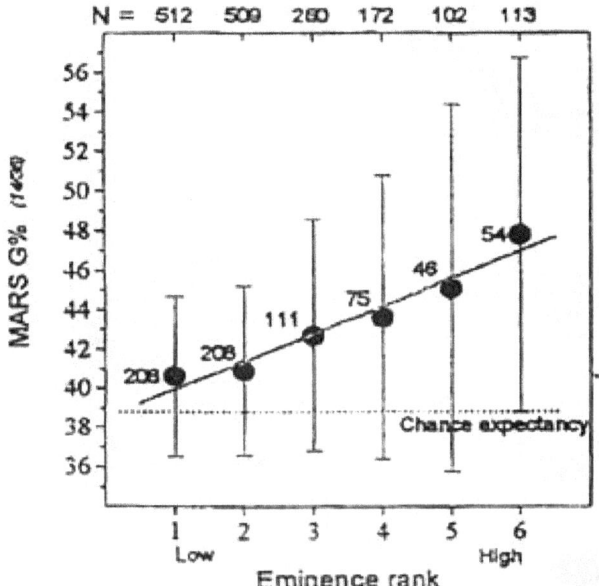

statistically-significant level.[23]

<u>Figure 5</u>: Ertel's 'too good to be true' graph, in which he claimed to have combined together three lots of sceptics data (n=1668), then graded them for eminence by Mars-score in Key Sectors using a 36-fold division. NB the totals specified in these six groups do not remotely add up to his total.

Ertel obtained a copy of the US sceptics' data, which they never published. His university position would have enabled him to do this.[24] Thierry Grafff obtained a copy of the data from Ken Irving, who co-authored the book with Ertel, and the data is now up on the opengauquelin.org website.

---

[23] Only just significant: Ertel, 'Debunking with Caution – cleaning up Mars Effect Research' *Correlation* 1999, 18,2 9-41 p16. Kurtz had averred otherwise, JSE 1997.
[24] Ertel let me have the Belgian Para data (n=535), which has his eminence-grading newalchemypress.com/gauquelin/ Page 3, Note 13, Excel spreadsheet: column J.

French Sceptics see the Mars effect

A year or two before this graph appeared, in 1994, Ertel had commented on the French sceptics' treatment of their data, though it had not formally been published. They had assembled birthdata on over a thousand sportsmen, and were reporting that no Mars-effect could be found in this data[25]. He made the rudimentary observation that eminence-grading using some well-known French reference-books such as *Stars du Sport* and *La Fabuleuse Histoire du Sport* showed that the more eminent sportsmen mentioned in these books did show the Mars-effect, while the less eminent did not. One would have thought this was fairly simple. They also set an unduly high chance-expected level, and may have showed bias in favour of omitting the more eminent athletes.[26] Two years year later the French book appeared, with no response to Ertel's already-published critique of their argument.

The US sceptics did not publish their data and one had assumed it was lost. I had written to the office of the US Sceptics but to no avail. Then in 2023 Thierry Grafff posted it up on his new, data-only website, opengauauelin.org. Where had he got it from? Why, he had written to Ken Irving. As Ertel explained: "CSICOP's data (n=408) was provided as hardcopy printouts by members of the Committee's research group" (*The Tenacious Mars-Effect*, 1996, p.13), whereby Irving as co-author obtained his copy.

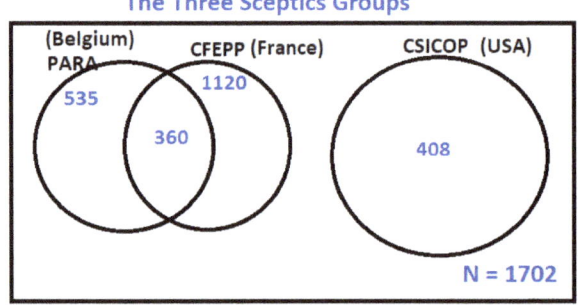

I asked Thierry Grafff if he would combine the three data-sets of the sceptics, Belgian, French and US and he did so, obtaining a total of 1702. That is somewhat more than Ertel, whose group from combining

---

[25] See, eg, Nienhuys, J. 'Science or pseudoscience? The Mars Effect and other Claims', 3rd Euroskeptics congress 1991 Amsterdam. The French book appeared in 1996.
[26] Ertel, S.: 'Mars Effect Uncovered in French Sceptics Data,' *Correlation*, 1994/5 13, 3-16. Use of the 12-sector division had been agreed in the 1982 protocol: see Chapter 6.

the three added up to 1683. A 'Venn diagram' highlights the large overlap between the two European studies, viz. 360 birthdates of sports-champions:

Taken as a whole the 'sceptic's group' showed a merely 8% excess of Mars in the two key-sectors. Removing the post-1930 data makes this larger, a 23% excess, then removing all post-1920 birthdata it becomes even larger – a 33% excess with a chi-squared of ten as shown below. Did the sceptics publish articles saying, 'How wrong we were!' or maybe, 'Rock-solid demonstration of astral influence by three sceptic groups'? Or, they could try a title like, 'What a shame we drove that French fellow to suicide, he was right all along!'

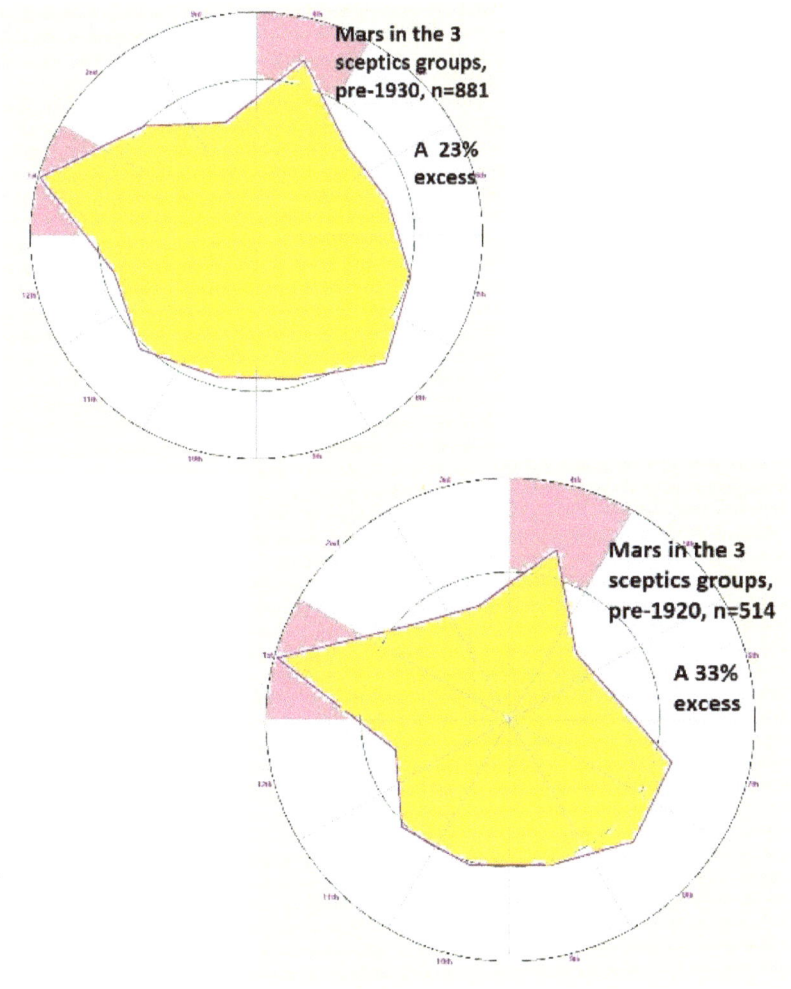

7

A SEARCH FOR 'PROOF'

Did the 'Gauquelin effect' result from Michel Gauquelin selecting the data? The great debates which raged, before and after Michel's suicide in 1991 – most terribly with his request that his personal database be destroyed – failed I suggest to reach a meeting-point on this question.

If science concerns objective knowledge, we require the establishing of data-sets which do not depend upon the person who selected them. It's fine for MG to have *collected* the data, but we don't want him to have *selected* it. The intense but unedifying debates between MG and the Sceptics over the 'Mars Effect' revolved around this database. I'd like here to develop the case I proposed in 2006[1], that as far as possible one should steer clear of who said what to whom, and rather focus upon the intersecting of defined sets, three intersecting sets being required (see figure on page 131).

Some eminent-professional groups will here be evaluated, of champions, writers and physicians. Psychology departments uploading this data will need reassuring about their objective validity, if that can be established.

The French *Dictionnaire Encylopaedia des Sports* (DES) by Bernard le Roy of 1973 has 3302 'sportifs' from all nations, arranged in categories from 'Alpinisme' to 'Yachting'. Most had a date of birth, at least two-thirds, giving somewhat over two thousand with known birthdate.

One could start off with just two intersecting sets: {all sportsmen in DES}, and {reliably known birth-data}, which would give an agreed-upon definition.

There couould be a third set to be applied, which sceptics may not be happy about, but seems to be a part of the intrinsic hypothesis the Gauquelins put forward. There is a period, when European births start to be induced, maybe around the end of WW2, and after that does any

---

[1] NK, 'How Ertel Rescued the Gauquelin Effect,' *Correlation,* 2005, 23 (1).

'Gauquelin effect' fade away? That *terminus est* limit needs to be ascertained by the computer – MG put it at around 1950. It may be ascertained by looking at the solar-distribution diurnal pattern here shown. The applying of that set would filter out a portion of the data, maybe one-fifth. Or, we could say that it divides the data into two parts, the earlier data where the Mars effect will tend to be present – if it is present anywhere - and the later data where it is absent.

We examine how the 'Mars Effect' has varied over the half-century or so of the birthdates, by breaking it down into a number of equal portions. A curious peak appears around 1910-1920. What, if anything, does this mean?

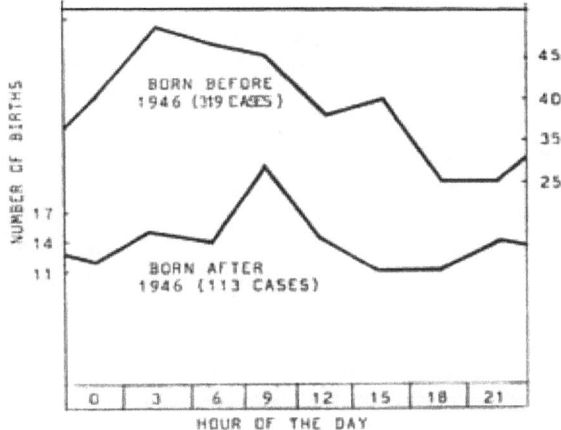

Figure: Graphs[2] showing pre- and post- 1946 birth-data for sports champions, plotted by time of day, showing the natural pre-dawn peak for births prior to 1946.

The Gauquelins took a pessimistic view that disruption of the natural timing of the birth-process (as shown by the change in the nycthemeral curve') had caused the effect to fade away. Hospital- induced births tend to peak around noon.

The scoring of eminence could be a lot easier today, by e.g. counting the number of web-citations for each name. Or, as newspaper-collections are becoming digitised one can search through them for name-citations. Such eminence-grading, over which there has been so much disagreement and bad faith, is only appropriate within a group

---

[2] MG, 1979, Series B, *The Mars Effect & Sports Champions.*

A search for 'proof'

that has been objectively defined, which was I suggest hardly achieved in the 20th century.

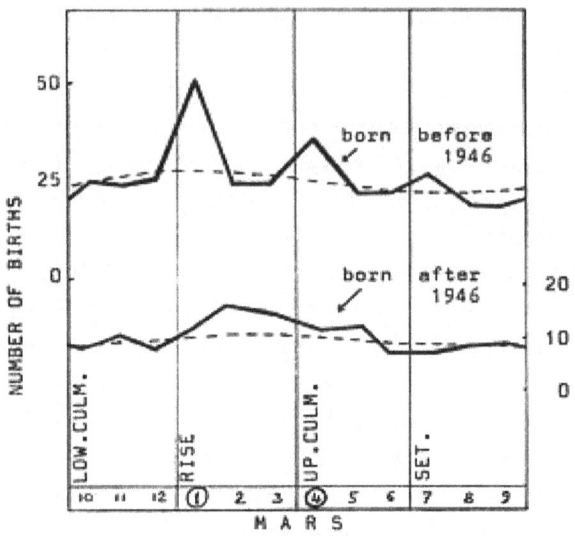

Figure: same data plotted by Mars-Sectors, showing how, when births are natural, a Mars-effect is present.

EMINENT SPORTSMEN

There was a later collection of French sportsmen by MG in 1979 which had the graph shown above concerning the effect of induced births.[3] What, we may ask, is this group?

He collected 'renowned European sports champions, that is athletes who not only succeeded in national, but in international contests,' selecting those born between 1940 and 1950, so as not to include those in his earlier publications. As a control MG gathered 423 'non-famous sportsmen' – also listed in the DES! This is where things start to get confusing.[4] 82% of MG's group of champions come from the DES. He did not want too many French champions in the group, so had to select from other sources. He took sportsmen who had 'more

---

[3] Ibid, p.13. For comments on how MG selected the data, see Ertel, *Journal of Scientific Exploration* (JSE), 1988,2,1 'Raising the Hurdle for the Athlete's Mars-Effect,' p.60.
[4] For scathing comments by skeptic Paul Kutz, see Kurtz et. al., JSE, 1997, 11,1, 'Is the Mars Effect Genuine?' p.29, 'The 1979 Test:' "the criteria by which Gauquelin selected notable sports champions seemed to vary from test to test."

than ten selections in the French National Team' or cyclists who were the yearly winners of a race. Also other sports books were consulted. Overall a selection-process is sketched out, which no-one else is going to be able to replicate, i.e MG is asking us to trust him. He ends up with a higher percent excess of Mars in key sectors than in any of his previous data:[5]

MG Sports data of 1979 vs earlier samples			
Year	Total	KS Score	Expect
1970	2088	435	358 => + 25%
1979	432	106	74 => + 43%

- which does strain our credulity. For comparison, in his published group of military (n=3046) Mars scored 18% in excess for the Key Sectors. His comment on this result, far higher than any of his previous groups, was:

> This fairly good proportion most likely is due to the particular care we took to gather, through all Europe, only highly successful sports champions. (1979, p.12)

Maybe, but *Ce n'est pas la science* - its uncheckable.

Gauquelin had previously gathered two thousand famous sportsmen (whose births were prior to 1945, and nearly all after 1870), and we would like to have been told how many of these were in the French reference book. Going back to the above intersecting sets derived from the *Dictionnaire,* one would have expected most of its members to have featured in his published sportsmen, would one not? The French Skeptics' account of their endeavour[6] described rather vaguely how 1066 eminent French sportsmen were selected by using two textbooks:

> A sample group of French athletes was put together from sports dictionaries listing the best athletes of the time (Le Roy's encyclopedic *Dictionary of Sports* and *L'Athlege*).

That is all it tells us, except that they went on selecting until they had over a thousand. Could someone else have chosen to select a different group? For example, MG wrote complaining to the French committee,

---

[5] MG 1972 series C, 'Profession-Heredity, Results' p.66.
[6] Claude Benski et al., *The "Mars Effect" a French test of over 1000 champions,* 1996, p.14.

A search for 'proof'

that they had chosen too many rugby players (327 of them), but only 192 footballers. He also complained that they had selected too many (30%) from one decade, the 1940s.[7]

Professor Suitbert Ertel applied his eminence-grading method to the groups of champions, using various textbooks, of which the first five, in descending order of citations, were:

> Le Roy *Dictionnaire des Sports* (1973),
>
> Garcia, *La Fabuleuse Histoire* (4 volumes) 1973, *Die Stars des Sports* von A bis Z 1970,
>
> Kamper, *Lexikon der 2000 Olympioniken* (1974) and
>
> Fassbender, *Sporttagebuch des 20 Jahrhunderts* (1984)[8].

There would be a good case for using any two of these, so that eminence meant being cited in both of them. It wouldn't matter greatly which volumes are used, one only requires a collective agreement which is then adhered to. One could prefer not to use an English-language primary-source since UK birthtimes are unrecorded. MG complained about the French sceptics using only the 1973 *Dictionnaire* by le Roy on the grounds that it had an undue number of French champions: in that case, one might prefer to use it together with one of the German textbooks: together they would have given a group of top sportsmen that everybody could agree upon, n'est ce pas? Alas, no such procedure was used.

The recriminations were mutual - the sceptics accused MG of improperly selecting his high-eminence cases, while Ertel described how the sceptics had used an undue number of low-eminence cases. Neither side attained an objectively-defined basis, in selecting their 'eminents,' so – unsurprisingly, nothing much was established. One may not be in a hurry to believe that either of the Gauquelins cheated, but scientific theories are not built upon trust. To paraphrase Ertel, Michel didn't cheat, but he did have bias.

FRAUD FROM THE SCEPTICS

If the French skeptics spent a decade figuring out how to do their test, you might have thought they could have told us a bit more about

---

[7] Ibid, Letter from MG, pp 76-8. The CFEPP data (n=1066) has 29% from that decade.
[8] Ertel, 'Raising the Hurdle for the Athlete's Mars-Effect' (JSE), 1988,2,1, p. 63.

their selection procedure than the above-quoted single sentence.[9] They finally told us that their 1066 sportsmen had scored Mars in Key sectors 200 times, an above-chance result of merely 9%.[10] That may not have been significant, but did *not* allow their conclusion that, 'The test does not show any evidence of the influence of Mars in terms of athletic champions.'[11]

Was a Mars-effect present in the entirety of DES champions? In 1982 MG commented: 'My reply to Kurtz was a proposal ... Let Kurtz himself consider all the names of the athletes listed in this *Dictionnaire* without any selection at all and see if the Mars effect still shows up when all the athletes in the book are included (the Mars effect does, by the way).'[12] If indeed that is so, then we should have been told that more coherently, and not merely as a casual remark. We'd like to hear what the size of that group was, and how the excess appeared.

Data-sets were available whereby the sceptics could have checked up on some of MG's claims without much trouble - had they wanted to. for example, they could have taken his 570 French 'sportifs' which he published in his first book,[13] taken from the French *L'Athlege* of 1949-50, and see whether he had indeed extracted all those of known birthtime, as he indicated. Then we would have had a reference-book and a data-set which fitted each other, so the task would have been simple. Ditto for French physicians, MG's very first endeavour: that comprised the group of 576 French doctors he extracted from a biographical index of French Academy members.[14,15] One need only check through say half of these data-sets, to ascertain any errors and establish whether data had been omitted. Thereby, objectively-agreed

---

[9] Some detail was provided by Nienhuys a few years later, in *Correlation* 1999, 8,2.
[10] Benski, *The Mars Effect*, 'Analysis of the Results' p.15; I'm here using Mark Pottenger expected frequencies (CCRS): see APP 1994,10,2: Pottenger, 'Gauquelin Sector Expected frequencies'.
[11] Ibid., p.15
[12] http://tricksterbook.com/truzzi/ZS-Issues-PDFs/ZeteticScholarNo9.pdf 1982, 9 *Zetetic Scholar*, p.55, commenting on Patrick Curry's article 'Research on the Mars-Effect,' Ibid p.34.
[13] MG, *L'Influence des Astres*, 1955, p.144.
[14] *Index Bibliographique des Membres, Associés et correspondents de l'Academie de Medecine de 1820 à 1939*, Ed Masson, 1939. MG, *L'Influence des Astres*, 1955, p.105.
[15] Towards the end of the 1980s, German psychology professor Arno Müller checked though this list of French physicians birthdata, and found quite a few errors, but concluded that bias was not there present: 'A Study of the G. Effect with 402 Italian writers,' APP 1993, 9,2.

upon databases would exist. That would have done so much to dispel the miasma of distrust and uncertainty.

The sceptics decided that they wanted fresh data, and so the several parties came to agree upon the more modern encyclopaedias. The more recent sources brought with them the problem that the effect tended to fade away as births became artificially-induced in hospitals. In the fine words of Françoise Gauquelin, 'The higher the economic level of a country, the sooner the natural nycthemeral birth distribution evolves towards the medically influenced distribution.'[16] One of the graphs above shows the pre-dawn peak for naturally-occurring births, which gets displaced towards noon in the more modern data-set, once hospital-procedures become standard.

We turn next to two objectively-defined data-sets that were established by the German psychology Professor Arno Müller, but not published.

WRITERS AND THE MOON: A REPLICATION

MG's first book had nothing about the Moon, then in 1960 his *Les Hommes at Les Astres* collected data on European writers, over eight hundred of them. Poets, literary critics, novelists and historians were thrown together and their data showed, he reported, a huge 30% excess of the Moon in key sectors.

The Gauquelins had used the Italian Who's Who *Chi è?* of 1948 to obtain their Italian sample, totalling 192 Italian writers. Checking through this, Professor Arno Müller was able to obtain far more, in fact he found no less than 402 Italian writers of reliable birthdata. The huge number omitted by the Gauquelins were excused, Françoise explained (rather apologetically) on the grounds that "our omissions were related to time pressure, shortage of funds for this particular research, language problems in this foreign country, but not to a conscious or unconscious desire to manipulate data."[17]

---

[16] Astro-Psychological problems, Edited by FG, Paris, (APP) 1992, 8,1, p.17. See also, *The Tenacious Mars-Effect*, Ertel & Irving, 1996, p.21: 'The Gauquelins first took issue with CSICOP for having used cases born after the cut-off date of 1950.'
[17] FG 'Answer to Prof Müller', APP 1993, 9,2, p.23.

Müller's Italian group of 402 Italian writers showed a 22% excess of Moon in Key Sectors that was just significant.[18] *But,* his data lacked female writers 'because their birth date was politely omitted'.[19] Let us hope that someone can re-check this data-set as given in the 1948 edition of *Chi è?* and obtain the relevant female birth-data. Could Italian astrologers locate such female writers of known birth-data? A complete set thus defined could then become of great interest to psychology students – not to mention, probably pushing the numbers up enough to give a significant result. A two-by-two division of that data could become feasible, of a male-female division or a division by imaginative writers versus factual-historical writers,[20] which would enhance the meaning of this survey. Students are not going to want to hear about some bureaucratic reason for gender-deletion.

Müller had no business to write, 'As long as no further positive results are obtained, no relationship between the Moon positions at birth and the future fame of a writer can be considered as proven.'[21] MG was depressed to be told this in 1989 by a University psychology professor![22] Müller wrote to MG

> Dear Michel,   28 July, 1989
>
> Sorry I have no good news for you about the results of my investigation. The hypotheses you sent me with your letter of June 29 (thank you for it) have not been confirmed. A look at the two enclosed tables of result will demonstrate it to you. Of course the subsamples are very small, but there is also no tendency if one combines the groups according to your hypothesis.

In this he erred. He should have reported that, the earlier effect for imaginative writers had been well-replicated with a strong negative-Saturn effect and a slightly weaker positive-Moon effect that was just about significant, and, had he been able to collect just a few more cases

---

[18] Müller's data given on p.46 of his *Astro-Forschungs Daten*, Band 1 (privately published), Table 5 is now up on opengauquelin.org.
[19] Arno Müller, 402 *Italienische Schriftseller* (402 Italian Writers), 1991 (band 1 of his *AstroForschungsDaten*); and APP 1993, 9,2, p.15. He has published all the birthdata.
[20] For discussion of gender-differences see Ertel, 'Planetary Relations with Female notabilities, Two First Results' APP 1993, 9,1, pp.22-5.
[21] Arno Müller, 'A Study of the G. Effect with 402 Italian writers' APP 1993 9,2, p.13.
[22] Müller, *Astro-forchungs Data,* letter to MG 28.7.89, at front.

it would probably have been significant. It was quite false to say 'no tendency ...according to your hypothesis.'

Müller's data had a somewhat lower amplitude lunar effect than MG had previously reported: the sample showed a 21% excess of Moon in Key Sectors whereas a very high 30% excess for a total of 1352 writers had earlier been averred by MG (See Table 1 in Chapter 1).

Arno Müller's secret positive result for the Moon and Italian writers (n=402)

Writers	Tot.	KS score	Exp.	Chi-Sq.	Signif.
Moon	402	82	67 => +23%	3.3	P < 0.05
Saturn	402	61	67 => -9%		

A tenured university professor could well have been reluctant to support a neo-astrological theory. Investigating the matter is fine, so long as one comes out in the end with a negative result. How many times have we heard that one before!

Michel never disputed that negative result claimed by Arno Müller, negating one of his most important discoveries: the link between the Moon and imaginative writers. After Michel's death Müller in 1993 published the allegedly-negative result in APP, and Françoise published her 'answer' in seven pages, which had in common with Müller's article that the data was not actually presented. Then some years later, the book by Ertel and Ken Irving reiterated that 'Professor Müller ... did not replicate the Gauquelins' results for the Moon and writers,...'[23]

Let's look at the figures. The original finding had found positive Moon and negative Saturn for writers, and Arno Müller found *exactly the same*. A chi-squared test measures (observed-expected)^2 / expected, and was just significant, at around 1 in 20. There are different views about how to do this – with obscure discussions about degrees of freedom and contingency tables, but let's say the significance hovers around the 1 in 20 figure.

---

[23] Tenacious, p.Ki-43.

For comparison, the group of Novelists (n=465) had Moon +42% and Saturn -18%.[24] And so, as one might have expected, Saturn was unhelpful for imaginative writers.

Michel had two eminence-grise psychology professors denying and/or invalidating his major discoveries, both of them carrying an aura of credibility due to being lecturers. We may be sure that both of them would have scored bonus points in their departments for investigating the 'paranormal' and coming up with a negative result. The combination of these two, one after the other, did they drive Michel to suicide? Michel did not have any mental illness or imbalance that caused his end. If only his wife has still been with him, then maybe together they could have coped, but these things came to him after the divorce.

PHYSICIANS

There is a little-appreciated German 'parapsychology' journal, *Zeitschrift für Parapsychologie* in which Ertel published seven articles and Arno Müller published ten, on the subject of the Gauquelin research. The very first edition, in 1958, had these three articles next to each other:

- Carl Jung: *Ein Astrologische Experiment,* p.81- 92
- Arno Müller: *Eine statistiche Untersuchung astrologischer Faktoren bei dauerhaften und geschiedenen Ehen,* p.93-101
- Michel Gauquelin: *Der Einflus der Gestirne und die Statistik* 102-123.

Jung was here reporting his famous marriage-synastry experiment, a propos of his theory of 'synchronicity' and Müller was commenting upon it - his article had nothing to do with Gauquelin's, which followed on. Books and articles about Gauquelin never mention this curious juxtaposition of Jung and Gauquelin. That little-known article by MG – by a Frenchman writing in German - was surely, his first.[25]

In 1986, Arno Müller published a report in that journal on a huge and careful replication of the Gauquelin work on physicians which he had done, and this was the one and only positive-result replication of

---

[24] For this data-set see 'Poets and the Moon' section posted up here http://newalchemypress.com/gauquelin/research8.php
[25] I've posted it up (with kind permission from the *Zeitschrift* journal) one the first page of http://newalchemypress.com/gauquelin/index.php

the Gauquelin effect published in Michel's lifetime, i.e. the only one he ever came across. It used '1,288 well-known German doctors.'[26,27] One finds no references to this, apart from Müller's briefly-stated conclusion that: 'Overall the findings of the present study [i.e., by Müller] mostly can be understood as a confirmation of the Gauquelin planetary effect.'[28]

Müller used two source-books for physicians: *Biographische Lexikon hervorragender Artze* (1962), of which 95% of them were born before 1890, plus also the less eminent *Kurschners Deitscher Gelehrtenkalendar* (1961) which had generally later births. This gave him a total of 2016 male doctors, of which he found birth-data for 1,288. There was some degree of overlap here with the Gauquelin data published earlier.

His 18-page report published in the *Zeitschrift fur Parapsychologie* gave graphs of his results but no data, which could be why this study remains unknown. His self-published volume of his researches *Astroforchungs Daten* strangely did not allude to it,[29] - one might have expected to find the raw data there - nor did an article by him in the *Journal of Scientific Exploration* (1990) make any allusion to it.[30]

He found an excess of Mars and Saturn in key sectors and a deficit of Jupiter, just as the Gauquelins had reported for their French data. It's not easy to apprehend how such an important and substantial replication of the Gauquelin theory could have become forgotten, and its data lost.

Müller's next replication concerned the Moon and writers, as we've already discussed, which he reported in *Zeitschrift fur Parapsychologie* in 1991. One would like to have a sequence of these articles available, or at least viewable, but that does not seem likely to happen anytime soon. Some discussion of this result took place in subsequent issues. A translation was published in Francoise's *Astro-Psychological Problems* in 1993.

---

[26] Müller, 'Lasst sich der Gauqelin-Effekt bestagen? ...*Zeitschrift fur Parapsychologie,* 1986, 28, 1,2, 87-103.
[27] Müller, 'Can the Gauquelin Effect be confirmed? Results with a sample of 1288 eminent physicians.' NCGR Jnl, Fall 1989, 17-20. The current Editor thinks he has a copy up in his attick somewhere, and hopes to find it.
[28] Müller, Quoted by MG in *Written in the Stars, the proven link between astrology and destiny* 1988, p.158.
[29] Müller, *Astro-Forschungs Daten* 1995: it merely referred to the NCGR article.
[30] Müller, JSE 1990, 4,1 *Planetary influences on Human Behaviour,* 85-104.

In the early 1990s a collaboration between Arno Müller and Suitbert Ertel took place. They located the follow-up 1972 edition of the same volume of eminent Paris physicians that Michel had used. This new reference-book had a total of 1260 distinguished French doctors, including some of Gauquelin's original data, from which they obtained 915 cases having reliable birth-data.[31] There were 168 cases from MG's original group born in Paris, for which Müller was unable to re-check their birth data. It would be valuable if someone were to do that. Of his total of these *Academie* members, 224 were not in MG's original sample.

Müller seems not to have published any report on this, except in his privately printed *Astro-Data Forschung*. Clearly, no-one could imagine two tenured psychology professors co-authoring a positive-result 'astrology' paper!

These professors, using their headed notepaper, had the ability to access data from registry offices. Ordinary people cannot do that, and especially not astrologers. Six hundred registration offices in France received letters from him, on headed notepaper of the 'Institut fur Psychologie der Georg August Universitat, Gottingen', requesting help 'in a study of biorhythms.' (!) Much care was needed because, he found, the registry offices would tend to mix up birth time with registration time, or muddle am and pm ('du midi' and 'du matin'), or the tiny script was illegible. He nearly always received replies. Only for those in Michel's original group born in Paris (168) was he unable to re-check their birth data: someone would have to live there to do that, he explained. This new total of Academie members had 224 that were not in MG's original sample.

Of his total of these Academie members, it would be of value if a Parisien investigator could check at least some of the birthdata of those 168 born-in- Paris doctors included by MG but omitted by Müller? It would mean that an objectively-defined group would exist, who were members of the Academie of Medicine, with reliable birth-data, and French. Psychology students investigating this set are not going to want to hear obscure reasons why a German professor could not manage to re-check some Paris data.

---

[31] Müller, A and Ertel, S., (1994) '1083 Members of the French Académie de Médecine' Band 5 of *AstroForschungsDaten,* Waldmohr: A.P. Müller Verlag.

A search for 'proof'

Arno Müller was more or less the only person to have collected data for an independent replication of the 'Gauquelin effect', and then claim a positive result. He was certainly the only person in the world to have done so, and published the data. In 1994 he and Ertel concluded a new survey of French physicians, self-published in Müller's *Astro-Forschung Daten* manuscript. Journals such as *Correlation* or APP would have been delighted to have a positive-result replication by two German psychology professors, of Michel's very first discovery, but perhaps for that reason it was not to be. They never *published* their result in any normal sense, as one would normally expect with a key scientific replication.

The two German psychology professors Ertel and Müller working together were able to *confirm* in 1994 what MG had reported as his first discovery four decades earlier - namely that Mars and especially Saturn were significant for eminent French doctors. Let us here summarise:

<u>Arno Müller's positive result for Mars-Saturn and French physicians (n=915)</u>

Mars: 180 in KS 1&4, exp. 159.5 => 13% excess, $\chi^2 = 2.6$, $p < 0.1$
Saturn: 187 in KS 1&4, exp. 151.9 => 23% excess, $\chi^2 = 8$, $p < 0.005$

What a shame they could not have come out with a positive report like this while Michel was still alive!

In addition they discerned a lunar deficit of -15% which Michel had not reported. Suitbert Ertel who co-authored this study concluded: 'In view of the empirical evidence obtained so far I can see no reason for doubting the existence of planetary effects.' (Band 5, p.27). Would two German psychology professors be seen to co-author a paper demonstrating an independent replication of the Gauquelin effect, with a highly significant result for French physicians? The report was self-published in a volume having no date or name of author on its cover and its date '1994' only scratched in ink onto 'Band 5.'[32] That volume contained five data-collections, and its Band 5 had data and results for the total number of cases here checked, namely 915. Very few got to hear of the fruits of their labours.

---

[32] I am grateful to Prof Ertel for loaning me his copy of it.

There were some cases where Müller had to correct MG's birth-data (n= 76), and he there noted no evidence of systematic bias, as one would expect if MG were cheating.[33] However, if we compare the new physicians data gathered by Müller to that gathered by MG, we see a slight difference:

Arno Müller evaluates French Physicians data, using 36 sectors

		Mars	Saturn
Müller-Ertel only	(n=224)	46 in KS => 20.5%	61 in KS => 27.2%
MG only	(n=168)	39 in KS => 23.2%	49 in KS => 29.2%
Total	(n=915)	234 in KS => 25.6%	254 in KS => 27.8%

The data collected by Gauquelin has higher scores, for both Mars and Saturn, than that only collected by Müller and Ertel.[34] They cited this breakdown using thirty-six sectors, with eight Key-Sector totals given as a percentage of the whole.[35]

In his very first book, Michel had gathered over a thousand eminent physicians, from two different sources, and found a 22-23% excess of Mars and Saturn, both roughly equal in the two Key sectors, plus a deficit of Jupiter though the latter failed to reach statistical significance. Comparing that with the Müller data – which is a separate collection but does overlap somewhat with the Gauquelin data – we see a weaker effect, that his 1,083 more recent eminent French physicians gave a 13% excess of Mars but a powerful 25% excess for Saturn (Chi-squared = 14) plus a deficit of Jupiter.

Then, six years later, an article not authored or co-authored by Müller, in the *Journal for Scientific Exploration*, featured a short section containing their results - using oddly enough the larger number of physicians viz. 1,083 cases. The article, by Irving and Ertel,[36] (though Ken Irving had had nothing to do with the investigation) included a short, not too accurate couple of paragraphs explaining where the data had come from. Müller was then seventy years old (he died in 2005).

---

[33] Müller, Band 5, comment by Ertel, p.27.
[34] There were 691 physicians cited or collected by both of them, and they scored 27.2% of Mars in Key sectors.
[35] Ibid, Table 6, p.18, citing expected frequencies as 22.9% and 22.2% for Mars & Saturn.
[36] Irving and Ertel, 'The Mars Effect is Genuine,' JSE 2000 14,3

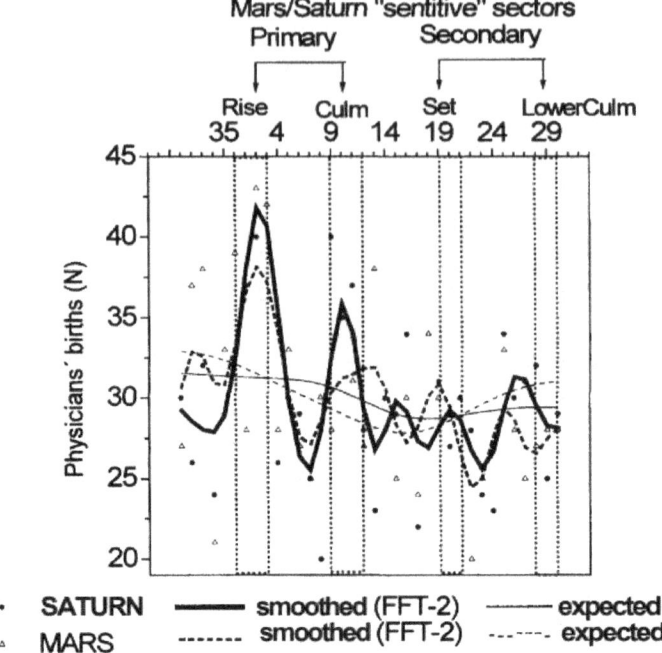

Figure: A dramatic view of Müller's French physicians data, as published in 2000.

It featured the above rather enchanting graph. In the JSE text, the significance levels are cited as being 0.06 for Mars and 0.00007 for Saturn, using the two Key sectors. That for Mars is about right, while that for Saturn is high, such that it's hard to calculate.

We have here a clear and strong positive replication,[37] using a 36-fold division with the two key sectors showing huge peaks for Saturn and lesser peaks for Mars. After so strong a positive result had been obtained - of much the same magnitude as the Gauquelins had earlier found for physicians – then why did not Arno Müller wish to publish it, or even to co-author an account? He had helped to collect and check the data, after all.

The graph shows the two extended key-sectors that are used in the 36-fold division of the circle, each covering four divisions or one-ninth of the circle: the first (rising) counts from 36 to 3 while the second (culminating) is 9-12. We see how Ertel plotted the 36 sectors by shifting them along so that his graph begins with 31, counting to 36,

---

[37] For how wrong I was, see my online 'How Ertel rescued the Gauquelin effect.'

then it starts again at 1 going onto 30, in order to highlight the rising position peak.

Ertel kindly gave me his copy of the data (identical with that in Müller's *Astro-forschung*[38]) enabling us to re-check these results. That data has here been plotted as for the Müller and Irving graph, in 36 sectors and with the data smoothed with a 3-point moving average, where separate dots are the unsmoothed data: and yes, the graph looks the same! 'Key sectors' are highlighted in yellow, of rising and culminating for Mars and Saturn, each comprising 4 out of 36 sectors.

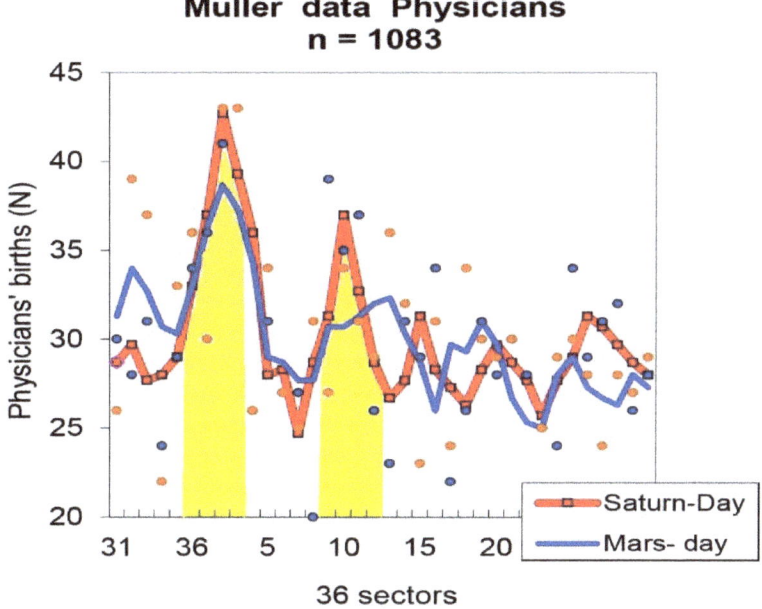

Figure: The Arno Müller physicians graph (36 Sectors) for both Mars and Saturn, as replicated by the Author.

If we take the larger number 1083 as plotted by Ertel and Irving, then using the 36-sector division a 24% excess of Saturn appears in the two Key sectors: Chi-squared =14 which is highly significant; while a mere 13% excess appears for Mars (Chi-squared = 4). We are relieved to endorse Ertel's maths for once. That is much the same as we saw earlier for the twelve-sector division and the number used by Müller, 915. A slight lunar deficit appeared of -8%, but the earlier Jupiter-deficit has gone.

---

[38] His book has a printout of the 1083 lines or birthdata; for digital values go to newalchemypress.com/gauquelin/, section 5, The Work of Arno Muller' and download.

A search for 'proof'

****

If one asks, "Are there any objectively-defined data-sets on which the Gauquelin effect can be tested?" then the answer has to be, yes: the 402 Italian writers and the 915 French doctors, collected by Müller. By 'objective' we here mean, that anyone else using the same reference-works would be bound to end up with more or less the same groups. We have seen how neither of these groups were published in the normal sense.

Müller's scrupulous care in acquiring and collating the data was not matched by his manner of reporting his results. We have here conjectured that a tenured professor could have got into trouble from reporting a positive result in this area. The births were over the period 1800-1920.

Michel's selection criterion for his group of physicians had been, membership of the prestigious French Academy of Medicine, whereas Arno Müller's survey of German physicians in 1986 did not select for eminence by membership of a prestigious society.[39] What he found displayed only a weak Saturn-effect: they scored 286 hits in the key sectors, and that was 24% of the total, whereas for his later 1994 survey this figure reached 28% (303 out of 1083 French physicians) - the expected mean value being 22%. This again shows an eminence effect, unfashionable though that notion may be today.

His survey concluded: 'Where G's data had to be corrected, this left the significance of his results unaffected...there exists, in my opinion, no solid reason that G's findings should not be acknowledged as objective ones.' Years later, an article by him in Francoise's journal, which re-checked MG's data on physicians, likewise concluded: 'This eliminates any suspicion of intentional tampering with the data by the Gauquelins.'[40] Thus we can say that Müller has independently validated the earlier MG data-collections.

When years later, Arno Müller discovered that a second edition of France's Academy of Medecine index had become available,

---

[39] Arno Müller, 'Last sich der Gauquelin-Effekt bestatigen?' *Zeitschrift fur Parapsychologie* 1986, 28, 87-103.
[40] APP September 1993, 'A Study of the G. Effect with 402 Italian Writers' p.13-21, 20). FG's commented on pp.22-28.

unnoticed by the Gauquelins,[41] he and Ertel used it as a basis for rechecking the hypothesis. A collection of 1086 member of the Académie de Medicine, of reliably-known birthdata, was thereby gathered, independently of the original Gauquelin collection, but with some overlap. Published in 1994 and co-authored with Ertel,[42] it confirmed a dominant Saturn-effect – as shown in the figure[43] - in the two key-sectors.

The traditional, Saturnine image of the doctor – i.e., one who can be safely allowed into one's home, on whose judgement one can rely, and whose profession had routinely to face death – that had thus been confirmed, by a separate gathering of data and fresh analysis. The strong Mars presence also confirmed what MG had found in his first publication, about French physicians.

What MG had found in his first book *Les hommes et les Astres*, had been replicated.[44] This is surely the firmest, most solid evidence we are going to come across: the effect for physicians replicates across various data-sources for eminent physicians, where no choice of data-selection exists, which rules out bias. It could not have somehow resulted from Michel collecting the data.

PROSPECTS

A good way to test the much-debated Mars-effect, which seems to have gone through some sort of anguished death and resurrection, would be to collect birthdata of Olympic gold, silver and bronze medallists every four years, collaborating with the sceptics in this endeavour.[45] In terms of how such a collaboration would work, one side (which one might wish to call, 'the believers') would be concerned to ascertain that the champions scored did indeed have 'the soul of

---

[41] Maurice Genty, *Index Biographique des Membres des Associes et des Correspondents de l'Académie de Médecine*, 2nd Edn., 1972 Paris (lists 1894 members); compare 1st Edn, 1939, Ed. Masson. Arno Müller discovered this volume in a Berlin library. He only scored the entries coming after 1792, when the French registration of birth-times began.
[42] Müller, A & Ertel, S, '1083 Members of the French Académy de Médecine', *Astroforschungsdaten* (Vol 5), Waldmohr: A.P. Müller; see also Ertel and Irving, ref.16, p.36.
[43] This graph appeared in JSE 2000, 14,3 p.425 using the earlier- published data (ref 28).
[44] To MG's original collection of 576 eminent French physicians which he published in 1955 he had added another 283, then Ertel and Müller collected 224 more; their rechecking altered 78 of MG's birthtimes.
[45] Concerning Olympic winners, see Ertel, *JSE* 1993, 7,2.

A search for 'proof'

hardened steel characteristic of the true sports champion'[46] as Michel put it, wherein lies the Mars-quality to be tested – and, as such, one might be uneasy about including some modern Olympic categories, such as diving or sailing, where this quality might be absent;[47] thus, one would be concerned with the *meaning* of the phenomenon. The 'sceptics', on the other hand, who see themselves as upholding science and reason, would be more concerned with procedure and whether something specified in advance could be demonstrated.

Does no Gauquelin-effect exist in modern populations, did it fade away in the mid- 20th century? It was irritating for the sceptics to be told this by MG. If so, the above proposal for Olympic winners might not work. We'll return to this theme, which involves the notion of influencing the birth-hour.

INTERSECTING SETS

Set theory uses the operations of union and intersection, the former being used for pooling together of data-sets. In the future, statisticians wishing to check out these databases will not want to hear obscure stories about who said what to whom, and the language of set theory offers a simple way of explaining where a data-group has come from.

The MG eminence-group is a *triune* concept, an intersection between three sets: for persons of a given profession, we seek for the sub-group of those with known birthdata and having an acceptable level of eminence, which has to be defined in some way.[48]

Intense debates have come about from difficulty in specifying a boundary to one of these sets, viz. 'eminent' persons.

For his 'painters' MG published all of those coming from one French

---

[46] Gauquelin, M. *Cosmic Influences on Human Behaviour*, London 1977, p.100.
[47] Asked whether Gauquelin had excluded any category of sport, Ertel replied in the negative, but added: "I have always been amazed that Gauquelin took every sports category that he found in his two main reference books (sports champions are categorized there). Gauquelin found differences among sports regarding the Mars effect, for example basket-ball did not have much of an excess of Mars-born players. So he advised Paul Kurtz to avoid selecting basket-ball players in the USA because he reckoned they were not likely to have a Mars effect: the result of Gauquelin's suggestion was that Kurtz selected a large proportion of basket ball players!"
[48] $N = \{P \cap B \cap E\}$ 'N' being the total group: 'P' the members of a given profession, here painters, 'B' is the set of reliable birthdata and 'E' comprises all 'famous' persons.

source and of known birthdata, and therefore his method is, as Ertel pointed out, fully checkable.[49] His re-analysis in 1987 started with a larger such group (1473 painters, as given by CURA) but found that, for the eminence-grading procedure, only three-quarters of those could be included, on account of his source for citations only going up to a certain date.[50] The eminence-grading of the groups already collected of artists and musicians' birthdata could nowadays be replicated and maybe improved using web-citations instead of reference-books. Bias is unlikely in the group of eminent painters' birthdata, because one finds no agreement as to which planet is supposed to be predominant: it mainly gave a negative Mars-effect. The total numbers involved slowly increase, as access to reliable birthdata improves.

Figure: how set-theory defines the group of 'eminent painters'

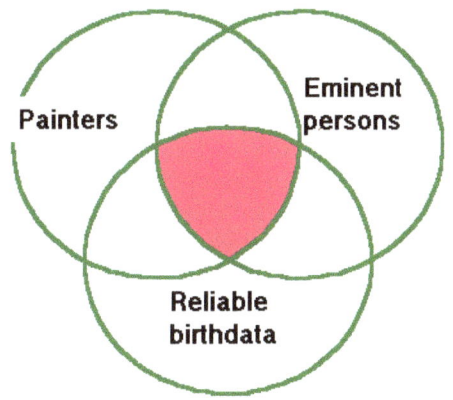

Here was Françoise's judgement concerning this Ertel-Müller replication:

> The idea behind this great effort was to check once and for all if the last CSICOP attempt to defame Michel Gauquelin's findings - by inventing ways in which our professional results might have been produced by devious (and actually impossibly complicated) manoeuvres - was justified by real cheating habits of my late husband ... the "Academiciens de Medecine" had been the first professional group collected by Michel, and therefore the only one gathered without my help. As CSICOP members seem to suspect me less easily of cheating than they do for Michel, checking the correctness of the birthdata as collected by Michel when he was alone was a crucial test of the validity of our data bases in general. It seems

---

[49] MG used the multi-volume *Dictionnaire critique et documentaire des peintres ... de tous les pays*, by Benezit E, Paris 1966: its first seven volumes were used for his 1955 *Les Hommes et les Astres*.
[50] Ertel Ref (11) p.8.

A search for 'proof'

> that this important control convinced the two German professors of Michel's absence of bias when he was collecting fficial birth records. Only a very few informations received by Ertel and Müller were different from the ones we had published. (APP 11,1 1995)

One regrets that MG did not live to hear that a university-based re-checking of his first, his original data-set, had fully confirmed it. Two German universities allowed their psychology professors to investigate the 'Gauquelin effect,' and in a sense, they rescued it. Science begins when data is replicated. By checking his data and developing the concept of eminence-testing using agreed reference-books, they left us a legacy of what can in principle become a new science of destiny. We here meditate upon the wise words of Ken Irving,

> A journey of discovery awaits those on both sides of the astrological divide who can put aside their hopes, fears and notions of what ought to be and who can instead look at what is.[51]

---

[51] *The Tenacious Mars-Effect*, Ertel & Irving, 1996, p.vii.

8.

A 'HEREDITY' EFFECT? NOT REALLY ...

Over several decades, both Gauquelins averred that what they called a 'Heredity' effect existed between parents and children of non-eminent people.[52] They amassed over a hundred thousand sets of birthdata of ordinary families, living in Paris, born around the turn of the 20th century. Some were single-parent families and all had children. For the Gauquelins, the point of this investigation was what they called 'heredity,' by which they meant, a relation between the birthcharts of parent and child.

From the 1960s right up to his last publication, Michel would keep alluding to it. He attended cosmo-geophysical conferences (ie, not astrological) where he would present papers averring that the fluctuating level of geomagnetism affected this heredity linkage![53] Based on this he would then theorise about how astrology, or what he had discovered about the matter, 'worked' – implying that some sort of 'mechanism' could be at last in sight. There are no less than thirteen documents by the two of them, now posted up on CURA, giving natal data of this kind, parents and children.[54] There are at least four books they published on the subject:

> M&F Gauquelin *Replication of the planetary effect in heredity*, Series D: Scientific documents (Vol. 2) 1977, Paris;

---

[52] M.G., *L'Hérédité Planétaire* 1966, English: *Planetary Heredity* 1988, ACS Publications.

[53] MG, 'A possible heredity effect on time of birth', Proc 4th Int Biometeorological Congress, *Int. Jnl. Biometeorology*, 1967, Supplement 11, p.341.

[54] Of the 13 data-sets put up on the CURA website, the first six correspond with what G. published in 1970, M&F Gauquelin, *Series-C Profession Heredity Results of Series A&B*, Paris 1972. The birth-data is here generally given to within the hour, but sometimes half-hour or quarter-hour. It is less clear where the second half of the data comes from. Most of it is described on the CURA site as 'unpublished' The 1984 publication M. Gauquelin, *New Birth Data Series Volume 2 Planetary Heredity A Reappraisal of 50,000 subjects* Paris 1984 had a small amount of data and said most was kept on magnetic tape at the San Diego Astro Computing Service.

A 'Heredity' effect? Not really ...

M&F Gauquelin, *Birth and planetary data gathered since 1949, Heredity Experiment,* Series B Vol. 4, 1970, Paris;

M.G., *Planetary Heredity: A reappraisal on 50,000 subjects.* New birth data series (Vol.2) 1984 Paris;

M.G., *Planetary Heredity,* 1988.

Here's how they described the effect:

> At the moment of birth of their children, they [the 'Gauquelin planets'] tend to lie in the same diurnal position that they occupied at the moment of birth of their parents. In particular there is a tendency for children to be born after the rise or culmination of one of the celestial bodies, if the same circumstances held for the birth of one of their parents.[55]

They added that, 'It is very marked for the Moon, Venus and Mars.' A decade later they described it thus:

> Children have a tendency to be born when a planet has just risen or culminated, if that same planet was in the same regions of the sky at the birth of their parents.[56]

A 1976 replication with another thirty thousand pairs of parent-child birthdata by both Gauquelins was reported as confirming the effect.[57]

Michel added, 'if both parents of the child were born at the rise or culmination of the same planet, the tendency in the child was doubled. But planetary heredity becomes weaker over the generations and is less marked from grandparents to grandchildren.'[58] Here is Francoise's definition:

> If we divide the parents' charts into two subsamples: (a) those in which a given planet is in a Key Sector, and (b) those in which it isn't, then we expect the children's planet to occupy more often a Key Sector in subsample (a) and more often not in subsample (b).[59]

---

[55] M&F G., Heredity Experiment, 1970, series B, Vol. 4, p.11.
[56] MG, *The Truth about Astrology,* 1983, p.43.
[57] M&F G., Replication of the Heredity Effect in Heredity, Series D, Vol II, 1977.
[58] MG Ibid, p46.
[59] F.G. 'Planetary Heredity: New Research Results,' APP 1992,8,1, p.11. MG had given much the same account of what they were looking for in 1984: a tendency for children to be born with [the Gauqulein planets] in plus zones if the same circumstance held for one of the parents.' Corr 1984 4,1, p.17.

It is similar to the above definition but not the same, i.e the maths would be slightly different. We would like, but do not get, more detail of what was actually done here.

L. Jean	21.2.1896,0h	Fontaine (Yonne)								
P. Angéle	7.11.1890,21h	Iffendic (I & V)								
fem.	6.2.1924,0h30	Créteil (Seine)								
	SO	MO	ME	VE	MA	JU	SA	UR	NE	PL
Father	27	17	29	30	30	12	36	36	16	16
Mother	24	29	25	22	17	17	29	25	5	5
child	28	27	30	25	33	33	2	25	10	13

The card here reproduced shows one of sixteen thousand parent-child data cards allegedly prepared, each having the data of mother, father and child, plus the ten planets given as 36-sector positions, to check for matches.[60] That would have been a vast amount of work, to find the 36 sector position for each planet, for such a huge population. And what for? The above definitions do not allude to the 36-fold sector division.

Their data-volume on Heredity[61] has each family as a unit, with just the five 'Gauquelin' planet positions quoted in their 36-sector division, plus a GMF value. If this data was ever kept on cards, they have all vanished now.

Michel's second from last book, egoistically entitled *The Truth about Astrology* (1983), all about his own work, devoted a chapter to the topic. It gave no hint that anyone else was helping him in this endeavour, it was just 'I, I, I'. Statistics are unlikely to be reliable if just one person does it all: several persons are normally required, or a minimum of two, for them to agree upon it, prior to publishing, if it is to carry credibility. The Gauquelins separated in 1982 and were divorced in 1985.

Now in this 21st century, when the *sturm und drang* is all over – the huge promises of a new *weltanschauung* - we are left with the largest database of reliably-timed birthdata on a specific theme, that has ever existed: over a hundred thousand lines of it, grouped in family units father, mother and children. Plus, each data-line has a 'Ci' value next to it, a geomagnetism index, all digitally transcribed in this 21st

---

[60] MG, *Planetary Heredity*, 1988, p16.
[61] M&FG, *Heredity Experiment* Ser b, Vol. 4, 1970.

century from the old books, onto the CURA site. This was a colossal amount of labour, and what does it show, does it prove some astral 'heredity'?

No, it does not.

For years I had wondered, about how one could check these claims, and how strange it was that no-one else had. Eventually, the Down Under investigator Ray Murphy (in Adelaide) put all the CURA 'heredity' data-sets together and thereby obtained four groups, of Mother-Son, Mother-Daughter, Father-Son and Father-Daughter, each having between twelve and fourteen thousand such pairs. Then I and my colleague S.R. became able to output the planetary house-positions (Placidus) for each of these, using the Solar Fire software (by Astrolabe, USA). It's a sobering experience to watch as Solar Fire outputs fourteen thousand charts in half a minute![62] Examining these huge groups, there was no tendency for planets to appear in the same houses parent-child, neither in the key sectors nor anywhere else.

This was a big shock to me.

For years I had wondered, how the great claim could be tested, but never did it occur to me, in applying for a grant to investigate the matter, that no such effect existed. There had been just too many conferences and books published, there were too many top virtuosos holding forth about the matter, taking for granted that some such effect was real.

Does the dream die? Up to a point, yes. We let go of that which does not exist, of a mere phantom. These negative findings endorse comments made by British psychologist David Nias. Thirty years ago he wrote in a review of Michel Gauquelin's new 'heredity' (i.e., parent-child) study:[63]

> In this replication of the planetary heredity study, Gauquelin presents data collected by registry office workers in five Paris areas. The results analysed by computer are consistent across the five areas: there is no indication of

---

[62] The 'heredity' results were generally depicted using 18-fold division of the diurnal circle: and our use of Solar Fire to do the calculations only allowed a 12-fold division.
[63] David Nias, 'Planetary Heredity: A Reappraisal on 50,000 subjects' book review Correlation Nov. 1984, p.45, reprinted in APP, 1985 3,2, p.33. David Nias was co-author along with Hans Eysenck of *Astrology: Science or Superstition?* (1982). He was reviewing MG's 1984 'Planetary Heredity a review of 50,000 subjects'.

planetary heredity, with all the results being clearly non-significant. Because of the large sample-size (totalling 50,942 cases) and the apparently rigorous manner in which the data were collected and analysed, this constitutes a serious failure to reproduce the results of the original study.

In his report, Gauquelin describes how he has checked the original analysis (published in full in 1970) and the first replication (published in 1977), which were both calculated by hand. Re-analysis by computer resulted in lowered significance levels. In the 1977 replication, this was sufficient to reduce the results to an almost non-significant level...The present study seems to confirm the conclusion that planetary effects apply only to famous people.

Michel wanted to make this mirage, this phantom a focal point for his huge endeavour and his second book on this subject (1988) affirmed:

> I consider planetary heredity, if real, to be a potential Rosetta Stone for all my findings ... It represents the best opportunity to integrate into modern science the 'neo-astrological' correlations discussed...[64]

Here is how Françoise summarised her position, after MG's passing, back in 1992[65]:

> There was good news to announce. First and foremost, it appears that the heredity effect is still valid. The non-positive outcomes obtained in 1984 have turned out to be related to the choice of urban areas for the data collection. A child's parturition is more and more often medically monitored there, so that the natural birth times that correlate with planetary positions are not given enough chance to reveal the planetary link between parents and children. But a new collection of three thousand timed births of parents and their children born in more rural areas provides a first significant outcome. Further similar data collections have already been started for giving a larger basis to the replicated effect.

---

[64] MG, *Planetary Heredity*, 1988, p.xv.
[65] *Correlation*, 1992,8,1,p.50, APP *Astropsychological Problems*, summary of issue 1992 Vol. 8., by FG.

A 'Heredity' effect? Not really ...

A quarter of a century after his death, we finally confirm the emptiness of this dream, the error of the huge endeavour.

But, for a different reason, we are glad that it was done.

The bar-chart is Geoffrey Dean's summary of these various surveys by the Gauquelins on this topic (the details don't here concern us). It shows how the first survey of Paris families claimed to have the most positive results.[66] Dean gives no reference for where this summary came from, nor any hint as to how what he is calling 'phi' might measure the 'Heredity effect.'

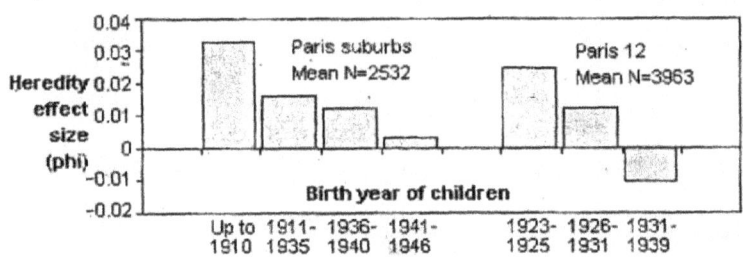

Figure: Geofrey Dean explains, 'Planetary links as effect size *phi* between parents and children tend to diappear as births become more recent, whether in Paris suburbs generally or in a single arondissement.'

The calculation is simple. The prediction is, that a planet turning up in one of the two Key Sectors of parents, using the original twelvefold division, will increase the likelihood of producing the same in that of a child. The expected frequency here is simply the square of the basic value, which in this case is 1/6. Thus, taking two of the twelve Placidus houses, the likelihood that the Moon, or Saturn or Jupiter will turn up in a key Sector is precisely 1/6, so likewise will the chance be of the child having that same feature, $(1/6)^2$: the coincidence will therefore be expected one in 36 times.

One is surprised that the Gauquelins never explained this simple square-ratio as giving the expected frequency, in any of their publications on the topic.

In their bulky data-volumes on 'Heredity Experiment' they recorded, for every mother, Father and child, the position in 36-sectors of five different planets. One is perplexed as regards the point of this.

---

[66] This bar-chart has been *thrice* published by Dean, twice in *Astrology Under Scrutiny* 2014 p.127 and, then in *Tests of Astrology* of 2016, p.

An easy-to use set of the heredity data has been posted up on the research page.[67] It consists of 20,916 groups of birthdata, Father, Mother and eldest child, in a form that can readily be copied and pasted onto a spreadsheet. Then, one at a time the separate columns can be fed into an astrology program eg Solar Fire. One could ask it to give e.g. lunar positions, for the Mother and child columns, in the twelve Placidus sectors. We then paste the two columns into an Excel spreadsheet, and the computer tots up all of the rows where the Moon is in the same house for parent and child.

We therefore expect to score around 20916/36 = 581 by chance, of the Moon being in that condition described by the Gauquelins as showing 'Heredity.' In fact there are 592, a mere 2% more, taking here the elder child of each family.

There is no effect.

One is here reminded of the conclusion drawn by the late German psychology professor Suitbert Ertel (1932 -2017):

> I first came across Gauquelin's research in 1976. I, too, was struck by is apparent golden glitter. But was it genuine? Today, after many trials, I believe that its original kernel is genuine while some of its later additions are spurious, as explained in what follows.[68]

For years, I was unhappy about that conclusion as being rather supercilious. At last, at the time of his passing, I came to agree with him at least in this respect. That conclusion of his was published, in the very last years of MG's life. Ertel could never do what I've done here, namely aligning the huge parent and child data-sets and counting them to detect any synastry.

---

[67] At www.newalchemypress.com/gauquelin/research7.php, right-click on the database, paste into a text file, open that in a spreadsheet eg Excel, copy one of the columns of data eg 'Mother', save it as a text file, then that can be fed into the Solar Fire to generate the zodiac longitudes.
[68] Ertel, 'Purifying Gauquelin's Grain of Gold' *Correlation* 1989 9,1 p.5

9

CHARACTER TRAITS

MOON

Very few scientists and sports champions are born with the Moon in a zone of high intensity. - M.G. [1]

The effect of the Moon in the group of imaginative writers was stronger than that for any of Gauquelin's other professional groups, scoring a huge 30% excess in key sectors (Chapter 1, Table 1). The Gauquelins claimed to discern the ideal writer's portrait as follows:

Doux, impressionable, nonchalant, parle bien, reveur, sensible, spirituel, subtil, sportif (pas)' [2]

(gentle, impressionable, nonchalant, well-spoken, a dreamer, sensuous, spiritual, subtle, not sporty). They found this modal personality most pronounced in imaginative writers, poets and dramatists.

To see how the effect, for the Moon and imaginative writers/poets, is larger than any other, here are the largest effects in descending order (% excess in the two Key Sectors):

Writers (n=1352) and the Moon	+30%
Sports (n=2088) and Mars	+26%
Military (n=3046) and Jupiter	+23%
Politicians and Jupiter (n=1002)	+22%

taken from Table 1 of Chapter 1. The significance levels are here in the region of one in a hundred thousand (i.e., chi-squares around twenty).

The group of writers and poets can be split into two groups, factual - historical and imaginative - fictional. From the writers' group,

---

[1] MG, *Spheres of Destiny*, 1980, p.124.
[2] M. Gauquelin, *La Cosmopsychologie*, Paris 1974, p.155

separating out poets and novelists[3] leaves a remainder of historians and writers on factual or philosophical topics. The sub-groups are thus:

    Novelists (465) and the Moon   + 42%
    Poets (420) and the Moon   + 31%
    Factual authors (536) and Moon +23%

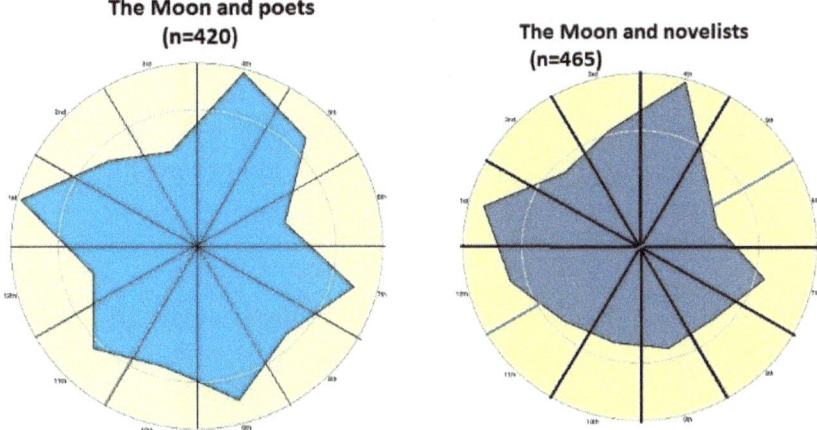

The graph for novelists shows an astonishing focus upon the MC position, or rather just after it (i.e., the 4th Gauquelin sector) - appropriate for people whose profession depends upon imaginative fantasy. Whereas, for poets and the Moon we see not quite so strong an effect (which is surprising), but a more fourfold pattern. Combining the novelists and poets gives an extremely high significance level of chi-squared at twenty. How strange that Michel never ever spoke about this, or wrote about it – his largest effect!

These groups have Saturn-deficits of around 10% in key-sectors, again in accord with tradition, and these are significant taken together (Chi-square = 6); whereas the remaining group of factual-historical writers, lacks any such Saturn deficit.[4]

Thus Selene's Sphere does - give birth to poets. How it does so is another matter, by no means within the scope of our enquiry.

---

[3] In the Writers & Journalists data of opengauquelin.org, select 'poets.' The *volume Series A, Volume 6 'Writers and journalists'* by M&F Gauquelin, 1971 has these poets on pages 43-47, novelists on pp.38-42.
[4] Saturn and the moon have expected frequencies just 1/6th of the total, as they have no degree of solar linkage (Chapter 1).

Character traits

A smaller lunar excess was found in the charts of eminent politicians (See Table 1, Chapter 1): here one could say that a politician aspires to reflect the feelings of the electorate, to express their mood, and may do so in a transient and changeable manner.

One would not expect to find these kind of character-traits in journalists, that being a different and more pushy temperament, focussed on the immediate present. Jupiter scored positive for this profession, the Moon being slightly negative. MG's comment here was: 'The group I set up is not made of simple reporters working to order, but rather those who direct and design Italian journalism, and whose fame is sufficient for them to figure in collections of prominent people'[5] - which could show more of a Jovian temperament.

MARS

Groups of basketball players, MG ascertained, hardly showed any 'Mars Effect.' Their skill does not involve aggression or nerves of steel and is more collaborative. The US sceptics, Michel complained, had collected undue numbers of such sportsmen. British psychologist Hans Eysenck, discussing this situation, here took the view that: "Gauquelin had noticed in his European sample that basketball players had a very low Mars effect, and the fact that the same was found in the American sample is really a finding that may be regarded as a replication of Gauquelin's earlier experience.'[6]

Some years later, Ertel found a gender-bias evident in the Mars and sports champion effect. Of his huge sports-champion database, of over four thousand, some 4% were female. For a given level of eminence his female sports-champions tended to have stronger Mars (i.e., scoring more frequently in their key sectors). He divided all the data into four grades of eminence and used the 36-fold division method, obtaining result as shown on the graph.[7]

---

[5] MG, *Written in the Stars*, 1988, p.137.
[6] Zetetic Scholar, 1982, 9, p.62, comments on article by Patrick Curry, 'Research on the Mars Effect'
[7] The expected value here is 22% (8/36=22.2%), see Chapter 2, Fig.2.

Figure: Sports champion data, grouped by four levels of eminence, gender-separated: 4391 champions, 186 of them female. Ertel 1988.[8]

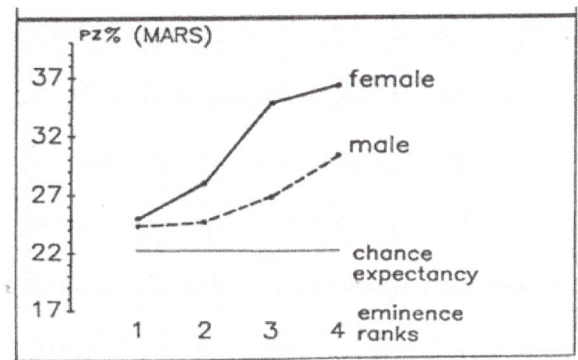

Likewise for actors, Ertel found that female stars needed more help from Mars to tread the boards so to speak, than their male counterparts. Although there was overall no Mars-effect for actors, he discerned a several percent difference:

Actors	No. in group	Mars in KS %
Male	1280	20%
Female	583	24%

(22% being the chance-expected level, using the 36 sectors). For Jupiter, the main planet for actors, no difference was found, so it was only Mars that responded to gender - in accord with millennia of tradition.

MG found a positive Mars-effect with French physicians, which is rather worrying. What has rough Mars got to do with the healing art? Physicians were then accustomed to carrying a knife around, a scalpel, in their doctor's bag, for the purpose of bloodletting. To quote Michel, pondering what he had found:

> *Sans doute Mars, dieu de la guerre, le violent et flamboyant Mars joue-t-il un rôle à la naissance des chefs militaires, et cela est curioux. Mais il serait logique de s'attendre à ce qu'il marque également la naissance des chirurgiens, puisque Mars est traditionnellement en rapport avec tout ce qui incise et découpe.*

'... everything that cuts and beheads'! Plus, the group was entirely masculine, the more feminine side of the healing art having been so to speak disposed of - or, one could even say, burnt at the stake - in

---

[8] Ertel, 'Planetary Relations with Female notabilities, Two First results,' APP, 9,1, pp.22-5.

centuries gone by. For whatever reason, a strong and somewhat anomalous Mars-energy was here present, and yes it did replicate.

SATURN

The temperament of great painters was found to be the opposite of scientists, in that Mars and Saturn scored positively in Key Sectors for science types, but reached a negative score of comparable amplitude for painters (Chapter 1, Table 1). The British psychologists Eysenck and Nias reckoned that Saturn best differentiated the artistic and scientific temperaments:

> He [MG] contrasted 5,100 successful artists with 3,647 successful scientists, and found that Saturn was the planet that best differentiated these two groups.[9]

A modern replication of MG's work might wish to compare the diurnal distribution of Saturn in groups of eminent artists and scientists, contrasting their Saturn distributions. Rotating the 'key Sectors round 45° one might see peak scores with the artists where one saw conversely low scores with the science-types. As discussed earlier in chapter 1, one might prefer a 16-fold division of the diurnal circle, to examine a fourfold pattern.

JUPITER

Michel collected birthdata of Nazi stormtroopers, and was startled to find a huge excess of Jupiter in their Key Sectors. It was a 42% excess - no other effect he ever found was as large as that! It was mainly around his 4th Sector, after the MC.[10] Was Jupiter as a Norse Storm-god - Zeus or Thor - turning up? Michel allowed himself to remark, in his second book:

> *La planète Jupiter ... prend ici un relief extraordinaire...Tout se passe comme si un déterminisme puissant avait présidé à la naissance des futurs dirigeants de ce qui fut le IIIe Reich...'*

---

[9] Eysenck & Nias, *Astrology Science or Superstition?* p.185. They don't give many references, and one may wonder where their 5,100 artists came from. Eysenck had had many conversations with the Gauquelins and had a good idea of what they had done.
[10] MG *Les Hommes et Les Astres* p.112-3, for English translation see *Written in the Stars,* 1980, pp.122-3: a group of 508 Stormtroopers and Nazis showed Jupiter 118 times in Key Sectors, expect 83.

Figure 3: Jupiter in 12 Key Sectors of 508 prominent Nazi officials and stormtroopers.

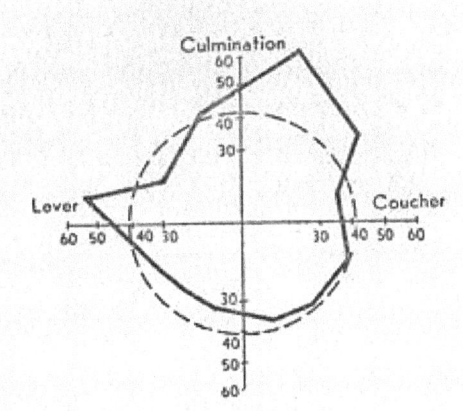

Jupiter tends to be portrayed by astrologers as Mr Nice Guy, as balanced, Jovial and benevolent, but the Gauquelins discerned this unexpected Thor-type 'dark side'; which tends again to suggest they were not cheating. I haven't found details of the birth-data from this early text (*Les Hommes et les Astres*), i.e. this is 'lost' data, so one cannot check it.[11] Let's hope someone re-collects that sample as it is so interesting.

We've twice quoted Michel in French, so let's note that character and soul-meaning is more readily expressed by him in his own native tongue, while his English-written books and articles are more dryly empirical. As a general comment, Michel declined to lecture on the intriguing variety of different archetypes that were turning up in his professional groups: it was always, the Mars-effect in sportsmen, which developed quite a level of tedium, in his visits to British astro-research conferences, as year after year he kept on with the same topic. There were some hints of Venus turning up in the artistic temperament, but nothing very definite.[12]

---

[11] The CURA data online does give 494 German military but its distribution does not much resemble the above - it's not the same data.

[12] For weak Venus-effect, see eg David Cochrane, 'Did Gauquelin prove astrology? Part 1' (online), 16 mins.

10

THE PRIMARY ARCHETYPES

The relationship between planet and character-trait could be observed without any need to take account of the professions.

Michel Gauquelin, 1983[1]

The Gauquelins published their big data-volumes, in the early 1970s, concerning the groups of eminent professionals, four of which had keywords extracted from biographies.[2] The so-called 'A' volumes gave the birthdata, while the four 'C' volumes had the character-traits,[3] as follows:

C2 Mars and Sports Champions…A1 Sports champions
C3 Saturn & Men of Science ….. A2 Scientists & Physicians
                                                     A3 Military
                                                     A4 Painters & Musicians
C4 Jupiter and Actors   … A5 Actors and Politicians
C5 The Moon and writers   … A6 Writers & Journalists

As well as six data-volumes of their different professional groups, which they labelled 'A1' Sports Champions to 'A6' Writers and Journalists, there were four where they extracted their lists of character-traits.[4] Only the Bibliothéque Natioale in Paris now houses

---

[1] Gauquelin *The Truth about Astrology*, 1983, p.63.
[2] There may also be a 5th volume based on US data: *Report on American Data, Series D*, Vol. X 1982. See MG, *The Truth about Astrology* 1983, p57.
[3] For a discussion of the process of extracting trait-adjectives from biographies, and the extent to which different persons concur on this matter, from a sceptical viewpoint, see Ertel, 'Why the character-Trait Hypothesis still fails' *Correlation* 1993 12(1) pp.2-9. He there disputed how many adjectives should be extracted from a given biography, where the Gauquelin approach seems to have been fairly minimalistic compared to others: since we are here restricting ourselves to John Addey's approach, whereby only four or five adjectives are used, I suggest that that old dispute does not matter very much.
[4] He selected (Dean explained) the four professional groups whose achievement was most strongly linked to a single planet and over ten year with various people assisting him he extracted traits for around one-third of each group. He took 60% of the writers' group but only 20% of the scientists, reflecting availability of biographies. Geoffrey

this complete set of data[5] - few books are so hard to find. Occasionally a second-hand copy will become available on the Web. No complete set of these volumes seems to exist.

We all feel that we know what a character-trait is, more or less. A psychologist might describe it as 'a relatively persistent and consistent behaviour pattern manifested in a wide range of circumstances.' Whatever they are, the Gauquelins began employing a team to extract them from biographies of eminent professionals in 1967, poring through designated encyclopaedias and compendia, of sports and music, etc. Michel describes how he would copy out details of sports biographies and then have a psychology student extract the traits.[6] There were a dozen paid helpers for this enormous task.[7] His work for the French psychology journal *Psychologie d'Aujourdhui* must have helped him here.[8]

Descriptive nouns and adjectives were selected. Thus, taking this excerpt (of a bio of a Nobel-prize winning French writer)

> One striking feature of this long career ... is the impetuous curiosity which turned him towards journalism where his reputation was soon established. Irritated – and for others irritating – the pen often ferocious, impulsive and indefatigable.

they selected from this the trait-words *impetuous, curious, irritated, irritating, ferocious* and *impulsive*.[9]

For the adjective 'Energetic' (the French word being similar) there is, in each of the four 'C' volumes, a list of names, for whom this adjective has been attributed. John Addey found that 'the word ENERGETIC was attributed to 187 different people (94 champions, 34 scientists, 42 actors, 17 writers).'[10] He is here giving the number of times this traits was cited in each of the four source-books, eg the Gauquelins found seventeen eminent writers of known birthdata who

---

Dean, 'John Addey's Dream: Planetary harmonics and the character-trait hypothesis', *Correlation* 1997 16(2) 10-39.
[5] The British Library has four of them: A2,C3, C4 and C5.
[6] MG, *The Truth about Astrology*, 1983, p.53.
[7] Dean et al., *Tests of Astrology*, p.88.
[8] Michel also had connections with the journal *Science et Vie*, see Chapter 5.
[9] *The Mars-Temperament and Sports Champions*, M&F G. 1973, p.23.
[10] JM Addey, *A New Study of Astrology*, 1996, p.118.

had been described as 'energetic' in a biography. I obtained the same count as Addey for this trait, which reassured me sufficiently to embark upon the present topic.[11]

TRAIT - CITATIONS

If one counts the number of traits having a decent score, i.e. that could be usable, one finds some 120 character-traits in the Mars and sports-champion data-volume:[12] many of which will appear likewise in the other three reference-volumes. Overall, there will be a maximum of around two hundred that could be usable. Traits 'having a decent count' could here mean, counted a minimum of forty or fifty times, in the different biographies.

A chapter-heading in Michel's 1983 opus was '50,000 Character traits.' Much of the general nausea that I used to come across, concerning the so-called 'CTH' or 'Character-traits hypothesis' may have come from this absurd number. Over the decade 1967 to 1977, he and a team of assistants had allegedly collected 'altogether 6,000 character traits for sporting champions, 10,000 for scientists, 18,000 for actors and 176,000 for writers. Eventually I had at my disposal an impressive catalogue of over 50,000 character-traits, an almost inexhaustible mine…'[13] No, he didn't! Likewise Françoise alluded, years later, to 'the complete catalogue of extracted traits, about 50,000 on the whole.'[14]

The Gauquelins are alluding here, to the number of times all the different traits were counted, in all the biographies, in other words a total, overall score and that could easily have added up to fifty thousand. The Gauquelins may have had fifty thousand *trait citations*. The number of their usable traits, ie having a decent number of citations, lies below two hundred. With that semantic quibble behind us, we proceed.

---

[11] In contrast, Francoise's *Psychology of the Planets* has 258 citations of the energetic trait in the four volumes (p.47). Maybe some multiple scoring was going on here? She named it: 'Number of birth data analysed for the trait' (p.43) as published in 'four successive volumes' (p.3).
[12] M&F G., *The Mars Temperament and Sports Champions* 1973.
[13] MG *The Truth About Astrology* 1983 p.55.
[14] FG, APP 11,1 March 1995, 'CTH Yes or No?' p.9.

The Gauquelins claimed that 'The abstractors of the personality attributes from the biographies did not know of the theory here tested.'[15] We'd like to have been given some details of these shadowy persons, and how they worked on the project.

We saw how the Gauquelins went over to California in 1980, where Neil Michelsen, Director of *Astro-computing Services* in San Diego undertook the huge enterprise of putting all of their data into a digital format, including the trait-words. Neil was not himself an astrologer but had a maths degree and is remembered for writing the programs whereby automatic horoscopes could be generated, so they did not have to be done by hand any more. He had started producing the yearly 'American Ephemeris.'

> We spent an entire year in San Diego, living in a white house two blocks away from Neil's computer. We also had the competent help of Thomas Shanks, ACS Director of Research,

recalled Françoise;[16] John Addey likewise recalled,

> In March 1979, Neil Michelsen very kindly and generously invited me to San Diego as his guest and placed at my disposal his computer which had been fully programmed with all the Gauquelin's data. In this way, with the help of Tom Shanks at the controls, I was able to repeat with much greater accuracy and with a larger set of character-trait words (enlarging the vocabulary from the top 87 words to the top 199) the work I had done in the previous two or three years.'[17]

This appears as the great moment of 20th century astro-research, as the Pythagorean philosopher John Addey scrutinised the Gauquelin data newly-uploaded into the powerful Californian computer. But alas no trace of this endeavour remains - all was lost![18] The magnetic

---

[15] M&F Gauquelin and Sybil Eysenck, 'Personality and the position of the planets at birth: an Empirical study' *Brit Jnl Clin Psy,* 1979, 18, 71-75, 74.
[16] FG, *Psychology of planets,* 1982, p.11.
[17] Addey, 'Harmonic Phase and Personal Characteristics – Part II' The Astrol Jnl., Winter 1979-80,pp.7-13, 8.
[18] We only have the rather brusque report given by Michel in his 1984 *Correlation* article (Chapter 1).

discs on which the data was stored did not make the transition into the 21st century.

Tom Shanks had input a couple of hundred trait words: roughly the number usefully extractable from the data. He occasionally emails me to say he's enquiring about the data, or where his old article might be, but his memory is gone. Years ago, back in the 20th century, after Neil Michelsen's passing, I recall visiting the ACS in Los Angeles and asking about any archives they might have, and encountering some kindly but blank faces. Let us hope that the present pilot-study may rekindle an interest in the subject, sufficient to get such a database online.

As a general comment, Addey's work was quite heavy on Pythagorean philosophising, with optimism about the big change that was to come - which never materialized - but it was supported only by a quite slender factual or empirical basis. Nonetheless I tended to believe him. He passed away while working on his trait-adjective theory. I used to drop in on him now and then and hear about it. Years later, Charles Harvey did his best to assemble the unfinished notes into a book, which emerged in 1996.[19] This chapter would not exist, without that opus.

Addey selected Mars key-words such as *active, courageous, rash* and *bold*, as well as *energetic,* and found that from these he obtained a fourfold diurnal pattern in the G-sectors.[20] This was supposed to be the same whether the biographies were from the Mars-types (athletes and military) or for others. What he called the 'pure 4th harmonic qualities (active, energetic etc)' gave a distribution such that

> ...there is no longer any tendency for there to be stronger peaks after the rise and upper culmination; all four angles are more or less equal in strength.

This point is very crucial and constitutes a huge difference, separating the character-trait results from that of the professional

---

[19] Addey, op.cit., 1996, Ch8 (he died in '82).
[20] While the Gauquelins were over in California, Tom Shanks did a computer study of trait-adjectives 'using the ACS computer on which the entire Gauquelin database was stored' (Dean *et. al., Astrology under Scrutiny*, p.235) –no trace of which now remains (nor does his Wiki site mention this). I have not even been able to find his report, Cosmecology Bulletin, 1980, 2(2) 81-86. Tom Shanks is still alive, but can't remember much.

groups. The Gauquelins did not comment upon this, i.e. that the phenomenon was manifesting as four equal peaks - in contrast to his professional data. Nor did anyone else in the 20th century, apart from Mr Addey.

In astrology the four 'cadent' houses numbered 3, 6, 9 and 12 become the Gauquelin-sectors 1, 4, 7 and 10, counted clockwise. These houses have always been regarded as somehow weak, for obscure reasons: "The Greeks called the cadent houses *apoklima*, which literally means "falling" or "decline," because the houses were seen to be falling away from the strength of the angular houses."[21] But, to quote Françoise:

> Each time statistically significant results showed up, they were maximal in those so-called "cadent houses". Present day traditionalists are shocked by these statistical results in Cadent instead of Angular houses. [22]

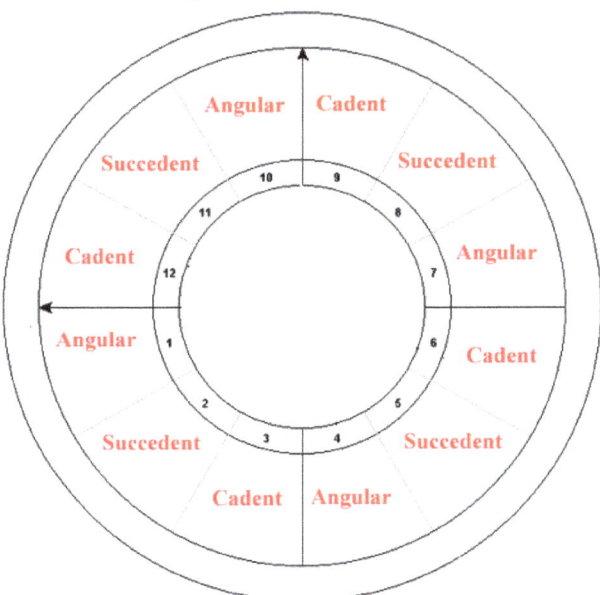

Figure: house system nomenclature: angular, cadent & succedent.

I selected a similar group of Mars-words to test: *courageous, active, energetic, combative* and *dynamic*, as being reasonably frequent in the 'thumbnail biographies'. I found that astrologers agreed upon them,

---

[21] Wiki, cadent houses.
[22] FG, APP September 1992 p.21. See further comments by FG in Appendix 1.

The Primary archetypes

viz that they were Martial not eg Saturnine. Also their French meaning was more or less the same as for the equivalent English word (there are fewer French adjectives, so this is not always the case). These traits are *coherent*, in the sense that all persons I consulted agreed in assigning them to Mars.

Here are the traits chosen, together with their 'citation counts' ie how many times they were selected, plus their net or mean percentage excess scored in the cadent houses:

Moon: {Imaginative (84), fantasy (77), dreamer 70, tranquil (57), pure (44)} => mean excess, 79%.

Mars: {Courageous (231), active (205), energetic (184), combative (109), dynamic (56)} => mean excess 78%

Jupiter: {Authority (125), joyful (90) director (81), organizer (71), pride (67)} => mean excess 68%

Saturn: {Solitary (105), deep (76) severe (64) cold (63), silent (45)} => mean excess 58%.

The basic archetypes here manifest, using just five adjectives. Jung would have understood.

Those traits were distributed unequally amongst the professions as we'd expect. We can see for example how 'scientists' had more 'Martial' traits but less pertaining to the traditionally-feminine planets Moon and Venus. The Table shows how these twenty traits were cited nearly two thousand times, in the four reference-books.

Profess^n Group	Luna	Mars	Jup	Sat	Total
Writers (2027)	174	116	87	133	521
Scientists(n=1094)	41	183	125	99	464
Actors (n=1409)	80	174	141	89	459
Sports (n=2089)	41	316	82	39	495

Table 2: Biographic sources of the above-selected trait-groups.

Here is another circular graph showing how, for overall citations of the traits *Active, courageous, Energetic, Combative, Dynamic* (altogether 789 of them), Mars came up with a huge 78% excess in the four Key Sectors, compared to the rest.

Just feel for a while the massive impact of this result: in its daily sojourn across the sky, this heavenly sphere is somehow affecting the future characters of people, expressed in their biographies, as seeded at their moment of birth!

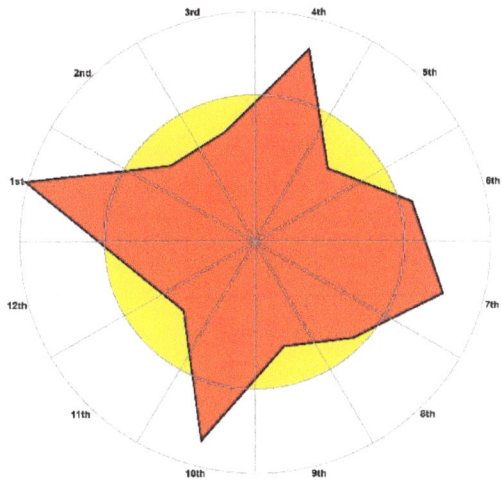

I scored some more traits, trying to look for Venus (which we'll come to later) and these included 'passionate' and 'ardent.' These two featured neither in Michel's NCGR list, nor in Addey's opus, however Françoise, in her book on the subject, does give 'ardent' as a Mars-trait - but not, 'passionate'.[23] These two traits score in quite large numbers – 230 for 'ardent' and 221 for 'passionate' so that's enough to plot each trait separately. 'Ardent' comes out twice as strong as 'passionate,' for Mars.

There are nuances of difference between these words, 'ardent' being more fiery while 'passionate' is more fluid and watery. The latter only scores twenty-five percent more in the cadent houses while the former shows a more than fifty percent excess. This tends to confirm what Françoise wrote in her book, with 'passionate' being only 'weakly' Mars.

We now have six strong Mars-keywords. Putting them in order of how frequently they were cited:

Courageous, ardent, active, energetic, combative, dynamic

How wonderfully do these express the fiery energy and dynamism of Mars! Overall these six, counted in 887 charts, gave a massive 75% excess in the cadent houses.

---

[23] FG, *Psychology of the Planets* 1982 p.44.

The Primary archetypes

Other traditional terms that could be worth a try here are: *Audacious, choleric, enthusiastic, fervor, force a, de la (full of strength), tenacious, foi a la (fervour), vif (lively), vigorous, vitality.*

Moon - For the Moon I initially selected, *Fantasy, imaginative, reflective, pure, tranquil, reveur* (a dreamer). These are not so coherent, in that people did not generally concur that 'pure' and 'tranquil' were lunar traits.[24] Checking the sources, i.e., the Gauquelins and John Addey, I noticed that none of  them cited 'reflective' as a lunar trait, and in fact Françoise said it was Saturnine. Removing it caused, I found, a huge *increase*: the effect become a lot larger, from a net 60% excess in the cadent houses it shot right up to 79%![25] I was having difficulty in believing effects of this magnitude.

So 'reflective' was not a lunar trait, contrary to what I'd initially surmised: yes physically the Moon is reflective - but this does not come through as a character-trait!

Over three hundred data-points were plotted using the traits *Imaginative, pure, tranquil, dreamer and fantasie*. We here see, as John Addey so rightly observed, a strongly fourfold structure and it shows a 79% excess in the four cadent houses compared to the others. The Gauquelins never saw anything of remotely comparable magnitude.

---

[24] Eg, if you wanted 'sensitive' as a lunar keyword, a problem would arise because 'sensible' is the nearest French word, and has by no means the same meaning.

[25] The excess here is of the four cadent houses compared to the eight others, which we may express as 200xA/(B-A), where A is the total score in the four cadent houses and B is that of the others.

So, the Moon is not reflective. I liked Addey's comment upon the lunar traits:

> How often we find, in the lunar spectra, words which are used of the Moon itself (*pure, chaste, clear, silent, secret, lucid, brilliant, cold, light, abundant or fertile*) or which are used in relation to watery surfaces (*tranquil, reflective*) or which refer to the image-forming capacity so often attributed to the moon, to water and to silver (*imaginative, fancy*).'[26]

One might also here try *'Naïve', 'poetic'* and *'spiritual'*.

Is the Moon pure? Some people queried this. The trait only turned up in 43 cases, deleting which, the percent excess dropped by five percent: so yes, the Moon is pure! One is here reminded of the 'pure, silvery Moon' and perhaps also of Shakespeare's 'celestial Diane, goddess argentine' (in the play, *Cymbeline*).

If one plots this group of lunar traits by the Mars-day, an overall deficit of 15% appears in the four sectors: so it's a kind of 'anti-Mars' character.

Jupiter keywords are 'Pride' and 'Joy' – I scored the keywords *Joyful (merry), Proud, organizer, director, authority*. Plotting them around the Jupiter 'day' (with 18-fold sectors) we here see a very significant result. A massive 68% excess appeared in the four Key Sectors compared to the rest.

So, the appearance of the terms 'joyful' or 'Jovial' in a biography, depends somewhat upon the position of a planet, four hundred million miles away. All European languages have words like jovial, jolly, which pertains to that distant sphere in the sky ... somehow related to being merry.

Anyone seeking to develop a philosophy of optimism will want to ponder these qualities of Jupiter. Jupiter here appears rather Zeus-like as the *merry boss*.

Persons consulted were dubious about the terms 'director,' 'authority' and 'organizer' as being Jovial. The Jupiter-traits seem to fall into two separate clusters: Joyful or merry and proud, and then *Authority, directeur, organizer*. People seem not to guess the latter as

---

[26] Addey, *A New Study*, p.167.

The Primary archetypes

being Jovial, but rather as more Saturnine.[27] Françoise did not cite 'director' as being a Jupiter-trait while Addey did. Removing 'director' from this group pushed up the net excess of the four 'cadent' sectors only a little, from 68% to 73%. Both of these sources cited 'authority' as a Jupiter trait, and sure enough deleting this trait caused a big drop, from 68% down to 53%.

Jupiter, for traits: Joyful, proud, authority, director, organizer

<u>Figure:</u> Jupiter's diurnal position plotted for 434 charts, of persons characterized as *joyful, proud, authority, director* and *organizer*

Jupiter is authoritative! Here one cannot do better than quote Michel:

Zeus ne preside-t-il pas aux autres dieux, du haut de son Olympe?[28]

Jupiter keywords	Cadent house(4)	Others (8)	% Exs
Joyful, proud, authority	145	156	86%
Organizer, director	63	89	41%
All five keywords(434)	198	236	68%

A table is helpful here, splitting the data into two groups. Removing 'director' and 'organizer' leaves 301 sets of birth-data for the three

---

[27] Traditionally-Jovial terms such as *expansive, regal, splendid* etc, are unsuitable because they are too infrequent. Commonly used trait-words, enough to count, are required.
[28] MG, *Les Hommes et les Astres,* 1955, p.225.

traits *joyful, proud* and *authority*. This gives a staggering excess of 86% in the four sectors. The trait-words 'organizer' and 'director' do respond to Jupiter, but at only half the amplitude of the others.

Other traits worth a try here would be: *Ambitious, personality, popular, self-confidence, smiling (souriant), verve.*

Saturn gets a bad press, and no wonder with keywords like *deep, cold, severe, solitary* and *silent*. Again these show a more than fifty percent excess in the four key sectors compared to others, despite which it's the least significant of the results.

If Saturn is the 'Wise counsellor', then some of these could also be worth a try: *Conscientious, distant, likes family, methodical, melancholic, modest, noble, prudent, precise, reserved, reflective, self-controlled (maitre de soi), serious, taciturn, timid, wise* (sage).

No shortage of gloomy Saturn-keywords have been put forward down through the ages, indeed one marvels at how two planets in the depths of space could express so great a polarity, of Jupiter as the exuberant Nice Guy versus somber, old Saturn. It's a very grey planet.

People tended to select 'authority' and 'director' as Saturnine rather than jovial, I found. So I took all of the birthdata with natives characterised as 'authoritative' and put them into the Saturn-group. It greatly declined in significance - i.e. it did not like being given the trait of 'authoritative'!

II - THE DATABASE

As a result of the foregoing endeavours, thirty-five different character-traits were logged in, comprising 4352 lines of birth-data from 1,142 people. This, after being checked meticulously by my colleague S.R., went up onto the UK's *Correlation* research web-page in November 2017.[29] Fifty years after the Gauquelins began the entreprise, it became the first online version of the character-traits. The Gauquelins had long insisted that these were more fundamental, more important, and showed stronger effects, than any of their professional groups. It is the second computerised version of the traits, the first having been that in San Diego around 1980, compiled by Tom Shanks

---

[29] Presently at newalchemypress.com/Gauquelin, '9. Character traits'

The Primary archetypes

on the big ACS computer (Astro-Computing Services) - of which no trace now remains.

Its list of character-traits has been compiled as explained from the four data-volumes which the Gauquelins published in the 1970s.[30] The number of times each trait-term was selected from the biographies is its 'citation count.' Here is my list of the 35 traits, ordered by that count:

> Simple (318), modest (287), friendly (268), courageous (231), ardent (230), passionate (221), charming (220), active (205), energetic (185), enthusiastic (148), gentle (145), loved (126), authority (125), combative (110), solitary (110), elegant (103), jovial (90), imaginative (85), graceful (81), director (81), noble (79), fantasy (78), profound (77), reflective (76), organizer (71), dreamer (71), seductive (70), proud (67), severe (65), cold (64), vitality (63), tranquil (58), dynamic (57), silent (46), pure (45).

Thus, the trait 'charming' appeared 111 times in biographies of actors, 55 times in those of writers, 28 times in sports biographies and 25 times for scientists – giving altogether a total of 220 citations.

Three pairs of French word have been combined: amitié (204) and aimable (102) => friendly, aimé (97) and amoureux (34) => loved and joyeux (24) and joviale (84) => jovial[31]. This helps where the numbers might otherwise be rather small; but for amitié and amiable, both over a hundred citation-counts, there seemed to be only the one English word (friendship, likeable). Thereby this list ended up with thirty-five English-word traits.

---

[30] To view this data, right-click on it, copy and paste it into a text file, then upload it onto a spreadsheet program. Column 'A' gives the professional group, column 'B' the notional planet – rightly or wrongly surmised – to which the character-trait may belong, and column 'C' has the character-traits, by which the data has been sorted by. Column 'D' gives the names of the eminent persons, and you may wish to sort this database using them, and thereby see how many character-traits have been selected for each name. Column 'E' gives the number assigned by the Gauquelins to each line of birth-data, which has been used on the CURA pages http://cura.free.fr/gauq/17archg.html as a reference. Other columns give birthdata, time and place, then on the right are five columns with numbers 1-12, the Placidus house sectors for each 'Gauquelin' planet.

[31] Some of the data is lost because the appropriate birth-data cannot be located. Thus 'jovial' here should add up to 106, but in the graphs shown here a mere 90 points are plotted for that trait. In the database at newalchemypress.com/gauquelin/ chapter 11 there are 90 lines given for 'jovial'.

The prediction is, that the four so-called 'Cadent' houses, 3, 6, 9 and 12 will show either an excess or a deficit for a given planet. In what follows we compare that excess, of one-third of the diurnal circle, with the other two-thirds, i.e. the eight other houses. In the language of yore, we compare how often it appeared in cadent houses, compared to its being in angular or succedent houses.

JUPITER

We now attempt a new thing, that has not been done since Time began. All previous accounts of planetary traits had authors telling us what they *felt* were appropriate, or what they had *heard* were the traits, whereas here they emerge objectively from a database, they arrange themselves from a frequency-count.

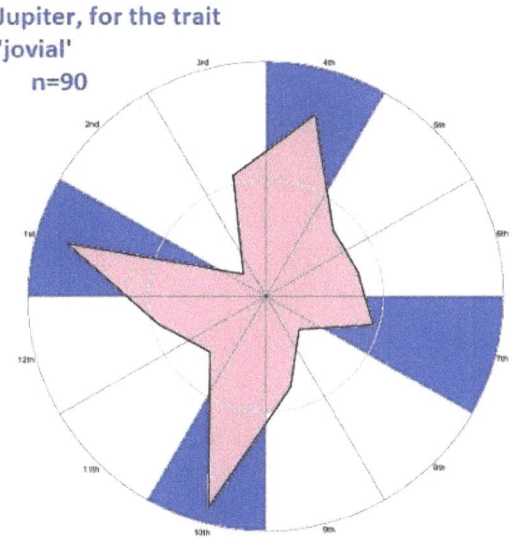

Each of the 35 trait-groups was scored by how many times Jupiter was in one of the four Cadent houses, at the birth of the native, expressing this as a percentage excess or deficit compared to the other eight.

The highest score here turned out to be the keyword 'Jovial.' This trait combined the two French words 'jovial' and 'joyeux.' It scored a 228% excess (48 out of 90 traits) which means, more than a hundred percent above chance level: and that is, the very trait-word named after the planet!

The graph shows this trait by itself – looking it must be said quite merry. Nothing could be simpler than this. Two graphs are here shown for the same data, when divided into 12- and then 18- fold

The Primary archetypes

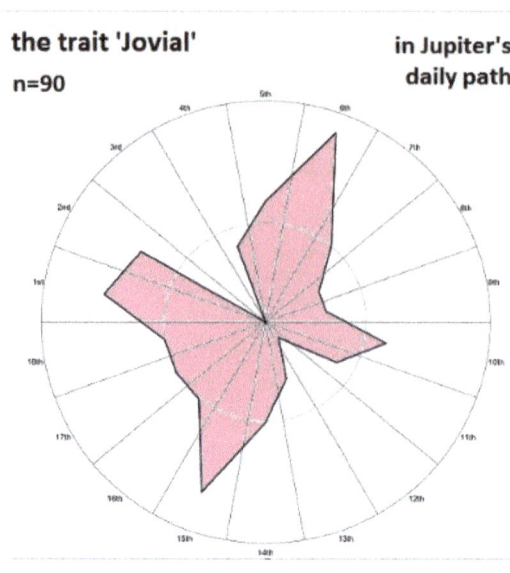

the trait 'Jovial'   **in Jupiter's**
n=90   **daily path**

distributions. The same data-set is expressed in these two different ways. Is this not the simplest astrological effect you have ever seen?[32]

Anyone looking for firm, concrete proof of astrology – here it is!

The next graph shows the distribution for five of the top-scoring Jupiter words – *Jovial, proud, authority, director,* and *energetic* – with overall a 78% excess. That is the sequence according to how well they scored. We see a strong vertical emphasis here, between zenith and nadir.

The next graph shows in contrast the three lowest-scoring Jupiter traits - *reflective, profound* and *solitary*. John Addey would have had a thing or two to say about the 1/8th angle through which the two fourfold structures here shown are rotated, with respect to each other.

The extravert character of Jupiter is here expressed, whereby these introvert traits scored lowest (a 25% deficit of the four sectors).

The manifestation of anti-Jupiter traits tends to indicate that the Gauquelins were not cheating – in case anyone were inclined to suspect such a thing. Major evidence against their having cheated has to be the simple fact that it never dawned upon them, that these trait-distributions gave a symmetrical fourfold-structure – nobody in the 20th century except John Addey ever realised that.

---

[32] That discerning investigator, Kyosti Tarvanien, checked out these ninety 'jovial' individuals because of his theory that the cadent-house effects were somehow caused by hard angles to the aspects. He did find such an excess of hard angles (quoted with permission): 'The above analysis seems to indicate that Jupiter's aspects with the angles make an individual jovial. But this doesn't explain why there is a clear surplus of Jupiter in the cadent houses. So, it seems to me that there is an additional, stronger, mysterious factor that makes people jovial and it somehow seems to work through the cadent houses. And due to this stronger factor, there is a surplus of Jupiter in the cadent houses.'

Four times each day, does Jupiter arrive in one of these Key-Sectors. During those times, people were twice as likely to be born who would later be described in their biographies as 'Jovial.' Clearly, this fact has far-reaching implications. It could lead to a new cosmology.

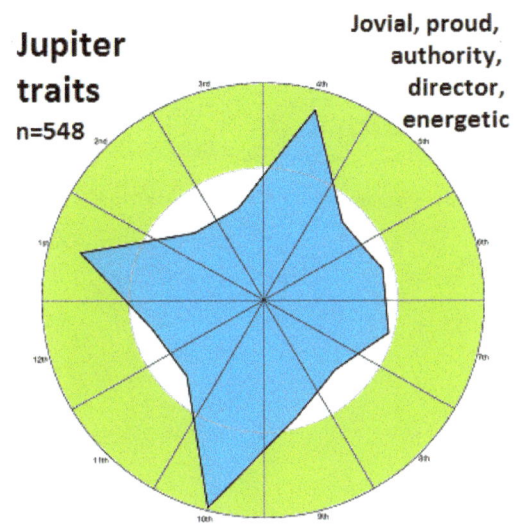

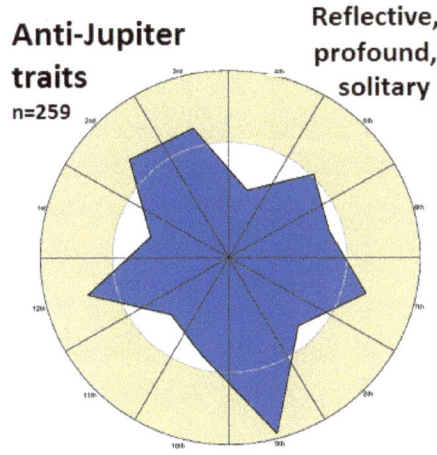

MARS

A graph of Mars-traits was shown earlier. There is little to add, except that the three top-scoring Mars traits -

Trait	Citation count	Mars score	% Excess
Combative	110	56	207%
Vitality	63	32	206%
Energetic	185	92	197%

The Primary archetypes

- give a 100% excess overall. There is nothing subtle about Mars-symbolism, it comes with a 'Pow!'[33]

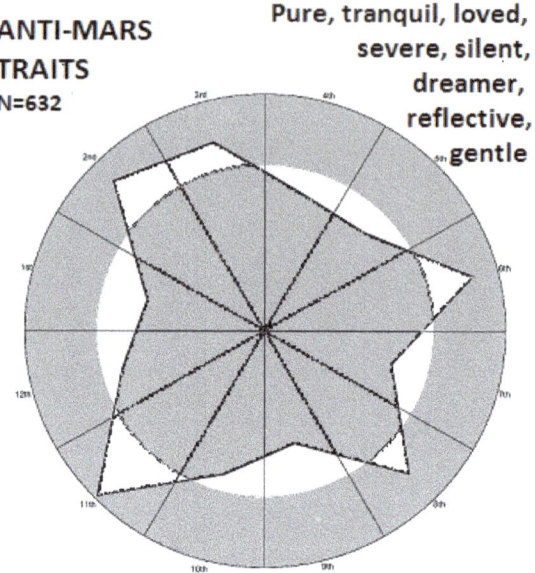

We contrast those with eight of the lowest-scoring Mars-traits which show a 25% deficit, overall. It takes one while to absorb, that these low-scores have actually been caused by the Red Planet's daily sojourn across the sky. These anti-Mars qualities help bring into focus the primary archetype:

    Pure

    Tranquil

    Loved

    Severe

    Silent

    Dreamer

    Reflective

    Gentle

---

[33] Explanation of Table: the trait 'combatitive' was found in 110 biographies, of which 56 had Mars in a cadent house. Therefore 54 were in the eight other houses. So the cadent houses had 56/27 = 207% more than the others.

The two anti-trait graphs here shown, display a kind of fourfold structure, only tilted round somewhat.

SATURN

The six top-scoring Saturn-keywords are shown in the Table, with the citation-counts plus Saturn-score. Ancient keywords, even from textbooks a couple of thousand years old, are here vindicated and validated - we do indeed sense here 'Old Father Time.'

The top Saturn keywords.

Trait	No. of Cita^{ns}	Saturn Score	% Exces
Silent	46	21	168%
Cold	64	29	165%
Severe	65	28	151%
Noble	79	33	143%
Solitary	106	42	131%
Profound	77	30	127%
Total	437	183	144%

Saturn here appears as slow to approach and maybe with some wisdom in his words: the Wise Counsellor. We may endeavor not to see him as the Gloomy Sage, pessimism being a deficiency of philosophic perception.

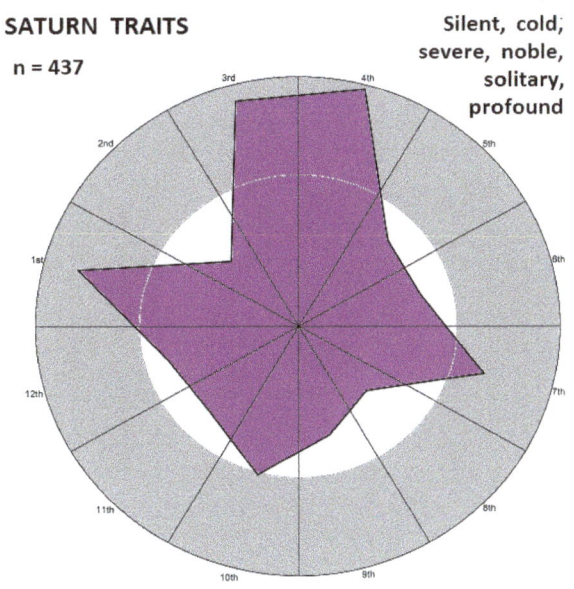

Notice how this *is the best list of Saturn-traits you have ever seen*, as likewise for the Jupiter-traits above. The reason for this is, not because of any talent which I

The Primary archetypes

surely don't have, but because these lists of traits have emerged objectively out of the data, not being guessed at or surmised by anyone.

Taken together these traits scored a 44% excess. They are all *introvert* traits. In contrast, here are the lowest-scoring Saturn-traits:

<u>Anti-Saturn (i.e., lowest - scoring) Keywords</u>

Trait	No.of Cita^{ns}	Sat Score	% Exces
Organiser	71	21	84%
Ardent	231	68	83%
Passionate	221	65	83%
Active	205	60	82%
Imaginative	85	24	78%
Combative	110	30	75%
Seductive	70	19	74%
Jovial	90	24	72%
Dynamic	57	12	65%

These all seem extravert – and youthful!

<u>Summary</u>

This chapter started off with surmise as to what the planetary traits might be, based on several different judgements. Gradually 38 traits were logged in from the four source-books, then six were paired together: the two French words joyeux and joviale became 'Jovial' as likewise 'friendly' and 'loved' emerged from two traits: thereby a final – for now – list of 35 traits was established. The objective selection and grading of the traits as scored for each planet thereby becomes possible for the first time ever in history; whereby the fourfold structure of the cadent houses assumes a new and startling relevance.

11.

VENUS FOUND

The Venus type was not linked to success in any of the professions which I looked at.

MG 1983 p.63.

Michel would now and then print a list of 'Venusian' traits,[34] although he was always equivocal on this topic and explained that they had not been 'confirmed.'[35] Here is one of these lists:

Affable, agreeable, ambiguous, attractive **beloved** benevolent, **charming,** considerate, courteous **elegant**, flattering gallant, **gracious**, juvenile, kind, obliging, pleasant, poetic, polite, **seductive.**

Those in bold are traits that I've logged in. The Gauquelins had found those five character-traits cited in 599 biographies of eminent persons of known birthdata. Plotting Venus positions for this group gives the pattern shown, with large peaks in the two Key Sectors.

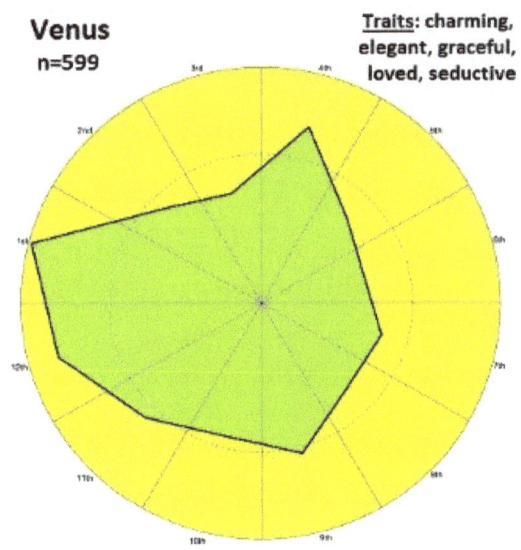

---

[34] *Spheres of Destiny* 1980 p.134.
[35] MG, *The Truth about Astrology* 1983, pp.64, 70: 'this description of the Venus-type has yet to be confirmed.'

Venus found

As this is the first time such an effect has been shown, let's also include an 18-fold division.

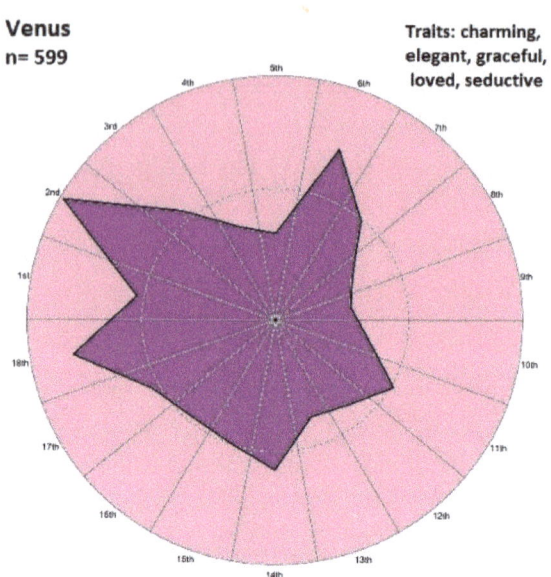

A faint circular line roughly indicates the chance-expected scores, but we recall that Venus has a very skewed distribution more than any of the other 'Gauquelin planets.' Turning back to Figure 1 in Chapter 2, the Venus-line is considerably more skewed than those of the other planets, owing to its solar proximity.[36] It will always show a bulge around the 12th house reflecting that proximity to the Sun, because natural births peak before dawn.

In the Key-sectors, we see a thirty-percent excess:

Planet	No. of charts	Venus in the KSs	Expect	χ²
Venus	599	139	105.8 => 31%	10

The chi-square figure indicates that, if anyone had predicted this effect in advance – which they didn't – it would have been highly significant.

Science involves hypotheses that are testable, and what is here presented can be tested using any or all of the other character-traits in the above list. It's also helpful to note, that all the traits in MG's list have a simple one-to-one correspondence with French adjectives.

Have the two Key Sectors here returned? Does not this contradict what we found earlier, that (quoting John Addey) the character-trait distributions had a symmetrical fourfold pattern? It would here be helpful if someone were to log in some more of the above-cited traits, such as attractive, pleasant, courteous, juvenile, polite, gentle,

---

[36] The graph gives expected values as 115 and 97 as percentages for the two Key Sectors, so the chance-expected value here is 599/12 x 212/100 = 105.8.

benevolent. Conversely a list of Venus anti-traits was given by MG in 1980 as aggressive, feverish, strenuous, frank, tough, choleric, hard, quarresome etc. What distributions would these show?

As a general comment, the Mars and Venus trait-terms are coherent and simple. Most people will guess them correctly, and that is not the case for the other Gauquelin planets. Readers are encouraged to make cards and write on each one, one of the 'top five' traits for each planet as we've here ascertained them, and then ask friends to place them in five piles according to the planets. There will be disagreement over whether traits are Jupiter or Saturn!

John Addey cited no Venus-traits, and one can say that during the 20th century no-one ascertained anything very definite in this respect. Françoise kept endeavouring to do so, as one can see in the pages of her APP journal, notably for groups of lesbians. MG merely cited a 'preliminary portrait' which had 'less statistical correlation' than the others.[37] We bear in mind that these professional groups are overwhelmingly male.

LUCIFER AND HESPERUS

Could the ancient distinction between Evening and Morning Star be relevant? The Greeks of old had used two different names for them, *Lucifer* and *Hesperus*. The Evening Star - which is seen dying down into the sunset - was more associated with romance and going to bed, with Aphrodite the adorable Goddess of Love and so would the gentle and sweet attributes of Venus be more linked to it? The Morning Star in contrast appears in advance of the sunrise, and it 'puts the stars to flight' in the early morning: could it be more strident being associated with Nike the Goddess of Victory, with more 'butch' and womans'-lib. type epithets associated with it? I found nothing much by way of classical references or astrological traditions to warrant this, but it seemed worth a try.

The two can be separated, by the Sun-Venus angle: the Evening Star has Venus ahead of the Sun.[38] To separate the data in this way, set

---

[37] MG 'The Gauquelin findings, their significance for Astrologers' *NCGR Journal*, Winter 1988-89,p81-2.
[38] One subtracts their zodiac longitudes and if {Sun − Venus} is negative then it is usually the Evening Star. The two spheres are always less than forty degrees apart. *But*, if 0° Aries is in-between them - eg, if the Sun is in Pisces and Venus is in Aries - then

an astrology program so that only the Sun and Venus appear in a chart, and try out several lines of data. One can soon ascertain whether it's Evening or Morning Star.

Some Venus traits were given in Michel's list in his NCGR journal of 1989,[39] one of the last things he ever wrote. For each of these sets of birthdata, the longitude values of the Sun and Venus were generated, (using the Solar Fire program). Subtracting them, half of these difference values come out as positive while the other half are half negative, and that is the basis for making the separation. Taking the list of five traits we started off with: for the Evening Star half of the data, a 25% excess appeared in the four sectors. Unsure what to make of this, I selected another group of likely-sounding traits:

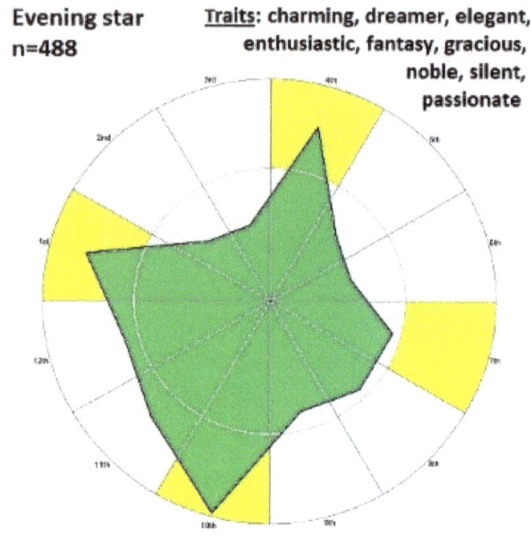

Ardent, gentle, passionate, amitié, amiable, amoureux, doux

These formed a bigger group, of which some four hundred were Evening Star. Checking the traits one at a time, it turned out that removing 'doux' (gentle) pushed the score *up*. Venus isn't gentle! (Think, thorns on a rose.)

In these two diagrams, the traits here plotted around the Evening-Star Venus-day, with citation-counts are: *charming* (108), *passionate* (95), *enthusiastic* (73), *elegant* (48), *noble* (35), *dreamer* (34), *gracious* (33) *fantasy* (33) and *silent* (24), totalling 488. Thus Venus as the Evening Star expresses traditional qualities, as shown for these nine traits – here depicted with both 12- and 36-fold divisions of the circle. It is of

---

subtracting the two will give around three hundred degrees, as a positive value, even though clearly Venus is the Evening Star: so then it's the other way round.

[39] MG, 'The Gauquelin findings: their signifricance for Astrologers' NCGR Winter 1988-9 pp. 81-82: MG says he obtained these from checking out individual charts, ie he was just guessing.

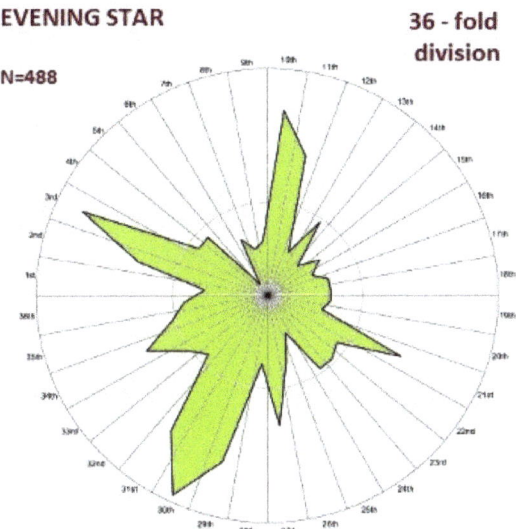

interest to look at a 36-fold division of the circle, although one might not (I suggest) wish to do numerical or statistical analysis using it.

These are very credible Venus-traits, and this is the first time they have shown up in the diurnal circle. The net excess here in the four houses is 60%, which is a lot.

And so, to discern properly the Venus-type, we separate the Morning and Evening Star data, and do so using the Sun-Venus angle in celestial longitude.[40] Here for comparison are the ten top traits for the Morning-Star - formulated *for the first time ever in the history of the world* - with numbers as before. Do they seem different from the earlier Evening Star traits?

<u>Top-scoring Venusian traits as Morning Star</u>

Loved	70,	32	+68%
Vitality	31,	14,	+64%
Severe	36,	15,	+42%
Profound	30,	12,	+33%
Proud	34,	13,	+23%
Pure	27,	10,	+17%
Authority	66,	24,	+14%
Director	45,	16,	+10%

---

[40] This Morning-star group consists of 2,260 person-character trait lines: with 718 individual birthcharts that means just over three traits per person, Each line of data has a unique {individual + trait}.

Venus found

Fantasy	45, 16	+10%
Tranquil	31, 11	+10%

<u>How its done:</u> The trait 'loved' for example scored in 70 different biographies of Morning-Star people, and for these Venus appeared 32 times in a cadent house. It therefore scored 70-32= 38 in all the others, so an average of 19 for the angular and succedent houses. The cadent houses therefore had a 32/19 = 68% excess compared to the others.

I combined two French trait-words *amoureux* and *aimé* into the one English word 'loved' – here starring as top of the list! The numbers are smaller, as we've split the data in half, so one cannot go too much by individual-trait percentages. We sense an inverse-correlation with the more traditional Evening-star traits: charming, passionate, friendly, ardent, seductive, enthusiastic, gracious, gentle, dreamer – these are *all in deficit*, that means they have been inhibited by the Morning Star. The biographical source-data is almost all male, so female qualities can be discerned only with difficulty.

Should astrologers start using these two opposite polarities of Venus? To help answer that, we contrast the scores for some traits, Morning versus Evening Star. The excess or deficit is given only to the nearest ten percent as the numbers per trait are rather small.

	Evening	Morning		Evening	Morning
Graceful, (grace de la)	+90%	-30%	Silent	+70%	-50%
Dreamer	+60%	-40%	Elegant	+40%	-20%
Deep, profound	-20%	+30%	Director	-30%	+10%
Passionate	+20%	-10%	Proud	-10%	+20%

The evening Star is graceful, silent, dreamy and elegant while the Morning Star is none of these things - quite the opposite! She's got work to do …[41]

She as Morning Star is neither tranquil nor 'friendly' (here adding together the two French trait-words aimable and amitié), nor is she

---

[41] Others not here used, together with their numbers of citations in the four volumes, which would surely throw some more light on this interesting question, are: self-willed 207, lively 163, faithful 146, gay 136, verve 135, always smiling 125, great-hearted 100, lyrical 83, funny, fantasist (fantastique + fantasist) 75, violent 74, laughing 67, poetic 63, naïve 62, moral courage 60, picturesque 50, romantic 45, young 39, exuberant 30, scandalous 27, beauty 26, enjoys life 26 and happy 25.

gracious (French, 'de la grace', having grace) or simple (note that this has a far more positive meaning in the French language, as being straightforward and direct, not duplicitous: with 318 of the biographies having used it). Nor is she *elegant, gentle, cold, silent* or *a dreamer*.

These traits could apply to a woman in charge who enjoys bossing people around. From tradition one might expect a more macho Venus-type to be here present as 'Bringer of the Dawn'. She appears before the Sun and 'puts the stars to flight'. She was *Phosphorus* and *Lucifer* (in Greek and Latin), whereas the Evening star was *Hesperus* and *Vespers,* and who remembers them? One finds remarkably little on this theme and astrology books do not treat them separately. There were no frequent-traits in common, between the Morning and Evening Star, for those here analysed.

The Morning and Evening Star traits correlate inversely, which indicates a real difference in their character. Scoring all of the traits for Morning Star then sorting them, the top-scoring six traits display an excess of 146% overall, while the Evening Star for the same traits scores low, at 89% - a staggering 50% differential in their scores. That effect is not astronomical, it's 'astrological'! Then, the bottom six traits for Morning Star score a mere 60% overall, whereas the Evening Star for these same traits scores a 128% excess. That's a huge 75% differential, between the 'two sides' of Venus. A strong anti-correlation is here present.

If we take the five 'adorable' traits: *ardent, charming, elegant, friendly, gracious* and *seductive* (total: 446), these score 121% with the Evening Star, but only 88% with Morning Star – again, a big difference.

Traits respond to more than one of the heavenly spheres. Thus 'Silent' and 'severe' were negative for Mars, but positive for Saturn, while 'pure,' 'tranquil' and 'dreamer' were negative Mars, but Moon-positive. It would be worth logging in a larger number of these traits to get a better focus upon how the archetypes are working – or at least, were working in Europe a century ago.

Françoise's book claimed to have examined a total of '253 separately-analysed traits.' (*Psychology of the Planets,* 1982, p.43) which seems a lot. She claimed to be following John Addey's sensible suggestion, of a minimum of fifty counts, for a trait to be included,[42] but that would have (it seems to me) reduced her total.

For example, the trait 'romantic' scored in 46 biographies (34 writers + 11 actors + 1 scientist + 1 sports champion), and would that suffice for inclusion?[43] A cultural difference appears here, in that nowadays many sports champions would probably be described as 'romantic' i.e. having some sort of sex-appeal, whereas mere pen-pushing writers would be unlikely to be so described, whereas they often were, for the French biographers.

Michel did not list 'dreamer' ('rêveur') as a Venusian trait: we saw how it scores oppositely for the Morning versus Evening Star, which is why he failed to see it. The trait showed a +60% excess for the Evening star – and there was a similar large excess for the Moon in the cadent houses. Although normally we require a couple of hundred values to construct a Gauquelin-graph, let's do this just for 'rêveur' as the effect is so large. All those songs you heard about sweet dreams and the silvery Moon, well here is an objective expression of that!

These are the harmonies of heaven, this is the Music of the Spheres.

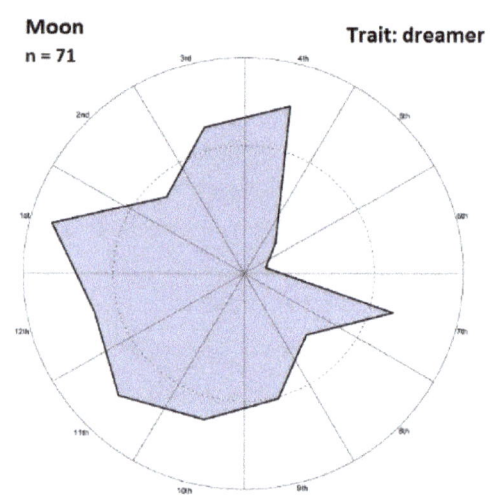

Especial thanks are due to Sven Raphael, computer expert and Astro-enthusiast, without whom I never would have been able to separate out the Venus data into the two groups.

---

[42] Addey, 'Harmonic phase and personal characterisics' the astrological journal, summer 1979 and winter 1978/80. Quoted in Gauquelin, F. 1982 p.43.
[43] Her book claimed to have scored 69 bios for 'romantic' (p.52), I've no idea how.

12

JOHN ADDEY'S DREAM

The first edition of *Correlation*, as the world's only astrology-research journal, appeared in 1981, with an article by John Addey about what he called 'harmonics.' They were some kind of wave-pattern which, he reckoned, could somehow transform or renew astrology. The Gauquelins never took any notice of this, not seeing what they had discovered as a wave-pattern. However we have now seen that where character-traits are concerned the phenomenon does greatly resemble a fourfold wave-pattern.

Let us suppose that the present work is taken further and that we acquired a couple of hundred of these traits, extracted from the Gauquelin data, all logged in, instead of just the three dozen used here. They are all in a computer, linked up to the birth-data sets, and we suppose that you, gentle reader, are able to adjust the controls. First of all, you select a threshold value that defines how many bio-references are needed per trait: i.e., the minimum number of birthdata of eminent persons assignable per trait for inclusion. That cutoff value could be as low as thirty, or as high as eighty. Your initial decision here determines how many traits appear in your group.

Concerning the low-scoring traits, if they have similar meanings you might wish to pair some of the the French words together, so that one English word includes them. The higher the threshold is set at (number of citations per trait), the more meaningful and reliable any ranking is going to be.

Then you select a planet, and the computer then gives you a listing of all the traits in terms of their score: that score means, the number of times that that planet appeared in one of the key sectors (the cadent houses, i.e. G-sectors 1, 4, 7 and 10), as compared to the chance-expected frequency. This would be simply expressed as a percentage excess, of the score of these four compared to the other eight. At the top of the list there one would see the traits relating most strongly to that planet in the G-sectors, while at the bottom one would see the anti-traits, those that were repelled or discouraged by that planet in the G-sectors.

You may then wish to select some group of these traits: you might want, for example, the top ten traits, or the bottom ten. Then, the computer can plot these in the normal Gauquelin-wheel. Thereby one can view how the typical traits here manifest, as we've been doing in the previous chapter.

The computer is able to distinguish the Morning and Evening star appearances, which gives us two options for Venus. If the thought-experiment proposed here were ever done, then the emergence of the two Venus archetypes would probably be the most interesting and important thing in the present study. There would be something in the Gauquelin data of especial interest to women. It would bring in a sex angle.

So far so good. In fact, you've heard it all before. But then, John Addey wanted to *rotate around* that fourfold structure in four clicks. The following diagram may help.

Addey reckoned that he wanted to be able to rotate the four sectors around in four different steps – I don't know why. He had no option (that I ever heard of) for a sixteen-fold division of the diurnal circle, as required for such a procedure. Thereby, he reckoned that a *spectrum of qualities* would appear. Let us suppose that we tell the computer to divide the diurnal circle up into sixteen intervals, making each 22 ½° of the circle: we thereby obtain a more limited and focussed list of qualities, than we had before when the sectors were 30°. You, as the operator, thereby become able to inspect four different groups of adjectives, each time you click the wheel round one-sixteenth.

You would notice – at least according to the theory of the previous chapter – that the second step of the rotation, i.e a one-eighth rotation, produced the anti-traits, in other words the adjectives that came bottom of the original list now come top.

What would this show? It would strongly indicate that the Gauquelins weren't cheating, for a start. Examining the four lists of traits, you as the operator would want to mull over the question, is this useful? Is there here a continuum or a spectrum of four different ways in which

Mars or Saturn expresses itself - or not? If the answer was 'yes', then this would give philosophers something to ponder, and could well lead to a reformulation of what astrology was about (as John Addey believed).

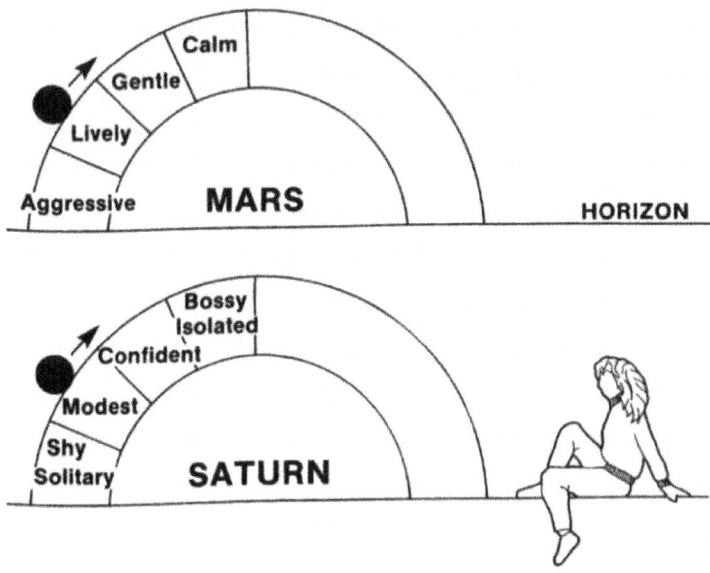

Figure: four different 'phases' of character, as envisaged by John Addey: Used with kind permission from: Geoffrey Dean, Kelley and Saploske 'Astrology: A Critical Review' in *Philosophy of science and the Occult*, Ed Patrick Grim 1990, p.67.

We saw in Chapter One how eminent artists – painters and musicians – lacked any planets scoring positive in the Gauquelin sectors. Is this maybe because persons who score positively in the Key sectors tend to be people who stand out in an active and forceful manner, upon the stage of history? Artists in contrast draw inspiration from some interior, imaginative realm which does not involve using words or establishing facts. John Addey's approach of rotating the fourfold structures with respect to the main Key Sectors, could give some more insight into this matter.

A FOURTH HARMONIC

Here is John Addey's diagram of Jupiter in the large group of

Scientist and Physicians.[44]

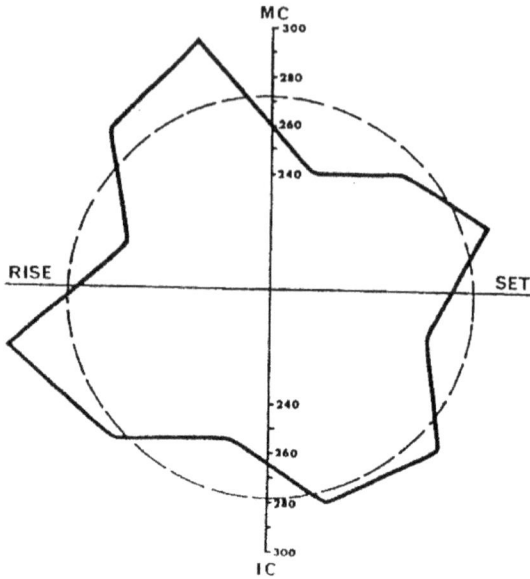

Figure: John Addey's (posthumously-published) graph of 'Diurnal distribution of Jupiter for Scientists'

We've earlier looked at a similar data-set as a twelve-sector bar-chart in Chapter Three. Have another look at that (page 50), and then compare it to the sixteen-sector bar-chart given here, for the same data. The idea here is, that if a fourfold effect exists, then a sixteen-point bar-chart would be preferable for viewing it. Are you convinced? We compare these with the above circular chart published years ago by John Addey, for a similar data-set of 'scientists.' Using the sixteen-fold division, the Jupiter-score here appears as: 281 ± 12 in the four Key Sectors, compared to the opposite four sectors which give 315 ±12. That is an 11% difference overall, and a t-test of significance between those two groups gives t=4.3 which is significant at around 1 in 200. If the Saturn and Jupiter scores are subtracted, then the four Key sectors gives 36 ± 13 while the four in-between positions give -25 ± 12: a difference significant at t = 5.9 - which is impressive.

We may compare these with a data-set selected by the qualities of Jupiter, and plotted using the same 16-fold division. This is based on

---

[44] Addey, *New study*, p.45: he's used about 3,200 from the {Scientists and Physicians} group. I infer the number from his mean value given of c.270.

the Jupiter-group we looked at in Chapter Ten, but a couple more traits have been added in to increase the numbers. We see here an effect four times larger than the above professional-group effects: the four peaks in the data show a huge 72% excess on average, compared to the four in-between values (i.e., we have compared sectors {1,5,9 and 13} with {3,7,11 and 15}.

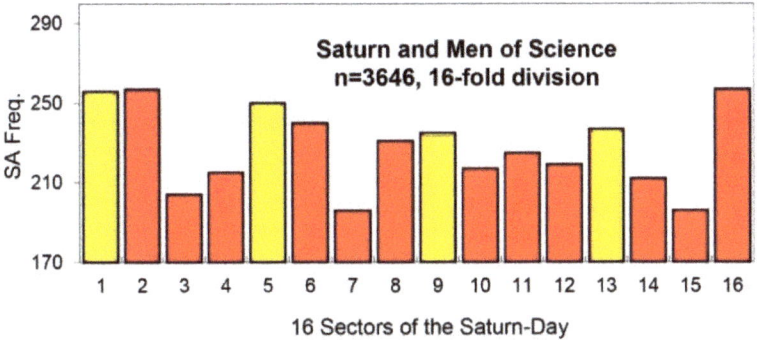

One may prefer to remove the traits 'energetic' and 'dynamic' from this larger group, because, as we found earlier, they only score weakly for Jupiter, being primarily martial. That would bring us back to the earlier group selected in Chapter 10, of just five Jupiter-traits. The four sectors then show an even larger excess of 90%, compared to the four in-between values.

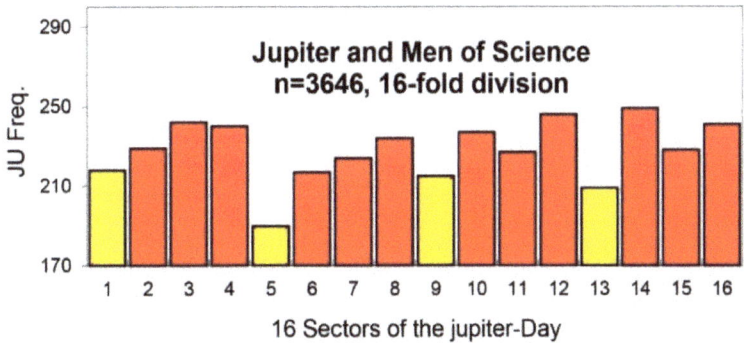

Thus a stronger effect using the 16-fold division is observed. Earlier, we found a 78% excess for this group of traits using just twelve sectors, in Chapter Ten.

Some birthcharts occur more than once in this group, as the biography of one person can be scored with several of these Jupiter-traits. There are somewhat over four hundred natal charts in this plot of their character-traits.

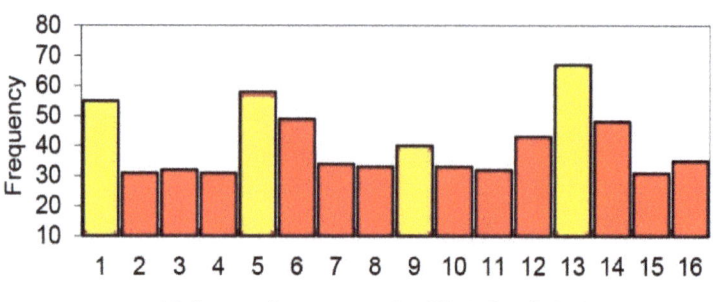

Likewise with Mars and its five traits we looked at in Chapter Ten: *active, combative, courageous, dynamic, energetic* (n=789), they show an even larger effect using a 16-fold division, a massive 93% excess of the four peak values compared to the four intermediate ones. This effect is *four times larger* than the biggest Mars-profession effect the Gauquelins found, which was with sports champions.

NO 3RD HARMONIC

Mistakenly, John Addey reckoned he had found a 'third harmonic' in the diurnal circle. Mars, he averred, could display such a triune waveform with certain character-traits. He here selected *simple, modest, noble, enthusiastic* and *vitality*, plus some others.[45] As Geoffrey Dean explained: 'this suggests there are two types of sports champion, one modest (third harmonic) and the other aggressive (fourth harmonic).'[46] Supposedly, this waveform was symmetric about the horizontal axis, ascendant-descendent. He drew up the two graphs here shown in 1981, which were published in the first issue of *Correlation*, after he had returned from San Diego, where he had access to Niel Michelsen's computer. He had evidently done some trait frequency analysis while over there.

I logged these five traits (adding up to 982 trait-citations), expecting

---

[45] Addey, 'The True Principles of Astrology and their bearing on Astrological Research,' *Correlation* 1981, 1,1, 26-35; *A New Study* 1996, p.127.
[46] Dean, 'Astrology: A Critical Review' in *Philosophy of Science and the Occult* 2nd Edition 1990, Ed Grim, p.26.

to find what here looks like being a more domesticated and mild form of Mars-energy, in a triune and not a square pattern – an attractive notion. But, there was only a slight effect, barely significant which did not resemble the above graph. Addey was doing his calculations with a pencil and paper. I'm in the judgmental position – which I don't much like – of correcting the theorists and dreamers of the last century! However, that endeavour was worth it because it led me to build up a large enough list of traits having a decent 'critical mass' size, where one could start to derive useful information from it, as has hopefully here been done. One would like to be able to put the clock back, and ask anyone at the San Diego ACS if such a triune pattern could be obtained, or indeed had been obtained, using the traits specified for the Mars diurnal circle?

Figure: Addey's claim contrasting 3rd and 4th harmonics of the

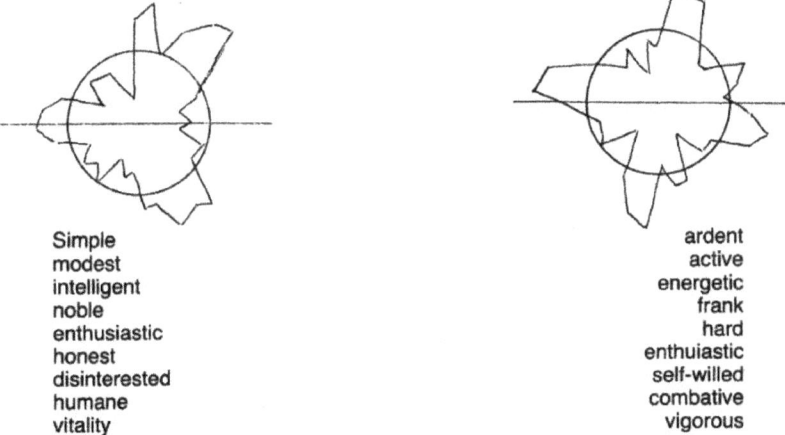

Figure 5. The traits defining the two types of sportsmen isolated by Addey, based on the 3rd and 4th harmonic of Mars, respectively, shown above. (after: Addey JA. Figures 5 and 6. *Correlation* 1981;1(1):31-2).

Simple	ardent
modest	active
intelligent	energetic
noble	frank
enthusiastic	hard
honest	enthuiastic
disinterested	self-willed
humane	combative
vitality	vigorous

Mars-day[47] as republished by Prof. Peter Roberts

The identical two graphs were then reproduced sixteen years later by Professor Peter Roberts (above), in the same journal. Roberts had worked closely with Addey. This also tends to imply that no-one had reconstructed or checked those two graphs – triune and fourfold – over all those years. This is puzzling and surprising to me, as I knew both of them, and am unable to reproduce any such effect. I don't have

---

[47] *Correlation*, June 1997, Peter Roberts, 'Harmonic Analysis of the diurnal distribution of Gauquelin's professional groups, pp18-25.

John Addey's Dream

all the traits logged in, but the five above-mentioned should have been enough to show the effect, were it present.

I did not log in the trait of 'intelligence' – here averred to be a Mars 3rd harmonic trait – for two reasons. Firstly there are a huge number of biographies in which this this trait appears, some five hundred, and I baulked at this because no-one has ever assigned a planetary affinity to it, except possibly to Mercury which does not here count. I don't want to discourage anyone from doing this in the future, but that is why it is not in the list of three dozen traits here used.

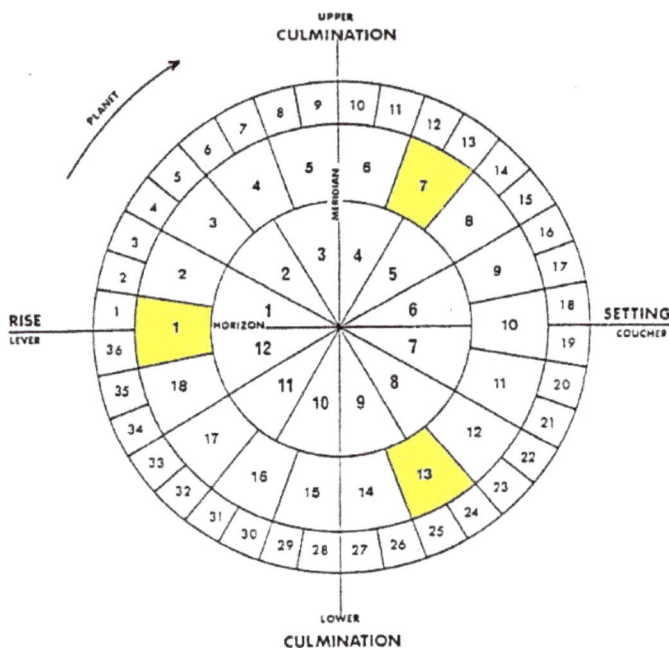

Figure: the Gauquelins' diagram of their diurnal divisions, twelve, eighteen and thirty-six fold.

The normally-used Gauquelin-sector divisions, as found eg in the modern Jigsaw program, are 12, 18 and 36, these being all multiples of three, as if someone felt that a triune division was important. Their use of the 18-fold division (here shown[48]) could be used to inspect Addey's claim. But alas the Jigsaw program offers an 18-fold division divided with nine above and nine below the horizon, and so does not permit evaluation of a pattern symmetric about the horizon as Addey

---

[48] APP September 1992

claimed. Gauquelin's 18-fold division has the first sector bisected by the Ascendent (See illustration), required to detect a pattern having such a symmetry.[49]

I will be happy to be proved wrong on this matter if anyone re-checks the data and can confirm it. But at present I suggest that having both third and 4th harmonics working in the daily round for five different planets would be an unduly complicated form of celestial influence.

John Addey advocated a wave-harmonic approach to the subject. By way of honouring what he tried to do, here is a best-fit waveform put though a summation of the Gauquelin data, as explained in Chapter Two (page 37). Mars-professional data has been excluded because its diurnal pattern is much affected by solar proximity. We saw earlier how there was a primary or 'first-harmonic' waveform,

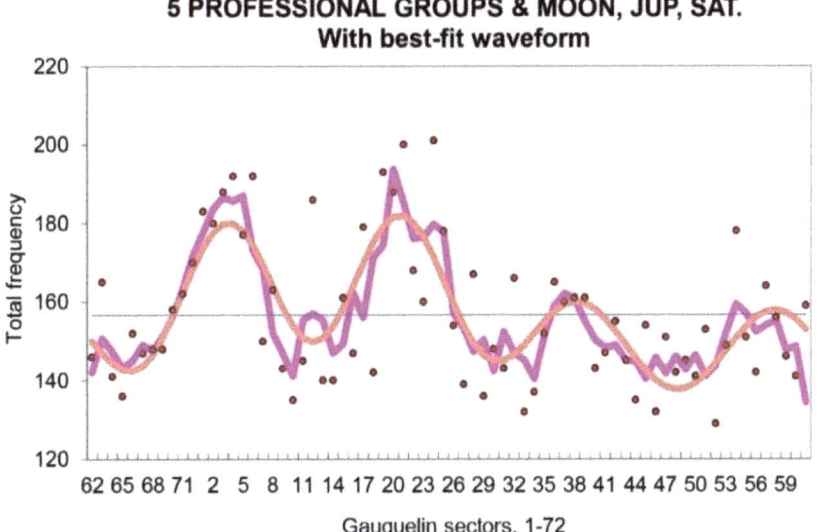

which distinguished between above and below the horizon. A fourfold ('fourth harmonic') wave is here added onto it, which has been amplitude-modulated to allow for the 'minor' nature of the third and fourth peaks.

We here discern the primordial, *Ur*-form of The Gauquelin Effect.

---

[49] The astrology-research program *Pegasus* developed by David Cochrane does offer both 24-fold and 16-fold divisions of the diurnal circle (at my request) See astrosoftware.com/Products

13

INTROVERT / EXTRAVERT

In 1974, Michel Gauquelin met Hans Eysenck, Britain's top psychologist, in Paris, in the office of the psychology journal for which he worked. The two of them mulled over use of the Eysenck Personality Questionnaire to discern the difference between Jupiter and Saturn types - the former being extravert and the latter, introvert. A year later Eysenck published an article on this subject in the weekly *New Behaviour*,[50] proposing that a hypothesis on this matter should be testable.

A few years later, the following paper co-authored by Eysenck on the subject used his EPQ on students:

> Geoff Mayo, O. White and Hans Eysenck (1978) 'An empirical Study of the relation between astrological factors and personality' *Jnl. Social Psychology*, 105, 229-236

which we return to later, soon followed by:

> Gauquelin, M& F. and Eysenck, S. B. G. (1979) 'Personality and position of the planets at birth: An empirical study' *British Journal of Social and Clinical Psychology*, Vol:18: pp.71-75.

> Gauquelin, M& F. and Eysenck, S. B. G. (1981) 'Eysenck's personality analysis and position of the planets at birth: A replication on American subjects' *Personality and Individual Differences*, Vol 2(4) pp.346-350.

These were and still remain (I believe) the only positive-result astrology-research papers ever published in academic psychology journals. The latter two did not have Hans Eysenck's name in them, but that of his wife Sybil.

---

[50] Eysenck: 'Planets, Stars and Personality' *New Behaviour*, 1975 p.246.

They used the character-traits which the Gauquelins had been extracting from biographies.[51] Sybil Eysenck felt she could make a judgement about each trait-term, deciding whether it was introvert or extravert. For example, she reckoned that 'arguer, athletic, attractive' were extravert while in contrast 'accurate, awkward and confidence (lack of)' indicated an introvert.[52]

A year later in 1982, Hans Eysenck summed up these results:

> Extraverts are significantly more frequently born when Mars and Jupiter had just risen or had just passed their upper culmination; introverts when Saturn had just risen or just passed its upper culmination.[53]

There has never been any follow-up to these papers: perhaps because readers were not unduly impressed by having one person make a rather arbitrary judgement over trait-terms?

The next year in 1983 Françoise analysed a group of drug addicts, which she reckoned showed the opposite of the customary 'Gauquelin effect.' Rotated at one-eighth of a circle with respect to the four 'Gauquelin sectors,' did they show four 'introvert' sectors of non-achievement so to speak?[54] As Françoise put it,

> ...peaks in "Succedent houses" with drug addicts are in obvious contrast to the low frequencies in "Cadent houses" (our "key-sectors" numbered 1, 4, 7 and 10, in the direction of the daily motion of the planets).[55] With prominent professional notabilities, we obtain the exactly reversed graph (see continuous line in our Figure 1). This "anti-correlation" is statistically significant. It finds its causal justification in the personality differences of both groups, the successful celebrities obtaining recognition by fighting efficaciously the difficulties of life, and the drug addicts

---

[51] The authors averred that: "The abstractors of the personality attributes from the biographies did not know of the theory here tested." *Brit Jnl Clin Psy,* 1979, 18, 71-75, 74.
[52] Gauquelin, *The Truth about Astrology* 1983, p.77.
[53] Discussion in *Zetetic Scholar* March 1982, 9, p. 63 (online).
[54] FG, APP 1983,1,4 pp.26-28:'Comments about Wolfgang Martinek's "Drug addiction and Horoscopes.'
[55] Reminder: see page 162 for 'Succedent houses' in the diurnal circle.

receding from these difficulties into the blissful oblivion of narcotics.[56]

That was probably Françoise's first statement about how the 'Gauquelin effect' could apply to ordinary people and not just the very elite eminent groups as her former husband had claimed. She found a similar contrast in the professional groups:

> There is a result, in our professional groups, which offers a similar contrast (see our Figure 2): the painters, musicians and poets form a group of artists oriented more towards contemplation than action, while the sports champions and military men prefer action to contemplation; their planetary results on the whole show the same "anticorrelation" as the drug addicts compared to the successful celebrities; and the anticorrelation reaches its maximum if we consider the results with the planet Mars (Figure 2).

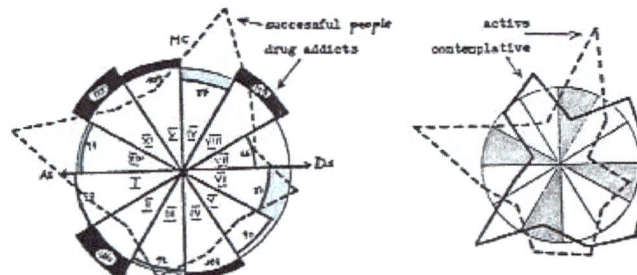

Figure 2: The Gauquelin results with very successful people (broken line) are in obvious contrast to Martinek's results with drug addicts (black bars). The anti-correlation is significant.

Figure 3: Similarly, Mars placements for active people (sportsmen, military men) are in sharp contrast to Mars placements for contemplative characters (painters, musicians, poets).

For comparison, here is John Addey's version of that polarity. He put together the Mars and Saturn distributions for two different groups of professions: the heavy line is that for scientists and physicians while the shaded area is that for writers, painters and musicians. He explained, 'We have superimposed the two graphs so

---

[56] F.G. et. al., 'Drug Addicts-A Replication' APP 1986,,4.3,p.6; see also F.G., 'Statistical Results with Ordinary People', *APP* 1994, 10,1, p.13.

that the opposite phasing of the two 4th harmonics can be clearly seen.'⁵⁷

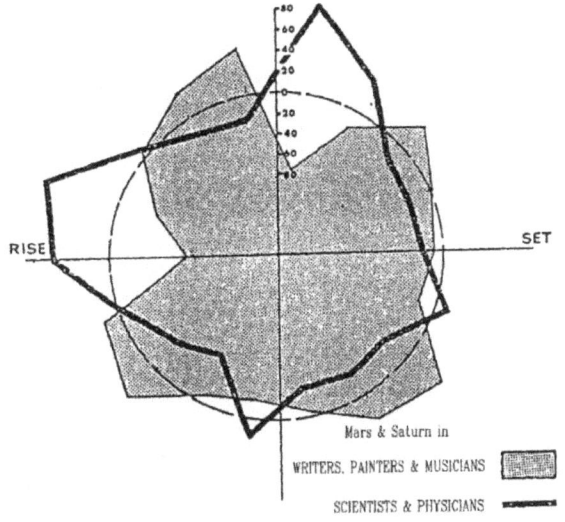

Fig. 27 Saturn & Mars distribution comparing different professions.

I have not confirmed this dramatic-looking graph but its included to show the limits of what could be achieved the last century, before modern programs became available.

Concerning the absence of any 'positive' (so-called) results for artist or musicians, in the planetary-day results, the psychology professor Arno Müller surmised:

> Artists differ from all other professional groups in that for them no higher-than-expected planetary frequencies have ever been reported. We may perhaps generalize as follows: Talent associated with positive planetary effect = power-exerting personalities (men of action, sportsmen, doctors etc.), talent associated with negative planetary effect = non-power-exerting personalities (e.g. artists). History shows that artists were rarely drawn from ruling or dominant classes (Müller 1990, p. 195). Thus, in the case of highly

---

⁵⁷ J.M. Addey, *A New Study of Astrology* (posthumous) p.89-90. He used huge numbers for making these two contrasting graphs: 1059 scientists plus 2552 physicians, contrasted with 1352 writers, 1473 painters and 1249 musicians.

talented artists, a temperament associated with Mars, Jupiter or Saturn is less likely to be present - excluding individual personalities of artists who may deviate from their respective group.[58]

A TEST OF THE EYSENCK-GAUQUELIN CLAIM

It was Dr Carl Jung who developed the introversion-extraversion concept. Introversion, he said, was an "attitude-type characterised by orientation in life through subjective psychic contents" while extraversion was "an attitude type characterised by concentration of interest on the external object." It's the one bit of psych-language that everyone feels that they understand.[59]

To test the idea which Eysenck and the Gauquelins had proposed, I reckoned that several persons scoring the traits as introvert or extravert were needed, and not just one: there is after all no 'right answer' on this matter. Also it seemed inappropriate to impose a yes/no dichotomy upon each trait. Therefore, I and three other people gave an introvert-extravert rating to the thirty-five character traits described in the previous chapter, on a scale -2 as Introvert, -1 as maybe introvert, 0 as neither introvert nor extravert, +1 as maybe extravert and +2 as extravert. Then, mean were values derived from these, per trait. Some of the scores they thereby obtained were -

$$\begin{array}{lll} \text{Active} & 1, 1, 1, 2 & \Rightarrow 1.25 \\ \text{Ardent} & 0, 0, 2, 0 & \Rightarrow 0.5 \\ \text{Authority} & 0, 0, 1, 2 & \Rightarrow 0.75 \end{array}$$

Etc.[60]

The average score for each trait was then plotted against the strength of a planet in terms of the percentage excess or deficit (in the four cadent houses at birth, as compared to the other houses) as

---

[58] Arno Müller, 'The Gauquelin Effect Explained? A Rejoinder to Ertel' JSE, 1992, 6, 255-259.
[59] For comparison, Mike Startup, in his University of London PhD psychology study, gave the 'Eysenck Personality questionnaire' to 468 subjects, and found that the scores of 'tough-mindedness' versus 'tender-mindedness' tended to correlate with Mars positions in the Key Sectors (4th astro-Research Conference, Institute of Psychiatry in London, 1984: reported in APP January 1985 p.9).
[60] For scores of all 35 trait-terms, go to Chapter 12 of 'Re-Evaluating the Gauquelin data' online, it's in a downloadable Excel file.

described in the previous chapter. The Mars graph is shown for the 35 traits.

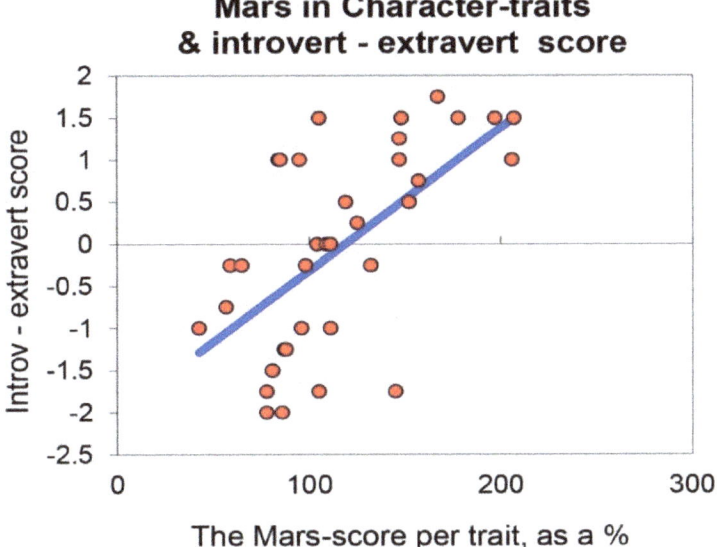

The correlation here is highly significant. If we look at the three strongest Mars-traits, around the 200 mark, as being strongly extravert: they were combative 207%, vitality 206% and energetic at 197%. That means that these three traits were found in biographies of persons having Mars in cadent houses at birth, twice as frequently as in the other houses (as explained in the previous chapter). At the other end, two of the lowest-scoring traits score around -1 on the vertical scale, ie judged as being introvert, are pure 43% and tranquil, 57%.

The Saturn-graph here shown goes in the other direction, i.e. the more frequently Saturn appeared in the four Key Sectors, the more introvert the traits tended to be. Thus in the Saturn-graph we see how the two 'strongest' (highest-scoring) traits were *silent* 168% and *cold* 165%, both rated as strongly introvert.

Thus we endorse the approach which the Gauquelins took on this matter in their 1979 paper, but hope to have improved upon the methodology. There is a strong anti-correlation between the Jupiter and Saturn scores: traits that score high with one, score low with the other. In general the high-scoring traits for each of the five planets do not correlate: which one may see as evidence for the authenticity of the phenomenon. But these two planets are antithetical. One of them is introvert, the other extravert.

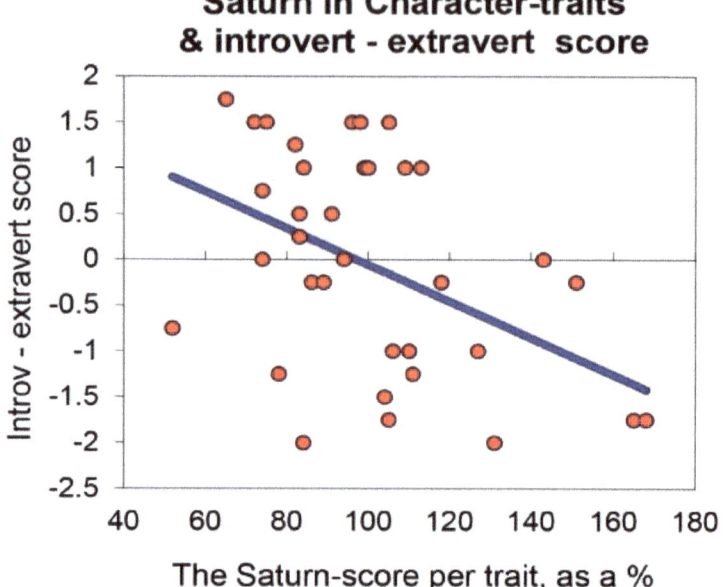

Taking all 35 traits, we find that Mars and Jupiter correlate together, ie traits that are strong for Mars will also tend to be strong for Jupiter, as here shown in the graph. In contrast and not surprisingly there is a negative correlation with lunar traits: as we saw

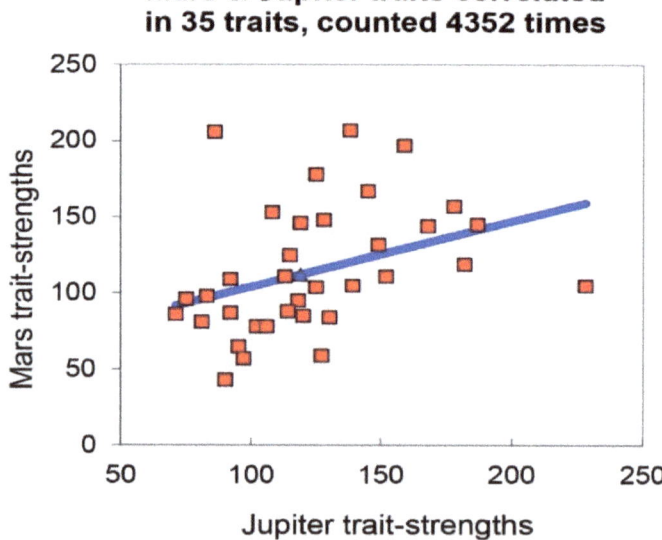

in the previous chapter, groups of birthtimes of people with lunar traits scored negative when plotted around the Mars-day.

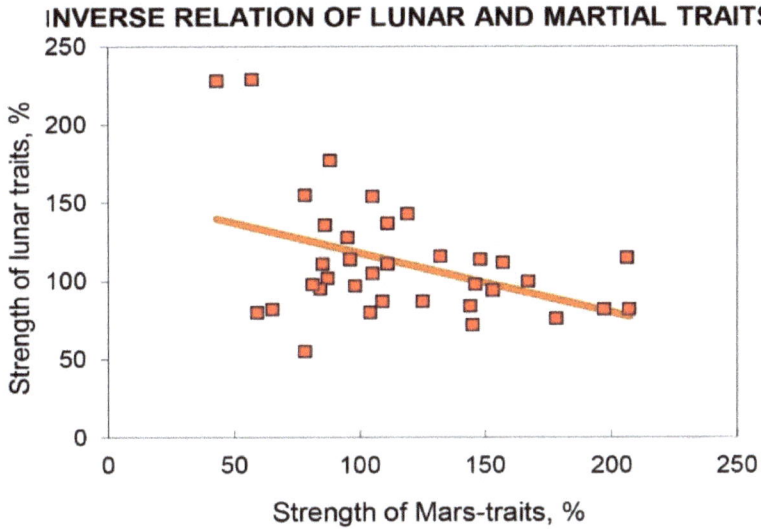

The above two graphs use no introvert-extravert score: we are merely plotting the two different planetary scores in the cadent houses.[61] Thus, we confirm MG's finding of 'a negative correlation between those traits that went with Mars and those that went with the moon.'[62]

GEOFF MAYO STUDY REPLICATION

The Eysenck-Mayo paper published in 1978 was hailed as 'probably the most important astrology story of the century' by *Phenomena, The Bulletin of Astrological news & Information* (May 1977, p. 2). Malcolm Dean, its Canadian editor, had a breezy optimism, but alas his journal only lasted a few years.

Using the Eysenck Personality questionnaire, the authors found a quite simple effect, whereby alternate sun-signs tended to be extravert (Aries, Gemini, etc) and then introvert (Taurus, Cancer, etc.). Other academic psychologists were able to replicate this effect, eg Prof Alan Smithers and Heather Cooper found very similar results, published a

---

[61] The argument of this chapter and the previous one was published by the author in the AFA's Research Journal for 2018, pp.1-8: 'The Gauquelin Character-Traits: New Studies.'
[62] MG, *Spheres of Destiny*, 1980, p.124.

decade later in the same *Journal of Social Psychology*.[63] We are here looking at the only positive 'astrological effect' ever published and then replicated in academic psychology journals.

Some debate ensued over whether this effect only appeared with people selected because they knew about astrology. Well-known British astrologers such as Dr Nick Campion vehemently rejected this claim - which Eysenck and Nias had made in their book *Astrology Science or Superstition* - that the effect was caused by people reading sun-sign columns! Did these columns lead people to perceive themselves as introvert or extravert? The subject has been well reviewed, together with another positive-result confirmation using 992 non-astrological subjects, by members of a Dutch psychology department in 1990. [64]

This effect has nothing to do with the Gauquelins, but is here included because a test of it is feasible using their character-trait-data. The data-set here used has 35 character-traits (see previous section) cited altogether 4,353 times in biographies of 1,142 people: that gives us just over four traits assigned to each person, on average. To test the Mayo thesis, one needs a measure of whether each person is introvert or extravert. One could say that a minimum of three such traits per person are required, for such an estimate to be credible. Accordingly, all birth names were deleted of people who had only one or two traits assigned to them, and that left just 557 people with three or more character-traits. Thereby a mean value of these traits introvert-extravert was assigned to them. Their solar zodiac longitude at birth was ascertained.

The graph shows a best-fit 6th harmonic waveform put through the data, i.e. one going through six cycles per 360° circle of the zodiac. It extends over sixty degrees, so that if someone was born with the Sun at, say 2° Gemini, i.e. 62° zodiac longitude, that appears as 2° on this graph. It has an amplitude of 25%.[65] A 'moving average' can be used

---

[63] Smithers and Cooper, 'Personality and Season of Birth', *Jnl. Soc. Psy.* 1987, 105, 237-241; reported in *Phenomena*, 1978 2.5 p.8, also see Eysenck &Nias, *Astrology: Science or Superstition?* 1982 Chapter 4.

[64] Rooij j. et al, 'Introversion-extraversion, Sunsign effect and Sunsign knowledge' Dept of Psychology Leiden, in *Geo-Cosmic relations, the Earth and its Macro-environment*, 1990, Ed. Tomassen, pp.267-271.

[65] The best-fit sinewave here shown has the equation $y = A + B\sin 6(\theta - C)$. A as the mean value is 0.22, B as amplitude is 25%, θ being solar longitude at birth. C is phase of the

to smooth the data, two of which are here shown, one of 100 points and the second of 50 points (for the latter, each point is an average of about one-tenth of the data). So, the effect does indeed exist and is quite significant[66] (More traits were scored as extravert than introvert, a feature one may assume of celeb biographies, which pushed the overall mean up to 0.2, with scores ranging from +2 to -2).

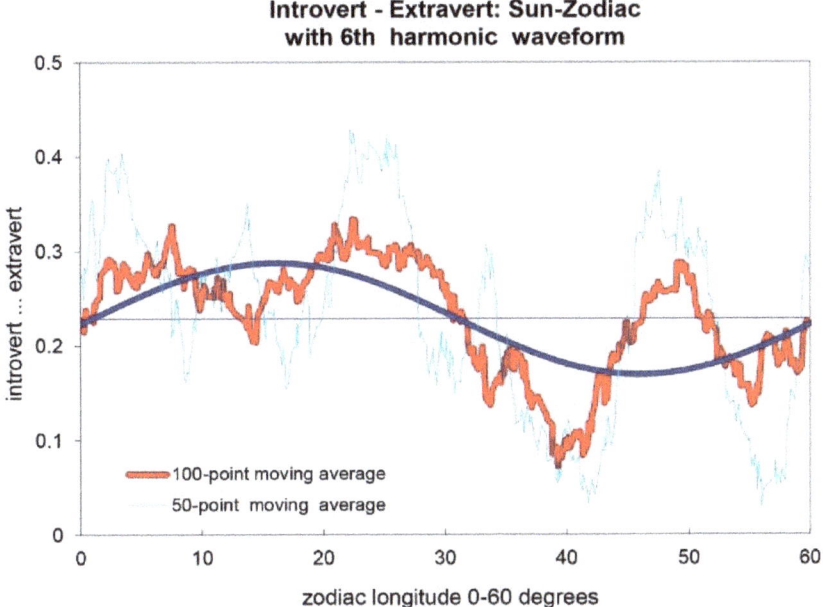

One of the volunteers who did the rating of introvert-extravert scoring for the traits, the Finnish K.T., took exception to the ratings for the trait, 'ardent' which were '0, 0, 2, 0' (see above). He assigned it a rating of +2, and wrote "I don't understand why all others gave 0 to the attribute 'ardent' since according to the dictionary it is clearly related to extraversion:

Ardent, adjective

1. having, expressive of, or characterized by intense feeling; passionate, fervent: 'an ardent vow, ardent love.'

---

waveform, which was basically zero, i.e. the best-fit waveform is here in synch with the Tropical zodiac and not any other. I hesitate to say how large this effect is for fear of being laughed at: the six extravert, 'plus' signs eg Aries have scored fifty percent more than the introvert, 'negative' signs eg Taurus.

[66] Using a t-test, for 0-30° scores averaged 0.29 ± 0.6 (n=270), for 31-60° they were 0.17 ± 0.5 (n=386) which gives t = 2.4, significant at around 1 in 100.

2. intensely devoted, eager, or enthusiastic; zealous:
   'an ardent theatregoer, an ardent student of French history.'
3. Vehement, fierce: 'They were frightened by his ardent, burning eyes.'
4. burning, fiery, or hot: 'the ardent core of a star.'

There is scope here for further discussion. But overall, it is clear that the introvert-extravert dimension of personality has much value in terms of demonstrating how the cosmos works upon the human psyche, and in being part of a language whereby astrologers and psychologists can communicate with each other.

I'd always taken a Keplerian attitude of scepticism towards the tropical zodiac, i.e. that no evidence had ever confirmed that it worked. Its definition always seemed to me illogical, as it was no longer aligned with the star-constelletions that gave it birth. That was Michel Gauquelin's view, which he used to use by way of dismissing astrology - something he did quite often. I was therefore surprised to find it confirmed by a simple introversion-extraversion test, just as Jeff Mayo claimed many years ago. We have here used the harmonic theory of John Addey, in putting a best-fit sinewave through the data: what he would have called a '6th harmonic' of the solar year.

The proposal which Michel made to Hans Eysenck in 1974 appears as vindicated. The optimistic conclusion reached by Hans Eysenck

> Perhaps the time has come to state quite unequivocally that a new science is in the process of being born[67]

was surely correct: or at least it could become so, if people wished to focus their minds on the subject.

---

[67] Eysenck and Nias, *Astrology: Science or Superstition?* 1982 p.209.

14

SYNASTRY OF PARISIEN COUPLES

From forth the fatal loins of these two foes,
A pair of star-cross'd lovers take their life
        Shakespeare, Romeo and Juliet

'Synastry' is about togetherness. It's about the relation between two people as seen in their natal charts. What kind of connection might we find there? We here examine pairs of natal charts, husband and wife, to seek for this in the huge database discussed back in Chapter 8.

In the course of collecting their 'Heredity' data, the Gauquelins amassed over twenty thousand pairs of birthdates, of married couples.[68] They thereby compiled the world's best synastry database. Their aim in so doing, was to investigate what they called their 'heredity' effect, not here confirmed. The Gauquelins never used their magnificent database to investigate marital synastry. Most of their important work came from a pre-computer age, which could be why they did not examine their data in this manner.

THE URGE TO MERGE

We scrutinise the 'urge to merge' using data from Paris of a century ago. 'Gay Paree' – its romantic affairs, its beautiful ladies, its happy music, its ardent passions and *les liasons dangereuses*! If synastry is going to work anywhere, it surely has to be here.

To create the database, children and single parents were filtered out from the 'Heredity' groups so that only married couples remained, denoted as Father and Mother. The Gauquelins had collected some thirteen different sets of such 'family' data (See CURA archive) of which eight were published. We've compiled it into one handy data-

---

[68] Search for 'CURA Gauquelin' and scroll down to 'Married couple data.'

set,[69] of 20,983 married couples.[70,71] Over the years, various people have weeded out errors, such that it may now be fairly reliable.

Such a large database of paired couples enables one to examine even individual celestial aspects in the synastry, which has never happened before.

The versatile 'Jigsaw' research program alluded to earlier is unable to handle pairs of charts, it can only score individual charts.[72] To get data for couples it is necessary to generate the columns of paired data one at a time by using eg the Solar Fire program.

SUN-VENUS

Using this Gauquelin data, synastry-frequencies for separate aspects were derived. Here is the data plotted for the *Sun-Venus opposition*. For each married couple, her natal sun's zodiacal longitude was subtracted from his natal Venus longitude. Iterating this through twenty thousand gives a frequency distribution, plotted around the zodiac. It shows up in the reverse way one might expect - her Sun and his Venus - and doesn't work the other way round![73]

We've selected a span of forty zodiac degrees, which means one-sixth of all the data. The overall mean was nearly sixty couples per zodiac degree.

Everything about this graph is mysterious. The very concept of Sun-opposite-Venus takes a while to assimilate! It is not happening in the sky, that's for sure. It is asymmetric about the point of exactitude, leaving us puzzled as to what 'before' and 'after' could mean in this

---

[69] 'We' here is Ray Murphy in Adelaide and this writer. Ray did all the computer work.
[70] For comments on this procedure see 'The Gauquelin married couple data' by NK, on the CURA site.
[71] The first synastry study using this whole database was by Kyosti Tarvanien: 'Classical synastry works in the Gauquelins' data' ,*The Astrological Journal*, volume 53, number 1, January/February 2011, looking at house systems. An earlier study using about a tenth of it was by Jan Ruis of Belgium, 'Indication for a Role of Synastry Aspects in a Gauquelin-Sample of 2824 Marriages', *Correlation* 1993, 12,2, pp 20-43.
[72] The more expensive US programmes, Sirius and Kepler, can handle these synastry databases.
[73] In my earlier article 'The Chemistry of Attraction' (*Astrological journal*, Nov/December 2015, www.thekeplerconference.com/TheChemistryOfAttraction.pdf) this was stated the wrong way round. I thank J.R. for noting this.

context. The five degrees after the opposition shows an excess of nearly thirty percent.

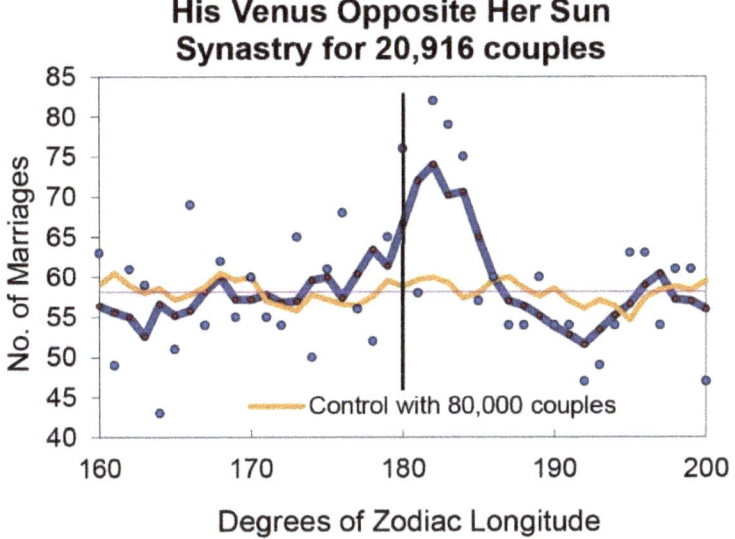

The graph has smoothed trend line put through the data with separate, one-degree values shown as dots. The Dutch astro-researcher J.R. has independently obtained this same graph for Sun-Venus synastry, using the same data, which is reassuring.[74]

Ray Murphy in Adelaide, Australia, was also examining this database and originally pointed out this result to me. He summed it up as:

> *Women marry men 15% more often if he has Venus conjunct or opposite her Sun within 2 degrees.*

If ever an astro-research result sounded like a newspaper headline! To check up on this Down-Under affirmation, the following Table compares the synastry at different orbs.

---

[74] For the 'control' or expected frequency: two columns of Sun and Venus were shifted with respect to each other, with the 'Dad' column moved down to six different positions, so that six control groups were thereby generated, each of twenty thousand. Thereby a hundred and twenty thousand 'control' values were generated, all having the same birthdata for husbands and wives, but shuffled around. Frequency-distributions of each of these six control groups were made, each having the same overall mean-per-degree as the sample. A mean value for each of these six distributions was plotted on the graph; which is - as one would expect - indistinguishable from the horizontal line of the overall mean.

Sun-Ve Orbs	Obs.	Expect[75]	Excess	χ^2
±1.5°	409	348	17%	41
±2°	533	465	15%	10
±2.5°	659	581	12%	9

<u>Table</u>: the excess of synastry conjunctions and oppositions at low orb, between his Venus and her Sun.

We can see it is highly significant (χ^2=10). The question of how such a tight orb can be so significant, between planets in the charts of people born at different times and places, we leave to philosophers. The question of how so absurdly high a significance level can be reached (χ^2 = 41 at ± 1.5°) is likewise baffling. But having the amplitude of the effect increase with decreasing orb, is the sign of a real effect.

The *conjunction* of the same two spheres shows a curiously different distribution. Once again the big change or swing takes place around the zero-point of exactitude, but here the swing goes in the other direction. The four degrees before exactitude score 30% more than the four degrees after it.

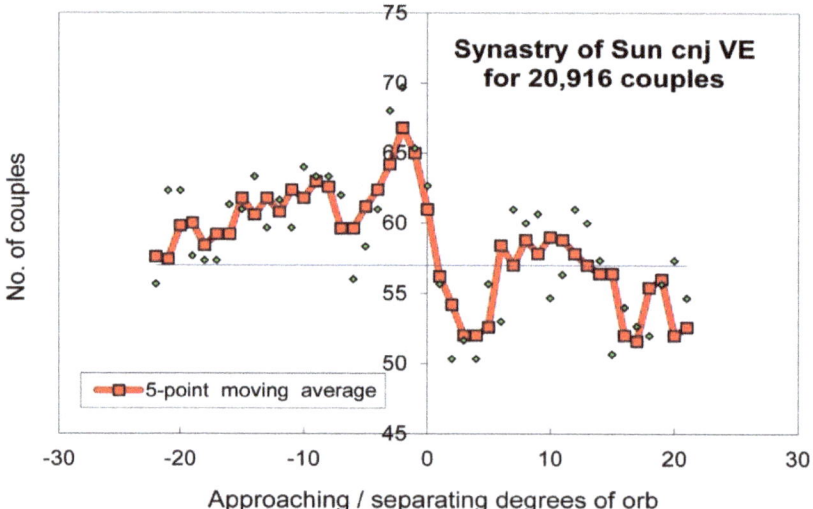

Here is the proverbial 'proof of astrology'. If anyone is looking for firm, concrete proof, here it is!

---

[75] The expected values are here respectively 6, 8 and 10 times the mean-expected value per degree viz. 58.1. Thus the ±1.5° gives a 3° span, and doubling that includes both the conjunction and opposition

SUN-SUN SYNASTRY

The most significant synastry link found here, was that between the two suns. Two major 20th-century surveys – first by Gunther Sachs of three hundred thousand Swiss couples then the even larger French survey by Didier Castille of sixteen million French couples[76] - have both claimed to show Sun-conjunct-Sun synastry. [77] They used untimed data, i.e dates only. In contrast, Jung's famous marriage-synastry experiment found mainly lunar links.[78]

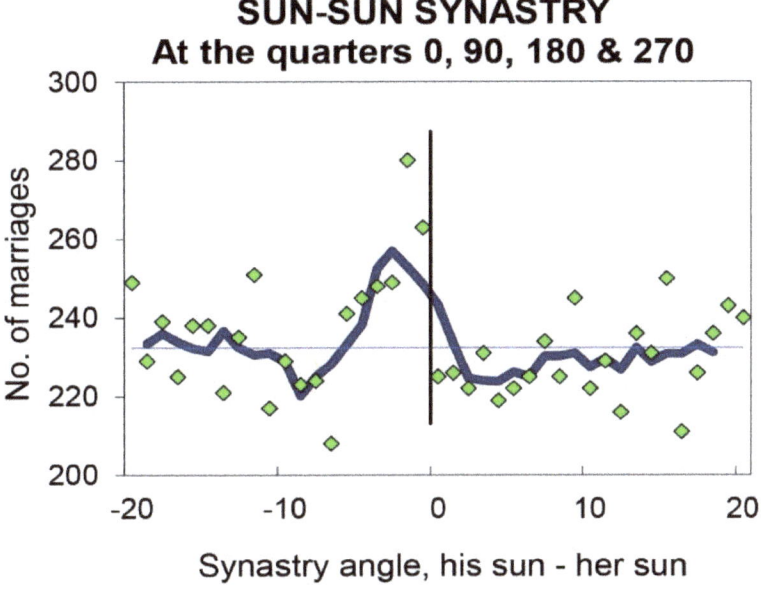

Subtracting the two natal suns, hers from his, showed a foursquare effect between all four angles of conjunction, opposition and the two squares. Squares don't normally show up, but here they are present.[79]

---

[76] N.K., 'Sun-Sign synastry in Marriage',*Correlation*, 30(2) 2016 38-48. Gunther Sachs, *Die Akte Astrologie*, Munich, 1997. Didier Castille, 'A Sunny Day for a Wedding', *Cahiers des RAMS*, 1999. Sachs found 3.5% excess of suns in the same sign for 176,381 couples and Castille found a comparable excess, but using decans i.e. 10° intervals

[77] Gunther Sachs, *The Astrology File*, 1998; Didier Castille, *Sunny day for a wedding*; both online.

[78] See N.K., Investigating Aspects, part 3 'Jung on Marriage Synastry' (in Pottenger, *Astrological Research Methods*, ISAR 1995.

[79] We may compare: 'Dr Kuypers of Apeldorm took 408 couples & saw that conjunctions, squares and oppositions between the suns, sun-moon and Moons were statistically significant (1:200) whereas the inconjunct (quincunx, 150 degrees) occurred far below average (1:500)': 'Astrology in Holland' by Rudolf Smit, *Phenomena*,

Synastry of Parisien couples

Thus, exactitude on this graph i.e. zero degrees of separation alludes to the four angles 0°, 90°, 180° and 270° between natal sun-positions. Again we see an asymmetric effect, but this time it's peaking a few degrees *before* the zero point.

The Gauquelins all their lives believed that no solar effects were present in their data, but, here it is! Never did it dawn on them that such results lurked in their data-sets.

We've seen how two kinds of aspects appear as significant, Sun-Sun and Sun-Venus. Let's compare these at two different orbs to see which works best. We find the 'effect' of the synastry-aspects at both 3° and 5° of orb. Assuming that all degrees of synastry are equally likely (the horizontal line in the graphs), we compare the two orbs :

Synastry aspect significance using 3° / 5° orbs

Synastry	Score	Expect	% Excess	χ^2
Sun opp. Sun	459 / 691	407 / 639	13% / 8%	7 / 4
Her Sun opp. His Venus	468 / 729	407 / 639	14% / 13%	14 / 17

The Sun-Sun opposition appears as significant at around 1% probability, using a 3° orb. But a higher significance is reached by her Sun opposite his Venus at a 5° orb.

The above graphs suggest that aspects somehow 'swing' around exactitude. The Table below compares the score of five degree-values before to that of five degrees after it. Mean values are shown. One is struck by the prevalence of Venus-aspects in this list - as traditionally related to 'true love' and marriage synastry.

The Gauquelins had Sun-conjunct-Moon in their synastry, to within three degrees, appropriate for all of the wonderful work they did together: his Sun at 21 degrees Scorpio and her Moon at 24 degrees Scorpio. That is what we are here calling 'after' the conjunction, so it is in accord with the above table.

The next Table shows such a swing for the Mars-Venus linkage: an alchemical-type effect, very traditional.

October 1977, 1.7, p.7. Smit published Dr Kuypers' findings in his book, *De Planeten Spreken,* The Planets Speak (1976).

The 'Swing', using 5° orbs

Aspects	His	Her	Before	After	Swing
Conj,Opp+Squ.	Sun	Sun	64.2±8	56 ± 5	-14%
Conjunct	Mars	Ven	64 ± 6	56 ± 4	-13%
Conjunct	N.Node	Sun	54 ± 5	61 ± 3	+12%
Conjunct	Venus	Sun	64 ± 10	52 ± 7	-21%

<u>Table</u> Comparison of five degrees before and after exactitude of celestial aspects, using {His - Her} zodiac longitudes, showing average number of marriages per degree, over four different synastry aspects[80]

Her Moon and His Sun – Again we see an archetypal link, for man and woman coming together. Alluded to by Jung in his classic study of marital synastry as his number one link, here it only scrapes in at the bottom of our list! It works both with the conjunction (Her moon subtracted from his sun) plus also the opposition (Her sun subtracted from his moon).

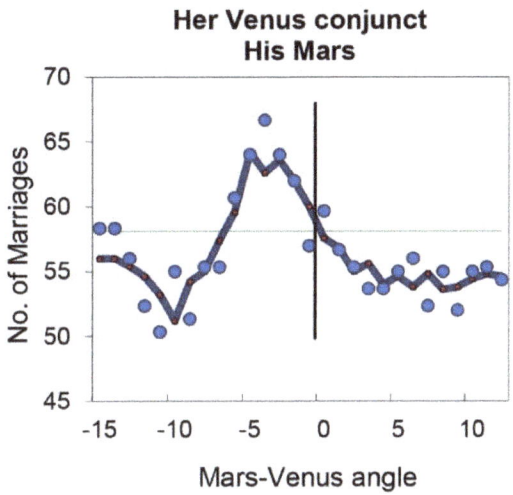

Sun-Node By tradition, nodes are related to fate and destiny. One finds a 'swing' as the Sun crosses over the nodal axis, counting her sun subtracted from his north node.[81]

---

[80] A wider orb effect was noted by Ray Murphy, for her Sun conjunct his Mercury, that taking fifteen degrees before and after, there were 13% more marriages before the aspect than after.
[81] An original paper by Mike O'Neill 'The Moon's nodes in Synastry' found a deficit of node contacts with the partner, for eminent persons, but concluded that the effect did not work for eminent persons (O'Neill, M. The Moon's Nodes in Synastry, *Astro-Psychological Problems*, 1986, 4:3, 24-30; The Moon's Nodes in Synastry – A

It is of interest to compare the aspects here found with the synastry-aspects published in Carl Jung's 1955 *Interpretation of Nature and the Psyche*.[82] The Sun has featured most often in the synastry aspects here found, while for Jung's marriage-experiment in Switzerland half a century ago, it was Venus.[83] The synastry aspects here noted are non-lunar, which means they should be testable on untimed data. It is far easier to obtain married-couple data that is untimed. But they differ strangely from Jung's results in which the synastry was primarily lunar.

The synastry results here described may not be universal: after all, the nature of the marital bond in Paris a century ago could be very different from that of today.[84] And yet, the synastry aspects here found do well accord with tradition: Venus as regards relationships, Saturn concerning Age and Time, and the Sun as signifying core-essence of one's being.

As the Moon crosses over the ecliptic each month, from southern to northern hemisphere, i.e. it reaches its North Node, one could visualise a 'swing' in the data around that moment of zero celestial latitude. But, how the Sun passing over that ecliptic point could show such an effect is harder to imagine! Astronomically the two nodes are opposite and rather similar, but astrologically that has never been the case. To quote Rob Hand "… the [lunar] Nodes relate to connections with other people: that is, they are an axis of relationship. In this context, the North Node has a joining quality, while the South has a separating quality."[85] The Sun's conjunction with the North Node is here found to be significant.

Replication, 1990, *Correlation*, 10(1), 10-18. KT, 'The Moon's Nodes in the synastry of the Gauquelins' couples,' *Correlation* 2016, 30 (2) 27-37, investigating the effect for ordinary people, using the present database. I haven't confirmed this.

[82] But NB no Moon-Moon synastry, conjunction or opposition were here found, as Jung did: for discussion see Eysenck and Nias, 1982 Chapter 5.

[83] For my comments on Jung's experiment, see 'Jung on Marriage Synastry': Pottenger, *Astrological Research Methods* ISAR 1995, online at www.astrozero.co.uk, pp.288-9, chapter, 'Investigating Aspects'.

[84] Didier Castille claimed to find strong Venus-Venus and Mercury-Mercury synastry links, which do not seem to be here present: see his 'Sunny day for a wedding' (2000), online. There was not give quite enough detail to follow this finding.

[85] Rob Hand, 1981 *Horoscope Symbols*. Para Research. p.90, quoted by KT in: 'The Moon's Nodes in the synastry of the Gauquelins' couples,' *Correlation* 2016, 30(2) 27-37,31.

The synastry aspects here found have a 'swing' around exactitude. That could be a general property of celestial aspects, not hitherto noticed.

It remains unfathomable to us, how two planets not in the sky but in the 'memory' of two birth-charts could affect a couple coming together - especially in the astronomically impossible aspect of Sun opposite Venus. But, they do! These results endorse the Shakespearean concept of 'star-crossed lovers' and indicate some heavenly meaning in the fate that draws a couple together.

Summary: In this chapter we've seen how the huge so-called 'heredity' databases acquired by the Gauquelins were of value, even though they did not show any 'heredity effect' as had been hoped. Instead, they can be used to demonstrate synastry. Pairs of charts between Mother nad Father were compared, and the large number meant that individual celestial aspects could be inspected for the first time ever. The links found were mainly solar whereas Carl Jung in a Swiss synastry study had found mainly lunar connections.

CONCLUSION

Figure: Moons of Jupiter passing across its 'Great Red Spot.'

It would seem that an opportunity lies in wait, of evaluating a wondrous new science in between Heaven and Earth. Human destiny does after all have some innate heavenly connection. That is the implication. If the results here are sound, they may strain our credulity as being rather large: stronger than they have any right to be, so to speak. The primary, ancient archetypes have emerged as alive and well, appearing as entirely traditional which is part of the strength of the Gauquelin thesis. However they have manifested in an unexpected manner, as a *fourfold daily pattern in 'Cadent' houses.*

How could astrologers have got it so wrong, for two millennia?

If Jupiter imprints itself into future biographies by virtue of its daily sojourn across the sky, affecting the moment of birth - or maybe affecting the future character at a moment of birth, depending on your theoretical bias – then this must have far-reaching implications. Also there is the question which Francoise kept grappling with in her journal, as to how this affects us ordinary folk. Or is the whole effect irredeemably elitist, only moulding the characters of those who come to be remembered, loved for their art or feared for their political effect?

Astrologers will generally prefer Jung to Freud and it's not hard to see why. We have here been examining basic archetypes, which anciently found expression in Greek mythology. During the 1980s, one Saturn-cycle ago, one could feel the mood of excitement amongst astro-researchers as if some new science was waiting to be born, which would relate such eternal or archetypal being-ness to various professions, and thence to character-traits. The Greek word *theoria* means an apprehension of *thea* the gods or divine principles and thus we may *theorise* about how it works.

The hoped-for new science featured an Earth-centred astronomy. It concerned zenith and nadir - the charming old, Arabic terms - and the time of day when planets 'culminated.' The planetary principles express themselves through a fourfold structure that is *compatible with* traditional twelve-house divisions but it gave them a different meaning. Thereby and at last we are able to respond to the astronomer Johannes Kepler's sceptical taunt:

> Demonstrate the old houses to me, explain their number; prove that there can be neither fewer nor more... show me undoubted and striking examples of their influence.[1]

Four hundred years later, we did that! Using house-divisions we explored the fourfold structures, and that brought us into a new *Kosmos* where major effects were perceived as working upon human temperament at the moment of birth. *Five* different heavenly spheres in their daily round did this, with an astonishingly large magnitude, acting at the moment of birth.

Sigmund Freud, in the intro to his magnum opus, *The Interpretation of Dreams*, quoted the Latin poet Virgil as saying

Flectere si nequeo superos, Acheronta movebo

---

[1] Letter of Kepler to the astronomer David Fabricius quoted in *Neo-Astrology: a Copernican Revolution* by Michel Gauquelin (Arkana 1991), p.92.

Conclusion

'If I cannot bend the higher powers, I will move the infernal regions.'[2] No doubt he was very successful in doing this. Whereas in contrast, the work of the Gauquelins brings us back to a more heavenly realm, it puts the *psyche* back into psychology. Is there an option here, of psychology departments offering a module on the subject?

That was the good news. The bad news is, that the near-universal induction of birth these days may mean that the useful data could possibly recede into the past. Are we now losing the most important time, that of the birth-moment, for hospital convenience?

> *Keeping time,*
> *Keeping the rhythm in their dancing*
> *As in their living in the living seasons*
> *The time of the seasons and the constellations*
> *The time of milking and the time of harvest*
> *The time of the coupling of man and woman*
> *And that of beasts. Feet rising and falling.*
> *Eating and drinking.*

Michel's suicide became the full stop at the end of the 20th-century astro-research enterprise. It juddered to a halt. Astrologers (in my experience) tend to shun deductive logic, as something which hurts. One can hardly blame them for this, because for several centuries they have been battered over the head by materialistic sceptics averring that factual, scientific logic refutes everything that they believe in! Theirs is a *feminine* art, which perceives symbolic meaning in the weaving of daily life. Understandably, this has to remain at some distance from things that can be measured, deduced or proved.

It is today hard to find anyone who even wants to talk about these matters. But, it's not over till the fat lady sings. To quote again from that T.S. Eliot poem,

> *What was to be the value of the long looked forward to,*
> *Long hoped-for calm, the autumnal serenity*
> *And the wisdom of age? Had they deceived us*
> *Or deceived themselves, the quiet-voiced elders,*
> *Bequeathing us merely a receipt for deceit?*

---

[2] Virgil, Aenead VII,312 '*Flectere si nequeo superos, Acheronta movebo.*'

Hell yes!

> *Do not let me hear*
> *Of the wisdom of old men, but rather of their folly,*
> *Their fear of fear and frenzy, their fear of possession,*
> *Of belonging to another, or to others, or to God.*
> *The only wisdom we can hope to acquire*
> *Is the wisdom of humility: humility is endless*

One should reject the feeble advice of the last two lines: rather, a Jupiter-type of wisdom is needed that can be optimistic and expansive. These days it is us, the old men, septuagenarians - who comprised the swinging - sixties generation, the baby-boomers - who are in some ways more discerning.

GALILEO AND JUPITER

The above image shows a couple of moons orbiting in front of Jupiter, passing by its Great Red Spot. In the 20th century, space probes descried huge Jovian magnetic storms which echoed across the solar system, even causing disturbances on the surface of the Sun and radio interference on Earth. Jupiter's surface consists of swirling storm clouds and cascades of lightning which cause the psychedelic colouring that endlessly churns and seethes around on its surface, reminding us of Thor, the Norse thunder-god. There could be no greater contrast with the grey, silent neighbour-planet Saturn, enclosed by its dead-level rings, and a mysterious hexagon fixed over its north pole. We saw how Jupiter was *energetic* and *expansive* in its being-essence; while in contrast the top Saturnine character-traits came out as *Silent, Cold* and *Severe*. (page 163)

The closest moons of Jupiter are the four discovered by Galileo, and they move round close to the planet in a marvellous synchronised rotation. One side of each ever faces towards Jupiter and three of them whirl around always maintaining a resonant rhythm, such that when two of them come together, into a conjunction, then the third will be directly opposite to them, or else in square to them. Complicated! They dance in perfect harmony. The periods of the three inner satellites are synchronised to a 1:2:4 ratio, so that Io goes round four times each time Ganymede revolves once.

Conclusion

We found the strongest attributes of Jupiter to be:

Jovial, proud, authority, director and *energetic*

while in contrast its anti-traits (i.e., the lowest scoring) were

reflective, profound and *solitary*

– these being quite Saturnine. These were selected from three dozen traits, and this astral personality-profile may be enriched as and when more are obtained. There could be up to two hundred of these, extracted the Gauquelin data-volumes. As astrologers associate wisdom with Jupiter, or maybe with Jupiter-Saturn, so they associate quick-witted intelligence with Mercury (which we failed to locate).

When Galileo discovered the four moons of Jupiter through his telescope in the year 1609, he called them the *Stella Medici,* because he was hoping to gain employment with the Medicis. He pointed out to the young Cosimo II de Medici (in a foreword to his report on the subject, the bestselling *Starry Messenger* that Jupiter held a strong position at the MC (i.e., the highest position) of his horoscope. It was, he felt sure, a special destiny that had enabled him to find these four new stars unseen hitherto. He then went on to list the traits or *qualities of Jupiter* which, he declared, were generally known and 'not to be doubted.' Addressing the young Cosimo de Medici, in the Preface of this bestseller, *Sidereus Nuncius,* he wrote:

> So who does not know that clemency, kindness of heart, gentleness of manners, splendour of royal blood, nobleness in public functions, wide extent of influence and power over others, all of which have fixed their common abode and seat in your highness – who, I say, does not know, that these qualities, according to the providence of God, from whom all good things do come, emanate from the most benign star of Jupiter?[3]

Those were his seven qualities of Jupiter! From whence did he get this glorious list of character-traits? These have been, it is fair to say, ignored by his biographers. Have you ever come across a history of science or of astronomy which pointed out that Galileo, the great Galileo, listed so well the *qualities of Jupiter*?

---

[3] *Sidereus Nuncius* 1610, Van Helden trans., Chicago, 1989, p.31.

He declared in the foreword to his *Sidereus Nuncius* that the 'Maker of Stars' had been speaking to him, during those chilly nights on his roof in Padua! Science historians tend to ignore that bit. Jupiter in the birthchart of Cosimo de Medici - as Galileo gave it - was *as we'd expect* in a Gauquelin sector: and maybe we need to understand how these qualities of Jupiter are more important that its rather boring physical properties: such as size, distance from the Sun, etc.

We surely concur with the great astronomer, that Jupiter is 'the most benign star.' As we'd also expect, Galileo the archetypal scientist had Saturn in a Gauquelin sector at his birth - it had just risen.[4]

Here is Galileo's explanation as to *how astrology worked*. He focusses upon the position of Jupiter at the MC in the Cosimo de Medici chart. Most of us might lack the confidence to hold forth upon such an arcane matter. But, as the Maker of Stars had been speaking to him ...

> Jupiter, Jupiter I say, at the instant of Your highness's birth had already passed the slow, dull vapours of the horizon and was occupying the Midheaven, from which point it was illuminating the eastern angle, from that sublime throne saw the most happy delivery and all the splendour and magnificence of the newly-born diffused in the most pure air, in order that your tender body and your mind might imbibe with their first breath that universal influence and power...

Jupiter at MC and as the most strongly aspected planet in this chart was in trine to the Ascendent where Sagittarius was rising, he explained, this being 'ruled' by Jupiter (expressed in the terse Latin of Galileo, '*Orientalemque angulum sua Regia illustrans*'): at the 'first breath' those very royal qualities were 'imbibed' by the future monarch from the ambient ether.[5]

THE MORNING STAR

We have located traits for Venus, that being an original feature of the present study, surprising considering that the biographies were

---

[4] He records his birth as having been at 16 Feb 1564 3.30 or 4 pm at Pisa.
[5] For a full account see *Galileo's Astrology* by NK and Nick Campion, 2003; or search for 'Galileo astrologer' for my Skyscript article. I gave a paper on the subject at the *Galileo 2001* Euro Symposium.

Conclusion

mainly male. The traits were at last distinguished by using the duality of Venus' being, as Morning and then the Evening star. The former appeared as being quite bossy: she was 'severe' and 'active', her 'vitality' score showed an excess of 60% – and yet, 'loved' was her top trait (!). To obtain that trait I combined the two French adjectives *amoureux* and *aimé*.

Whereas in contrast the Evening Star appeared as being 'silent' and 'dreamy', 'charming' and 'graceful' – i.e., quite traditional. *Nobody chose those traits*, in the present study, they emerged objectively from a frequency distribution. Thus a polarity is expressed in the trait-terms of the Morning and Evening Star. We are here rediscovering very traditional archetypes, which reach back millennia into European culture, and then further back into classical Greece.

The major Venus-traits we've just looked at -

Charming, elegant, graceful, loved, seductive

tend to reassure us that it is a good world we are living in, in spite of all its horror, or at least that there exists a principle of benevolence in the design of things, in the *Kosmos*. These traits are linked to the daily passage of the nearest heavenly sphere as it rises in the East, its *oriental* position, then as it passes across the zenith, which is called the midhaeven. It is pleasant to use these old, Arabic terms.

The ancients alluded to *Lucifer* and *Hesperus*, as the Morning and Evening Star. We've lost our experience of the Morning Star, arising in the East before sunrise, however we can still appreciate the Evening Star which sets in the Western sky after sunset: Venus goes through this cycle of its changes, appearing and disappearing, once per nineteen months, and if you want to remember that in days, it is $8 + 8^2 + 8^3 = 584$ days!

Here is a modern image of the mandala woven out by Venus around the earth, showing its pentagram structure. Astronomers alas don't talk about this and why not? *The Da Vinci Code* – the fastest-selling book ever - had its main character realise that:

As a young astronomy student, Langdon had been stunned to learn the planet Venus traced a perfect pentacle across the ecliptic sky every four years.

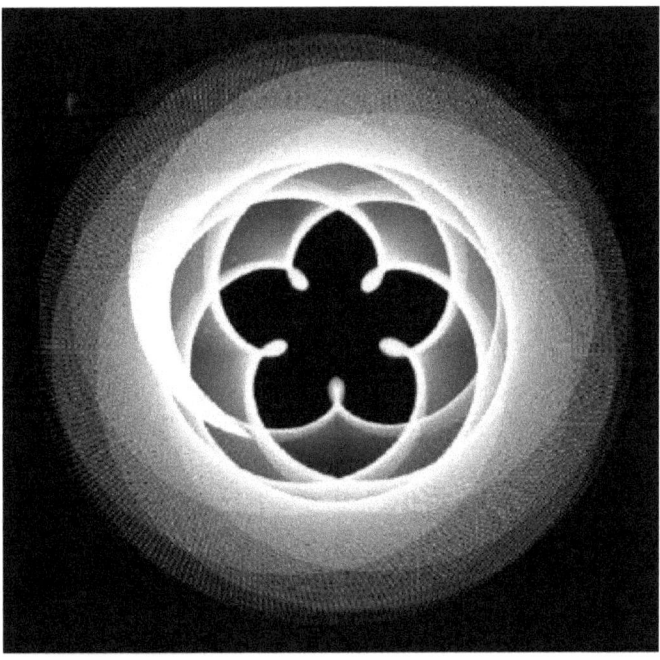

Figure: A reconstruction of Venus' sidereal motion over some decades, with Earth at the centre

Many believe that the eight-year cycle of Venus tracing out its pentagon pattern around the Earth, was first described in that book! It certainly did much to bring the matter into public awareness. Its story focussed on the Divine Feminine and Venus, with gripping plots interwoven around them.

The image shows how Venus draws nearest to Earth in the sky to form its loop of retrograde motion, and then moves away again, and thereby weaves out its pentagram over eight years. Those so-called 'retrograde stations' remain fairly immobile in the Zodiac and Venus becomes invisible to us at those points. She is then in-between Earth and Sun, after having finished as Evening Star and before she becomes the Morning Star: Her celestial dance. It's sheer poetry, really.

Much about Venus concerns what Kepler called the world-Harmony, *Harmonices Mundi*. It rotates very slowly in space in the reverse direction to all of the other planets, taking 243 days, which happens to be the fifth power of three –

$$3 \times 3 \times 3 \times 3 \times 3 \times 3$$

which happens to be two-thirds of an Earth-year, i.e. Venus rotation period / Earth year = 2/3 , quite exactly to within 99.8%. She revolves *just twelve times in space* every eight years, that *is every thirteen Venus-years*, while that pentagram pattern is being woven out. Oddly enough that synchronizes mathematically to make the same side of Venus face Earthwards every time she comes nearest to the Earth, at each inferior conjunction. It is a very slow rotation, slower than any other planet and in the reverse direction to all the others. We thereby sense much that is 'perfect' about the way Earth and Venus move together, in their heavenly dance.

A Venusian type of person can mean that you feel good sitting in their home, or you just like walking down the street with them. It can mean that you sense a kindly benevolence, and they are not about to say something horrible about you. And why should that be? Well, there are different levels of explanation here, and you might like a mathematical one. Venus and Earth form the Golden Ratio in their years, to about 1%, and the synodic period of Venus – that's the one we have just looked at, with five of them every eight years – does this more exactly, giving phi to within half of one percent, ie

$$\text{Venus synodic period / Earth year} = \varphi$$

i.e. the golden Ratio. The phi-ratio expresses the notion of perfection and harmony, and it has a connection with Venus, and the pentagram.

MICHEL'S VIEW

Michel was a materialist. He developed the following ultra-paranoid perspective:

> My work, which began with the 'astrological' notion of the birth hour, may find its eventual fulfilment in a biochemical formula to replace the information provided by the natal position of the major planets. Such a discovery would explain the sensitivity of the foetus to the cosmos at the time

of birth, in function of its heredity... 'Neo-astrology' is a frightening idea.[6]

It is indeed, and one can see why French astrologers wanted nothing to do with it. One is reminded of that above-quoted line "Do not let me hear / Of the wisdom of old men, but rather of their folly." I have endeavoured to critique errors made in the 20th century, by those who were doing their best, but did not have our modern facility of summoning the data up onto a computer screen to examine it. I wish I could go back in time to the big international conferences we used to hold, where the *cognoscenti* would sort things out, or try to – now that I at long last understand what the questions should be! For me the worst shock came from having to re-evaluate the contribution by that *eminence grise* Suitbert Ertel who had published so much on the subject.

We've seen how the German journal, *Zeitschrift für Parapsychologie und Grenzgebiete der Psychologie* ('Journal of parapsychology and fringe areas of psychology') carried articles by Carl Jung and Arthur Koestler as well as Gauquelin. Its various articles by Ertel and Müller had back-and-forth arguing between the two. If those could be put up online preferably with English translations then that might do a lot to clarify the matter. My rather stern judgements about Suitbert Ertel in Chapter 5 might then need to be revised.

We have examined what was initiated by a remarkable couple, who seemed not to get on well together, but who had integrity; and followed them over a vast transition almost like going from one world to another, as we entered the computer age. Their main work was done with pen and paper and they never really used computers except when they went over to California to have their work re-evaluated by Tom Shanks and Neil Michelsen. And the way all record of that disappeared, I continue to find rather baffling. Their work went off in too many directions as they tried too many things.

The world decided that the Gauquelins had cheated, around the time of Michel's suicide in 1991. We have now examined the historical record and checked through databases in much detail in order to resolve this matter. The answer we reached was, in the negative. They did not cheat. They were muddled, yes, and did show some bias, yes,

---

[6] M.G., *The Truth About Astrology*, 1983, p.178.

but cheating – no! The US sceptics, in contrast, clearly did, in a disgraceful manner.

APPENDICES

1. ANCIENT SEQUENCE OF THE HOUSES

Françoise checked out the earliest roots of astrology, found in the omen-texts of ancient Babylon. Scrutinising these millennia-old texts, she concluded that astrologers had erred in their use of house-systems:

> The first astrological texts we know…clearly indicate that those first observers of the sky predicted for strongly meaningful events to occur when the planets were situated after – and not before –the angles of the chart.[1]

From these early texts written on clay tablets she inferred that astrologers had been counting the houses in the wrong direction for two millennia!

> It seems that the modern statistical obervations are in agreement with the first traditions, when they indicate strong zones to be situated in houses 12, 9, 6 and 3. Shouldn't we therefore call those zones "Angular" rather than cadent?[2]

The beliefs of astrologers about the 'twelfth house' (just after a planet's rising) – that it is 'the house of self-undoing' etc, rather private and hidden - were radically incompatible with what the Gauquelins had discovered and indeed hardly compatible with idea of a planet having just risen. The counting was all wrong she reckoned, and it should rather be the first house, not the 12th![3]

> Fortunately the several thousands of years of intense observations of the sky and the related events on earth, by the less abstract peoples of Mesapotamia (where astrology

---

[1] APP 1992, 8,2 p.21, F.G. For further discussion see Micheal Baigent, *The Omens of Babylon*, 1994, p.180.
[2] Ibid. 'Cadent,' she explained, meant 'falling' in Latin.
[3] F.G., 'The Greek Error or Return to Babylon,' APP, 1985, 3,3 p.9. Online at: http://cura.free.fr/xxv/24app3-3.html A few years later Jacques Dorsan's book *Le véritable sens des maisons astrologiques* 'the True Direction of the Astrological Houses' appeared in 1989 – in English *The Clockwise house system*, 2011, shamefully making no acknowledgement to Françoise.

originated) have been summarised on collections of clay tablets. Alexander Sachs, specialist in deciphering cuneiform script, published in 'Babylonian Horoscopes' (1952) lists of such omens derived from planetary placements. Some of these placements are deciphered by Sachs, but cannot be translated because their meaning is still unknown ("dur", "mi-sir", "tallu"). But others are quite clear. Among them, many concern planetary placements after their rising and setting points, that is in the presently discussed houses twelve and six. In this tradition, there is no trace of bad omen attached to the placement in the twelfth house. For instance:

* If a child is born when the moon has come forth (i.e. has risen above the horizon), then "his life will be bright, excellent, regular and long.

* If a child is born when Jupiter has come forth, then his life will be regular, well; he will become rich, he will grow old, his days will be long.

* If a child is born when Venus has come forth, then his life will be exceptionally calm; wherever he may go, it will be favourable; his days will be long.

* If a child is born when mas has come forth, then … hot temper…!

* If a child is born when Saturn has come forth, then his life will be dark, obscure, sick, and constrained.

From all this, she concluded,

The differences in these omens are related to the different character traits linked to each planet, as tradition still transmits them, and as modern results confirm them.

The first house, in which these bodies are not yet visible, is of course not mentioned at all for Babylonian omens. The omens for placements in the sixth house are erased on the tablets from Uruk translated here; but other sources make them appear as less favourable than the omens attached to the placements in the twelfth house:

* If a child is born when Jupiter comes forth and Venus has set, it will go excellently with that man; his wife will leave.

Appendices

* If a child is born when Venus comes forth and Jupiter had set, his wife will be stronger than he.

The sidereal astrologer Robert Powell has endorsed Françoise's view:

> Undoubtedly the greatest contribution with regard to the house question—in terms of providing concrete evidence for the validity of some or other house system—has occurred in the twentieth century through the work of Michel Gauquelin (1928-1990) and his first wife, Françoise Schneider-Gauquelin. In some respects, the Gauquelin research represents a return to the Egyptian star-clocks. Just as the ancient Egyptians contemplated the rising, culminating and setting of the stars during the night, Michel Gauquelin spent much of his life statistically investigating the rising, culminating and setting of the planets at the time of birth of prominent people. And just as the special interest of the Egyptians was directed to the rising ("birth") and culminating ("prime of life") of the planets and stars, so the Gauquelins found empirically that the rising and culminating of the planets are the two most important phases of their diurnal movement. Also, the Gauquelin clockwise method of dividing the sky into sectors is reminiscent of the Ramesside star clocks.[4]

Françoise has no Wiki page and is now greatly forgotten. Her rational proposal for the houses to be counted clockwise shows no sign of catching on.

2. SYNASTRY NOTES

The following is unrelated to Gauquelin research, however it uses the Gauquelin 'heredity' database.

When Françoise had the synastry or so-called 'heredity' data posted up onto the CURA website, she used 'M' for mother and 'F' for father. Ray Murphy (in Adelaide) preferred not to use this nomenclature which quickly leads to confusion between {mother, father} and {male, female}. Instead, he labelled the columns, 'Mom' and 'Dad.' Ray who did the original computer work for the Chapter 14 synastry study has kindly allowed me to reproduce this summary of the results.

---

[4] Robert Powell, *History of the Houses*, 1997, p.20.

1. His Sun conjunct her Moon at 5° orb, 6% above the expected score all the way through. Also the same thing in reverse for the square - Her Moon less often on his Sun with a square.

2. The women had an aversion to marrying men with his Sun opp her Sat.: it is 14% lower at 3° of orb.

3. Women married men MORE OFTEN if her Moon was square or in opposition to his Venus, with the scores about 8% higher than expected

4. Sun opp Sun, orb 7° => 7% above the expected score,

5. His Venus conj. her MC, 6% above the expected score, 3° orb.

6. Moon conjunct Pluto 6° orb, consistently for both partners.

7. Partners had deficit of Saturn conj. MC synastry, to 7° orb

8. Husband's Moon con her VE/MA midpoint at 15% above the expected rate with a 3° orb being the best fit

9. The husbands' Moon is also opp. the wife's VE/MA midpoint - 5% higher consistently - 3° orb

10. Her Moon conj. His Asc 6% above expected.

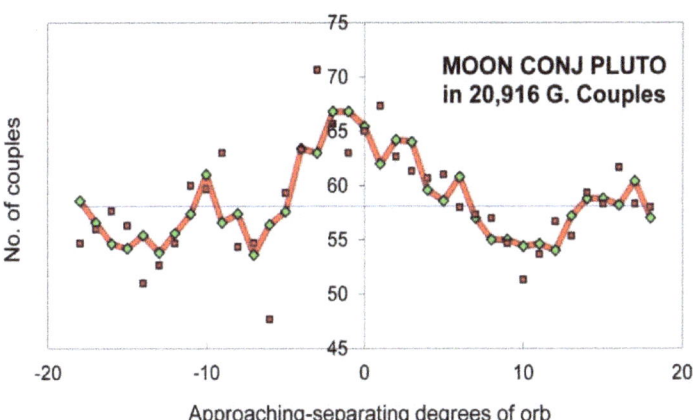

Jung's synastry study (1955), found mainly lunar synastry in a group of somewhat less than two hundred married couples.[5] The first synastry aspect on Dr Carl Jung's list, *her* Moon conjunct *his* Sun, only appears

---

[5] Carl Gustav Jung, *The Interpretation of Nature and the Psyche*, 1955: introduced his concept of 'synchronicity.' For my comments, see: 'Investigating Aspects' (online at astrozero.co.uk) *Astrological Research Methods*, ISAR, Ed. Mark Pottenger, 1995, pp. 287-302, section III.

weakly in the present data-set. That is an archetypal relation, i.e. it finds expression in traditional alchemy.

Moon-Pluto: Can Pluto affect marriage prospects? Her Moon was subtracted from *his* Pluto: the zero degrees (conjunction) then showed an excess of 14% for three degrees either side. The effect was slightly bigger before exactitude, significant at 3° orb ($\chi^2=7$). Astral philosophers will want to mull over this startling effect: could it be that she (Luna) was attracted to his 'plutocratic' wealth?

Mars-conjunct-Mars or Jupiter-conjunct-Jupiter synastry will appear to give a large excess, but this is merely an 'astro-demographic' effect: a control sample, made by shuffling days and months in one of the columns, will give much the same effect.

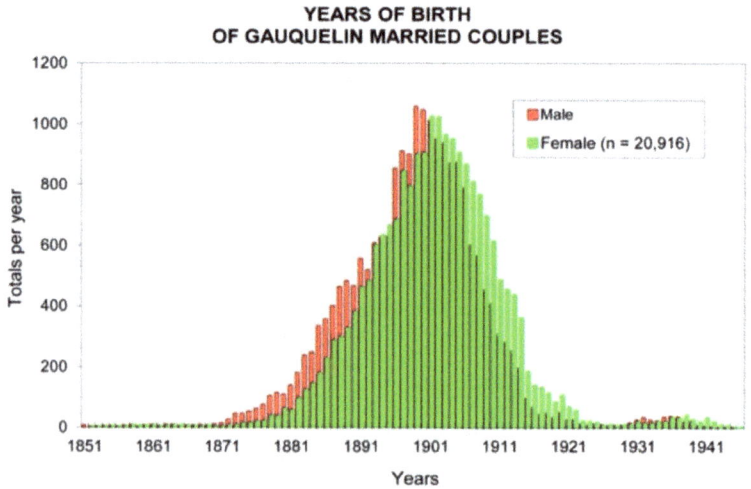

Figure: Age difference husband and wife, showing that wives were on average 2.8 years younger. 95% of the birth-data lay between 1980 and 1920.

VENUS, SATURN AND AGE

The Finnish investigator Kyosti Tarvanien has discovered that harmonious aspects between Venus and Saturn (i.e., trines and sextiles) in the chart of the *husband* tended to make him *older* compared to his wife's age.[6] To check this pleasantly simple result, the columns of Venus and Saturn longitudes in the husband's chart are subtracted. We can express

---

[6] KT, 'Effects of Venus/Saturn aspects in marriages,' *Correlation* 29 (2) 2014, pp. 7-14.

that as {Saturn – Venus}. Another column found the age difference between partners, {Wife's date of birth – that of husband}. The results of the subtraction must lie between 0 - 360°.

Sorting the columns by longitude, sextiles are at 60° and 300° and trines are at 120° and 240°. The columns are then aligned or

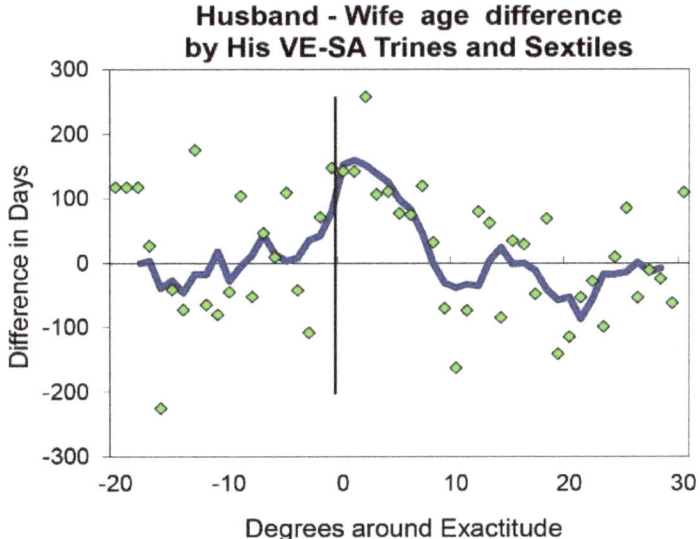

superimposed, so that those four angles, those four zero-orb positions, coincide. Thereby those four aspects will overlay each other, over say a fifty-degree span (see graph). Taking mean values of these per degree gives a startling increment, of over *one hundred days* increase in husband's age compared to the wife. That's for the Venus-Saturn aspects.

Age differential husband-wife, vs his Venus-Saturn aspects.

3° orb Aspects	Venus-Saturn	Venus-Moon
Trines & sextiles	+126 days	-6 days
Squares & oppn.	-3 days	-45 days
Conjuncn.	+78 days	-79 days

The mean age-difference per degree of that angular difference is here shown.[7]

---

[7] These aspects chime at 60°, 120°, 240° and 300° in the circle of the ecliptic, so the figure takes the values for 40-80° and 280-320° (sextiles), 100-140° and 220-260° (trines) and has overlaid them.

Appendices

Trines and sextiles between Venus and Saturn in the husband's natal chart confer upon him *an extra one-third of a year* in age, compared to his wife. The main effect appears *after* exactitude, i.e. after Venus has chimed with Saturn. There was no effect for hard aspects, i.e. the squares and opposition.

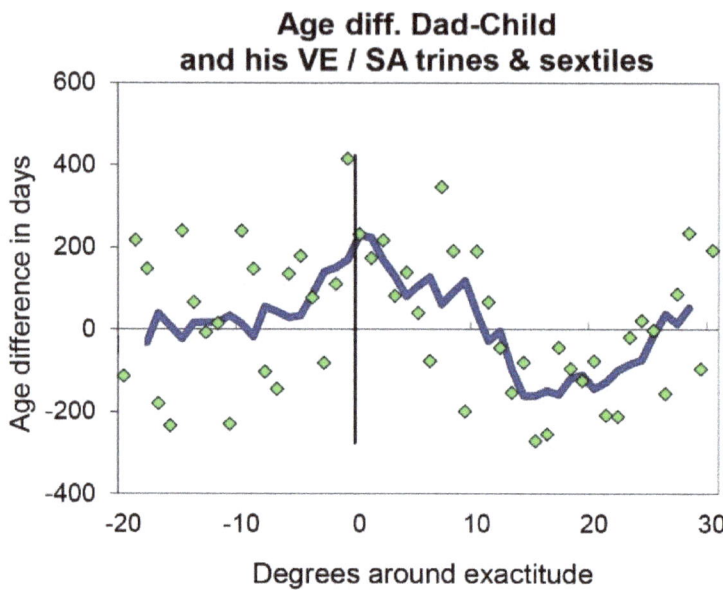

For comparison, KT used 7° orbs for trines and 5° for sextiles.[8] Thus we have replicated and confirmed what he found – except that he did not comment upon the big difference between approaching and separating aspects.

These same aspects caused the birth of the first child to be delayed: i.e., the father tended to be older at its birth. That again was linked to his Venus-Saturn aspects, as the graph shows.

Mean Increments in age differential husband-Ist child in days, vs. orb of VE-SA aspects.

Orb	age difference	t-value
2°	233 Days	2.7
3°	178 days	2.6
5°	165 days	3.1

---

[8] That is much the same probability-value as KT claimed, viz 1 in 500: 2014 (ref 13), p.10.

We see how the effect dramatically increases with decreasing orb, and that strongly argues for a real effect: up to two-thirds of a year is added to the Father's age, by virtue of having these aspects in his chart, when his first child is born.

This Venus-Saturn link to age-difference in couples appears as a significant 21st century astro-discovery.

UPLOADING THE GAUQUELIN DATA

For these synastry comparisons one has to move files back and forth between a spreadsheet program (eg, Excel) and an astrology program (eg, Solar Fire). Columns twenty thousand long on an Excel spreadsheet were fed into the Solar Fire program as 'text' files. It is quite an experience to see Solar Fire generating its file of twenty thousand charts, in one minute: bearing in mind the many years which it took the Gauquelins to compute such charts, by hand. But, that is progress. Only one planet is selected, e.g. the 'Mom' file may contain only solar longitudes. Solar Fire outputs this data as a column of zodiac longitudes in a text file.[9] The two columns are brought into an Excel spreadsheet and subtracted, to obtain differences eg [Sun – Venus] as degrees of longitude. Excel then makes a frequency distribution of these twenty thousand differences, 1° – 360°.

3. MISCELLANY

HEREDITY DATA

There are thirteen 'Heredity' files on the CURA site from which altogether 81,386 birthdates are extracted; with 20,916 'couples' i.e. families for which the birthdata of both father and mother have been obtained, or 30,025 family units, including those where birthdata for only one parent was obtained. The number of parent-child couples are:

	From CURA page	Analysed by MG
Father-Daughter	12,049	3,471
Mother-Daughter	14,283	4,296
Mother-Boy	14,931	4,433
Father-Boy	12,613	3,837
Totals:	53,876	16,037 parent-child couples.

---

[9] To import the text file, select Utilities/Chart Import-Export, which will make the Solar Fire chart, then export it as a text file using Chart/Open/Export.

Appendices

There were 33,201 child-birthdates.

The Gauquelin *Planetary Heredity* book of 1966 (1988 English edition) stated: 'The birth data allow 16,073 parent-child comparisons" (p.19) and the same number is given in his 1970 data-volume (p.vii).

CHARACTER-TRAIT DATA: COMBINING TWO TRAITS

Jovial: *Joyeux* {19,29,29,7} + *Joviale* {7,5,12,0} (of Sports, Writers, Actors, Science) => total, 108. Total with found birthtimes: 94

Friendly: *Aimable* {25,16,42,19} + *Amitié* {12,87,50,55} => total, 284. Total with found birthtimes: 286.

Loved: *Aimé* {5,11,62,19} + *Amoureux* {0,25,9,0} => total, 131. Total found birthtimes: 126.

For these three 'double traits' duplicates may exist, eg, writers described as 'joviale', could also be 'joyeux'.

Other traits of a possibly Venusian relevance could here be: *viv*/lively (207), *fidèle*/faithful (146), *Gai*/Gay (136), *verve (de la)* (135), *souriant (toujours)*/always smiling (125), *couer du bonté*/great-hearted (100), lyrical (83), *fantastique* + *fantaisiste* (75), violent (74), *fier*/proud (68), *rieur*/laughing (67), poetique/poet (63), *naif*/naïve (62) and *pittoresque*/picturesque (50). Traits of too low a score but possibly worth testing in combination are: youthful, young-looking (39), exuberant (30), scandalous (27), beauty (26) bon vivant (26) and happy (25).

PROFESSIONAL DATA GROUPS

Uncertainties over the sizes of the groups have been alluded to, thus:

Journalists: The CURA group of journalists contains 674 of them and gives a 13% excess of Jupiter in the Key Sectors. MG published in 1980 a group of 903 with a much larger 23% excess but never seems to have explained how he obtained that group, which cannot readily be derived from his two published data-sets of Journalists, one of them shown here (674)[10]. To those he added another 344 (Series E, Vol, 3, 1984) adding up to 1018: which does not correspond to the total of 903 given in his 1980 *Spheres of Destiny*; we'll ignore the latter (confirmed by Patrice Guignard of CURA).

---

[10] The group of Journalists first appear in MG's *Les Hommes et Les Astres* 1960: 824 from several European countries.

Military: MG in 1980 mixed top military (3046, his 1970 total and as given by CURA) with aviators to get the larger total of 3438: maybe, better kept separate.

Musicians: MG in 1970 grouped military band leaders (383) with his eminent musicians (866), to get 1248, but one may wish to separate these. In his 1980 *Spheres of Destiny* he there showed how the military musicians had a different profile (a stronger Mars) from the others.[11] Venus, although cited in the above Table for musicians (as +5%) was not significant.

Physicians: MG oddly grouped Scientists and Medical physicians together in his 1974 publication as well as his 1980 *Spheres of Destiny*, then in 1984 he gave a separate group of 975 eminent physicians.[12] He published 3647 'Science and Medicine' (Series A Vol. 2) of which 1094 were scientists and 2552 were medical doctors. It is useful that on the CURA site these can be separated.[13]

TIME IN THE GAUQUELIN DATA

Time in the Gauquelin data-volumes was given mostly to the nearest hour, whereas the old CURA data was confsingly given to minutes and seconds. The nearly-ready site 'opengauquelin.org' site has re-created the time data in its original form.

The CURA data gave the birthdata on each line but without names. The published G-volumes have the data listed alphabetically by name. To compare the two one has to rely upon the 'Gauquelin number,' given sequentially for the printed data-volumes in the same sequence as the alphabetical names.

---

[11] One can obtain MG's group of musicians from the 'Painters and Musicians' CURA page http://cura.free.fr/gauq/902gdA4y.html where it appears together with military band leaders.
[12] But NB they are separated in MG 1972 (ref.3). No copy of his 1984 text Series E, Vol.1 *Physicians, Army Leaders, Top Executives*; nor Vol.3 *French Writers, Artists, Actors, Politicians & Journalists* seem to exist anywhere in the UK, limiting my comments upon them.
[13] The first 2252 in that list are physicians, as stated on the CURA site, also in the 'Scientists A volume 2' data-book published by the two Gauquelins. MG's 1988 *Written in the Stars* has a chapter 'Doctors and scientists' which has 1084 doctors and 990 scientists, and does not really explain why he is putting them together. He there has 3,306 'Men of Science' p.106. The group numbers in that book differ from the published data totals used here.

Appendices

There are three kinds of time in the Gauquelin data. Starting around 1800, local mean time (LMT) was being used. LMT is converted to UT or GMT by subtracting four minutes for each degree East in longitude. From 1891 onwards, the LMT of Paris became uniformly accepted throughout France, a consequence of the developing railway timetables. French time was then GMT less 0.16 of an hour or nine minutes. From 1911 onwards French time became synchronised with GMT, making the time correction then either 0 or -1 hours, the latter for Summer Time. The data goes up to around 1920.

The 'opengauquelin.org' site has replaced the old CURA site of the late Patrice Guignard as data-source. Its author aims to re-check all the birth-data.

5. A LAST WORD ON THE SCEPTICS

There is no Wikipedia page about he Gauquelin work as such, only a brief 'Mars Effect' section dismissing it, with Geoffrey Dean getting the last paragraph. It alludes to alleged 'social effects' that explain the phenomenon.

As Robert Currey states in his critique of Dean's work (astrology.co.uk/tests/deantest.htm), 'Dean has been involved in almost every sceptical investigation into astrology since 1985.' That is quite a track record!

Dean holds a doctorate in chemistry. He used to turn up to astrology-research conferences, always polite and informative. But then, when back home at his desk his lengthy screeds would debunk any alleged results. His latest how-to-scoff-at-everything tome runs to some nine hundred pages of small print.

Totalling some two thousand three hundred pages, his four volumes are finding their way into university libraries. As a fellow of the US sceptics society CSICOP, this arch-skeptic has spent a lifetime publishing his negation – texts:

- Dean and Mather, *Recent Advances in Natal Astrology, A Critical Review* 1977, 575 pages;
- Heukelom, Dean and Smit, *Astrology Under Scrutiny* 2014, 360 pages;

- Dean, Mather Smit and Nias, *Tests of Astrology* 2016;
- Same authors, *Understanding Astrology A Critical Review of a thousand empirical studies 1900-2020,* 2023, 948 pages

These appear as having been well-funded by the skeptics and the last one is beautifully produced. One notes the deceitful titles: the first book *Recent Advances* was far from being about any advances, so the last, *Understanding Astrology* will surely not bring understanding, only scepticism.

His earlier books had endorsed the researches of the two Gauquelins but his latest dismisses the topic on the basis of 'social effects.' What might these be? More births, we learn, take place at the weekend while there are less at inauspicious days of the year such as Halloween or on the unlucky 13th day of the month. And, sometimes there was misreporting of birthdate. There is a huge 'midnight-hour avoidance' (as we saw on page 106), whereby fewer births are then recorded. But, so what?

No resonant periodicity exists between, say, Mars' diurnal period and any of these lucky/ unlucky days, so they simply average out, producing background noise but that is all. Because the birth data extends over several decades, the various solar and planetary imbalances – the midnight avoidance hour being by far the largest – don't show up in a planetary diurnal-frequency distribution.

The Gauquelin effect concerns *two* Key Sectors. That is so crucial because no physical or demographic effect can model or predict it - it's an *astrological* effect. Vainly, Dean writes in his final, weighty tome (page 189) –

"CONCLUSION

Do social effects explain the puzzles? In a word, yes. Nothing else comes close."

Mothers and midwives, he reckoned, had been figuring out in advance the rising and culminating times of the planets then would try to give birth at these times. Why woud they do that? I've never met anyone who took Dean's arguments seriously (except maybe long ago Charles Harvey, the *Astrological Association*'s President, who was responsible for initially promoting Dean) or who could even see the point of them. Mothers, he argues, didn't know on what day their child was born and also were liable to perjure themselves in filling out a birth certificate. Very occasionally that would have been so but would not affect the results.

Appendices

Dean put forward what he reckoned was a clincher argument based on the accuracy of birth times. The Gauquelin data had mainly been given to the nearest hour, but around a third of them were more accurate, being quoted to the nearest ten minutes. Dean convinced himself that groups having *more* accurate birth data showed a *weaker* effect:

> Now the big one. Why is the planetary effect for precisely recorded birth times half that for birth times recorded to the nearest hour? This is like saying the more we tune our radio the worse the reception. It is not what we expect. (page 190)

That claim can be at last evaluated thanks to Thierry Graff restoring the actual birth-times as given by the Gauquelins. (The old CURA page only had birthdata given in UT to the minute which meant that no-one could evaluate the claim by Dean. Time-zone corrections (in minutes and seconds) had been applied to the published data when it was converted into digital form and put online, so that no original data existed online for time of birth within the data-sets.)

Using the newly-restored local-time data on opengauquelin.org, I divided the sports-champion data into two groups, those accurate to the nearest hour (that was two-thirds of the data) and the remainder given to minutes. There was *no difference* in the magnitude of the Mars-effect between the two groups. I wrote to Geoffrey Dean about this but he did not reply. 'No astrologer, no skeptic, not even Gauquelin would have predicted such a result' he observes, which is true enough, because it doesn't exist. He uses this to support his argument about 'misreporting' as having somehow produced the effect. It's a totally bogus argument.

The great length with which Dean holds forth on these topics should not be mistaken for insight. His writing has a facile, fatuous tone which normally misses any important point. Suitbert Ertel wasted much time trying to debate the above issue with him. He has spent a lifetime to be remembered as Dr No, as the Master of Denial.

The core Gauquelin hypothesis which was formulated in 1951 on the basis of eminent physicians' data has been tested again and again on different continents and by various groups and persons and it has done exactly what a scientific theory was supposed to do: the effect was repeatedly demonstrated. The peaks it predicted were in accord with what millenia of tradition said were the two most important positions in the day: rising and culminating, the Ascendent and MC while the symbolism involved was fully in accord with tradition: the Moon for poets and Saturn for scientists, etc. It would help if sceptics acknowledged this and stopped pretending the issue was just about Mars and sports champions.[14]

ARTICLES PUBLISHED

ASTRO-PSYCHOLOGICAL PROBLEMS

1983 Mar, Vol.1 (2), Douglas, Graham: A Theoretical Prediction from the Gauquelins' Findings

Sept, Vol.1 (4), Martinek, Wolfgang: Excerpts from "Drug Addiction and Horoscopes" http://cura.free.fr/gauq/907app-mar.html

Sept, Vol.1 (4), FG: Comments about Wolfgang Martinek's "Drug Addiction and Horoscopes" http://cura.free.fr/gauq/907app-mar.html#cfg

Sept, Vol.1 (4), Reverchon, Jacques: Two Notes for Discussion (Demographic peculiarities & Planetary heredity) http://cura.free.fr/gauq/907app-rev.html

1984 Mar, Vol.2 (2), Eysenck, Hans: The Mars Effect and its Evaluation http://cura.free.fr/gauq/909app-eys.html

Mar, Vol.2 (2), Ashmun, Joanna: Critique of C.G. Jung's Astrological Experiment

1985 Jan, Vol.3 (1), Burmyn, Lynne: Preliminary Report on Lesbian Study

Jan, Vol.3 (1), FG: The Search for the Lesbians' Planet

Jan, Vol.3 (1), FG: The Nycthemeral Expectancy

May, Vol.3 (2), FG: Comments of David Nias's Review of "Planetary Heredity"

Sept, Vol.3 (3), FG: The Greek Error or Return to Babylon http://cura.free.fr/xxv/24app3-3.html

Sept, Vol.3 (3), FG: More Precisions about the Gauquelin Sectors

1986 May, Vol.4 (2), Costa-Ribeiro Anna-Maria & DeMarco Donna & Gauquelin Françoise: Drug Addicts - A Replication

Sept, Vol.4 (3), Stark, Franz: How Strong is the Gauquelin Planetary Effect Really?

Sept, Vol.4 (3), O'Neill, Mike: The Moon's Nodes in Synastry

1987 May, Vol.5 (2), Stark, Franz: Replication of a Study on the "Gauquelin-Effect" with Ordinary People

May, Vol.5 (2), FG & Costa-Ribeiro Anna-Maria & O'Neill, Mike: 231 Male Homosexuals from Brazil

---

[14] See review of the Dean *et. al.* opus at astrozero.co.uk/kollerstrom

May, Vol.5 (2), Blackwell, Arthur: Local Apparent Time
May, Vol.5 (2), Pottenger, Mark: Do you mean Apparent?
Sep, Vol.5 (3), FG & Lehman Lee & Costa-Ribeiro Anna-Maria: More Data of Homosexuals
1988 May, Vol.6 (2), Ertel, Suitbert: Planetary Relations with Female Notabilities: The First Results
1989 Mar, Vol.7 (1), FG: An Interview with Neil Michelsen
Mar, Vol.7 (1), O'Neill, Mike: The Moon's Nodes in Marriage - A Replication
Mar, Vol.7 (1), Ertel, Suitbert: Reversed Eminence Correlations
Mar, Vol.7 (1), FG: Answer to Professor Ertel's Comments
Mar, Vol.7 (1), MG: Comments on Prof. Ertel's Article
Sept, Vol.7 (2), FG: An Interview with Robert Hand
Sept, Vol.7 (2), Lehman, Lee: The Neo-Astrology Conference: Some Reflections
Sept, Vol.7 (2), Müller, Arno: Can the Gauquelin Effect be Confirmed?
Sept, Vol.7 (2), O'Neill, Mike: Analysis of Ballet Dancers in Gauquelin Sectors
1992 Mar, Vol.8 (1), FG: Michel Gauquelin, in Memoriam
Mar, Vol.8 (1), FG: Planetary Heredity: New Research Results
Sept, Vol.8 (2), Eysenck, Hans / Smit Rudolf: In Memoriam Michel Gauquelin (1928-1991)
Sept, Vol.8 (2), Ertel, Suitbert: References of Michel Gauquelin's Publications (Complete list)
Sept, Vol.8 (2), FG: The Gauquelin Sectors
1993 Mar, Vol.9 (1), FG: About the Accuracy of Birth Time Registration I
Mar, Vol.9 (1), Ertel, Suitbert & FG (References of their Publications)
Sept, Vol.9 (2), FG: MG's Planetary Temperaments versus FG's "Pure Types"
Sept, Vol.9 (2), Müller, Arno & FG: A Study of the Gauquelin Effect with 402 Italian Writers
Sept, Vol.9 (2), FG: Accuracy of Birth Time Registration II
1994 Mar, Vol.10 (1), FG: Statistical Results with Ordinary People
Mar, Vol.10 (1), Irving, Ken & FG: Pure and Mixed Planetary Types
Sept, Vol.10 (2), Pottenger, Mark: Gauquelin Sector expected Frequencies
1995 Mar, Vol.11 (1), FG: CTH Yes? or CTH No?
Mar, Vol.11 (1), Douglas, Graham: Planets in Semantic Space
Mar, Vol.11 (1), Pottenger, Mark / Gauquelin Françoise: Follow-up on the Neptune Factor

Sept, Vol.11 (2), FG: Can we Conclude about the CTH Controversy? Not yet it seems

CORRELATION

1981 1(1) 26-35 JM Addey, The True Principles of Astrology & Bearing on Astrol Research

    36-44 Mike Startup The Accuracy of Astrologers Keywords

    1(2), 4-14: M.G., "Planets, personality and ordinary people"

1982 2(1) 4-9 M&FG, Sybil Eysenck, "Eysenck's Personality analysis and Position of the Planets at Birth: A Replication on American Subjects"

    33-36 FG, "The Astrologer's Keywords Re-analysed – Part III"

    2(2) 2-4 Hans Eysenck, "Michel Gauquelin's `Suggestions for Studying Ordinary People'"

    5-12 MG, "An Empirical Study of the Accuracy of ancient astrologers' Keywords"

1984 4(1) 5-7 Mike Startup, Planets, Personality and Ordinary People: A Reappraisal"

    8-24   MG, "Profession and Heredity Experiments, Computer reanalysis"

1987 7(1) 4-17 Ertel, "Further grading of eminence: musicians, painters, writers"

    18-25   Peter Roberts "Harmonic analysis of the diurnal distributions of G. professional Groups"

1989 9(1) 5-24   Ertel, "Purifying Gauquelin's' Grain of Gold"

    24-28   Letters to the Editor – Comments by Müller and MG.

    29-31 Comments.

    32-33 MG, 'The Moon and famous Writers'

    9(2)   28-32, Ertel, S. "Birth time precision reconsidered."

1990 10(2) 3-19 Ertel, "Scrutinizing G's Character Trait Hypothesis Once Again"

    20-33   MG & Susan Tracs, "G.s Character Trait Hypothesis: The Fresno Experiment"

1991 11(1)   9-11   Patrick Curry, "Michel and the Scientists"

    12-23, Ertel, "The Publications of Michel Gauquelin, Complete list, 1955-1991."

1993 12(1) 2-9 Ertel, S. "Why the character trait hypothesis still fails."

    12(2) 20-43 Jan Ruis, "Synastry Aspects in a Gauquelin-Sample of

                    2824 Marriages"
1994 13(2) 3-16. Ertel, "Mars effect uncovered in French sceptics'data."
            31-39 J Ruis, "Planetary Gender Difference"
1995 14(1) 8-14. Ertel, "Gender of notables related to planetary positions."
            30-37. Ertel,. "Birth time precision and the Gauquelin effect."
            50-54, Ertel, "Reply to Dr. Nienhuys' letter."
1996 15(1) 2-16. Ertel, "How to suppress the Gauquelin Mars effect"
            53-4 Eysenck, Review of *Tenacious Mars-Effect*.
            54-60 Ken Irving, Review of Benski Report (CFEPP)
1997 16(2) 10-39 Geoffrey Dean, "John Addey's Dream: Planetary Harmonics and the Character Trait Hypothesis."
1998 17(2): 4-23 Ertel, "Is there no Mars effect? The CFEPP's verdict scrutinized"
       18(2) 50-60 Ertel, "Reply to Nanninga and Nienhuys on "Is there no Mars effect"."
1999 18(2): 9-41 Ertel, "Debunking with caution. Cleaning up Mars effect research."
2000 19(2): 37-46.Ertel, "Scrutiny of Geoffrey Dean's parental tampering claim."
2002 21(1): 35-39 Ertel, "Whence midnight avoidance? Scrutinies of Geoffrey Dean's parental tampering claim (4)."
2005 23(1) NK, "How Ertel rescued the Gauquelin eff€ct"
2005 23(1): 7-33 Ertel, "Gauquelin planetary effects - brought down to earth? On Geoffrey Dean's dealing with stubborn facts."
2006 24(1) 21-31 Graham Douglas, "Grains of Silver and Gold"
            33 The G. effect and birth order (online CURA?)
2007 25(1) 35-50 Graham Douglas, "Seasonal cycles in the G. data follow geomagnetic indices"
2008 26(1) 5-25 "Orbituary to Françoise Gauquelin"
            33-50 Graham Douglas, "Moving from Gauquelin to Classical Astrology"
2011 32(2) 24-46 Graham Douglas, "Some unexpected solar patterns in the Gauquelin data"
2015 30 (1) 53-7 N.K., 'Neptune & Alcoholics'

THE HUMANIST

1975 Sept/Oct 35,5 The original statement by 186 scientists & articles

1976   Jan/Feb 36,1 p2,46: Readers's Forum, by Carl Sagan & Rob Hand.
      Committee Para replies, Zelen 'Astrology and Statistics, A Challenge', astronomer Abell.
   Mar/April 36,2 p52-53: Sceptical comments by Jerome, MG on Fact versus Fiction.
   May/June 36,3 p28 Founding of CSICOP; 'The Gauquelins Visit the US,' p.32 Committee Para reply to MG.
   July/August 36,4 p2,42: M&FG, Truth about the Mars Effect,
   p.50 press coverage.
   Sept/Oct 36,5: p2, 60-63 G.O. & Abell ,
   p.60, M&FG Test of the Mars Effect.
1977 Jan/Feb 36,1, p2,57: French scientists support statement on Astrology, G-study continues.
   Nov/Dec 37, 6 p.29: Paul Kurtz, 'The Mars Effect and the Zelen Test'
   37,6 p30-35, M&F Gauquelin, 'The Zelen Test of the Mars Effect'
   37,6 36-39 Zelen, Kurtz & Abell, 'Is there a Mars Effect?'

JOURNAL OF SCIENTIFIC EXPLORATION

1988, 2,1 Is There a Mars Effect?   Michel Gauquelin
   2,1 Raising the Hurdle for the Athletes' Mars Effect: Association Co-Varies With Eminence   Prof. Ertel
1990, 4,1 Planetary Influences on Human Behavior ("Gauquelin Effect"): Too Absurd for a Scientific Explanation?   Arno Mueller
1992, 6,3 The Gauquelin Effect Explained? Comments on Arno Mueller's Hypothesis of Planetary Correlations   Prof. Ertel
1993, 7,2 Puzzling Eminence Effects Might Make Good Sense   Prof. Ertel
   7,3 Dutch Investigations of the Gauquelin Mars Effect   Jan Nienhuys
1993 7: 283-292 "Comments on Dutch investigations of the Gauquelin Mars effect."
1997, 11,1 Biased Data Selection in Mars Effect Research   Ertel & Ken Irving
   11,1 Is the "Mars Effect" Genuine? Kurtz, Nienhuys and Sandhu
   11,3 The "Mars Effect" As Seen by the Committee PARA J. Dommanget
2000, 14,3 The Mars Effect Is Genuine: On Kurtz, Nienhuys, and Sandhu's Missing the Evidence   Prof. Ertel & Ken Irving
   14,3 Bulky Mars Effect Hard to Hide: Comment on Dommanget's Account of the Belgian Skeptics' Research   Prof. Ertel

SKEPTICAL INQUIRER

1979 December Kurtz-Zelen-Abell: "US test results."

    Rawlins: "Report on the US-test" (criticizes Zelen).

    Gauquelin, M. & F.: "Star US-sportmen show the Mars effect".

Kurtz-Zelen-Abell: "Response."

1980 Summer 4(4) 58-62 MG: "The Mars Effect: A response from MG".

    4(4) 62-68 Kurtz-Zelen-Abell: "The Contradictions in Gauquelin's Research".

    Fall Jerome: "Mars effect".

    Winter Rawlins: "Remus extremus" (SI, Winter)

    Abell-Kurtz-Zelen: "Statement".

    Abell-Kurtz: "Response".

    Gauquelin: "Letter".

1981 6(2) 66: Spring Abell-Kurtz: "Statement by CSICOP executive Council in Response to Rawlins".

    Fall   Abell-Kurtz-Zelen: "Reappraisal"

    Gauquelin: "Comment" (SI, Fall).

    Kurtz-Abell: "Response" (SI, Fall)

1983 Spring 7(3) 77-82: Abell-Kurtz-Zelen, Mars Effect Experiments, a Reappraisal.'

    Fall 8(1) p.87: MG 'Reappraisal of Mars Correlation', reply 88-89 by Kurtz & Abell.

1992 Winter 16(2) 150-160 Ertel, 'Update on the Mars-Effect' Kurtz reply, p.161 (online).

1995 Jan/Feb 19(1) 4, 62 Kurtz, 'French Committee Announces Results of Test of the So-Called Mars Effect'

1997 November 21(6) 24-29 Nienhuys, 'The Mars Effect in Retrospect'.

THE ZETETIC SCHOLAR

1979, Vols 3&4: Astrology: A Review Symposium with G. O. Abell, Dane Rudhyar, H. J. Eysenck, Michel Gauquelin, Malcolm Dean and others http://tricksterbook.com/truzzi/ZS-Issues-PDFs/ZeteticScholarNos3-4.pdf

1982, 9 Research on the Mars Effect by Patrick Curry with comments by Michel Gauquelin, H. J. Eysenck, I. J. Good, J. Dommanget, and others http://tricksterbook.com/truzzi/ZS-Issues-PDFs/ZeteticScholarNo9.pdf

    10, 50-65, The True Disbelievers: How the Mars Effect drives Skeptics to Irrationality, by Richard Kamann. Online at discord.org/

10 On the Mars Effect Controversy -- comments by R. A. McConnell, T. K. Clark, Richard Kammann, Michel Gauquelin and others
http://tricksterbook.com/truzzi/ZS-Issues-PDFs/ZeteticScholarNo10.pdf
1983, 11 On the Mars Effect Controversy, II -- comments by Patrick Curry, Antony Flew, H. J. Eysenck, Marcello Truzzi
http://tricksterbook.com/truzzi/ZS-Issues-PDFs/ZeteticScholarNo11.pdf

PHENOMENA, THE NEWS JOURNAL OF COSMIC INFLUENCE RESEARCH, Toronto:

1975 H.J. Eysenck, 'Planets, Stars and Personality', *New Behaviour* 20 May p.246-9.

1977 1.6 September 1.6 'Gauquelin Scores Again: tests on Heredity Confirmed' p1-2; 1.8 Eysenck-Mayo-Gauquelin Papers back Planetary Influences p3,6.

1978 2.1 1-3 Humanist Attempts to Discredit Mars Effect; 2.2 pp,1, 6-7 Cover Up! Committee supresses documents, pressures against symposium'; 7-8, MG Getting the facts straight: The Committee and the Mars Effect'; 9-11, Hans Eysenck 'On Jerome's Astrology Disproved'; 12-13, Rob Hand, 'Science vs Scientism'; 15-16, interview with Paul Kurtz; 18-21 Erik Tarkington, 'Gauquelin's Travels Adventures (while shipwrecked in the lands of his various critics). 2.3 p.22 Dennis Rawlins, 'Memo on the relation of Mars solar proximity to MG's sports results.'

MISCELLANY

1967 *Int. Jnl. of Biometeorology* 11, Supplement p.341, MG, 'A possible hereditary effect on time of birth …its relationship with geomagnetic activity.'

1972 *Journal of Interdisciplinary Cycle Research*, 3,2,81-8, MG, 'Planetary Effect and time of Birth…'

1975 *Psychology Today*, MG, 'Spheres of Influence', October, pp. 37-50.

1979 *British Journal of Social and Clinical Psychology*, 1979, 18 71-75, M. Gauquelin, F. Gauquelin and Sybil Eysenck [wife of Hans], 'Personality and the position of the planets at birth: an empirical study.'

John Addey, 'Harmonic phase and personal characteristics', *The Astrological jnl*, Summer 1979 and Winter 1979/80.

1980 Tom Shanks, *Cosmecology Bulletin*, 1980, 2(2) 81-86

1981 *Personality and Individual Differences*, 2(4) 346-350: by M. Gauquelin, F. Gauquelin and Sybil Eysenck, 'Eysenck's personality analysis and position of the planets at birth: a Replication on American subjects.'

Fate, October, 67-98 Dennis Rawlins 'sTarbaby'

Science et Vie March, pp.39-45. Rouzé, M. 762 'Effet Mars: La Néo-Astrologie en échec.'

New Scientist, 92, p.294 'Paranormal Watchers fall out over Mars Effect' 1982, *Science et Vie*, October, 1982, 781, p.44. MG Protocol.

93, 4 March, p.40 MG letter; Curry, 93:601.

Psychology Today 16(7) 8-13 George Abell, 'The Mars Effect'

1987 *Jnl. of Amer. Statistical Assocn.*, 98: 697-8, Prof. I.J. Good, 'The Mars Effect' (book review).

'Searching for significant factors in the Gauquelin professional data', Tom Shanks, ACS, San Diego, CA.

1988 Michel Gauquelin, 'In there really a Mars Effect?' *Jnl of Astrol. Studies* Vol. 11, 4-7, online (N.B., I don't know of this journal)

1989 *NCGR Research Journal*, 'Can the Gauquelin effect be confirmed? 1298 eminent physicians' Fall 17-20, Arno Müller.

1992 Science or Pseudo? The Mars Effect and Other Claims. Proceedings of the Third EuroSkeptics Congress, October 4-5, 1991, Amsterdam; Koppeschaar, C.E. 'The Mars effect unriddled'.

2006 *Les Cahiers du RAMS*, 14, 1-8, Pierre Perradin, 'Effet Mars.'

2013 Geoffrey Dean and Rudolf Smit, *Astrology Under Scrutiny*, 2014; *Tests of Astrology*, 2016.

2017 *ISAR Astrology* jnl. December Vol 46. N.K. 'Is Mars Passionate?'

2018, *AFA Research Journal*, 18, 1-8, N.K., 'The Gauquelin Character Traits – New studies.'

2020 *ISAR Astrology* jnl., April, Vol. 49. N.K. 'The Gauquelin Mars-Effect: Did it Replicate?'

ZEITSCHRIFT FÜR PARAPSYCHOLOGIE UND GRENZGEBIETE DER PSYCHOLOGIE

2013 (?) "Gauquelins „erratischer Block". Können Müller (2005) und Hergovich (2005) ihn beseitigen?"

2007, in Band 49 (1-4), S. Ertel: Die neo-astrologische Entdeckung Gauquelins - Rückblick auf fünf Forschungsjahrzehnte (1955- 2005)

2007, 2006, 2005, Band 47-9, S Ertel, "Die neo-astrologische Entdeckung Gauquelins. Rückblick auf fünf Forschungsjahrzehnte, 182-207.

1997, in Band 39 1997 (1/2), F. Gauquelin: Stellungnahme zum Artikel von Arno Müller: "Ist die Character-Trait-Hypothese Gauquelins endgültig widerlegt?" Kritisches Forum

1996, Band 38 1996 (3/4), A. Müller: Ist die Character-Trait-Hypothese Gauquelins endgültig widerlegt?

1995, Band 37 (1/2), A. Müller: Der Gauquelin-Effekt: Antwort auf Ertels Stellungnahme

Band 37 (1/2), S. Ertel: "Die Stärke des Gauquelin-Planeteneffekts: Arno Müllers Bilanz korrekturbedürftig" (The strength of the Gauquelin planetary effect: Arno Müller's verdict requires correction 37(1-2): 3-27.

1994, Band 36 (3/4), A. Müller: Der Gauquelin-Effekt: Eine kritische Bilanz

1993, Band 35 (1/2), A. Müller, E. Lührs: Eine Untersuchung zum Gauquelin-Effekt mit einer neuen Stichprobe berühmter Männer und Frauen

1992, Band 34 (93/4), A. Müller: Gauquelins Mond-Effekt bei Schriftstellern - Entgegnung zu Ertels Stellungnahme, 232-4.

Band 34 (3/4), S. Ertel: Ist der Mondeffekt bei Gauquelins Schriftstellern zweifelhaft? Notizen zur Wiederholungsstudie Arno Müllers

Band 34 (1/2), A. Müller: Zur Erklärung des Gauquelin-Effekts: Eine Entgegnung zu Ertels Stellungnahme

Band 34 (1/2), S. Ertel: Ist der Gauquelin-Effekt zu erklären? Eine Stellungnahme zu Arno Müllers Deutung der planetarischen Effekte

1991, Band 33 (1/2) A. Müller: Eine Wiederholungsstudie zum Gauquelin-Effekt bei 402 italienischen Schriftstellern

Band 33 (1/2), S. Ertel: Nachruf auf Michel Gauquelin (1928-1991)

1990 Band 32 (3/4), A. Müller: Planetare Einflüsse auf menschliches Verhalten ("Gauquelin-Effekt"): Zu absurd für eine wissenschaftliche Erklärung?

1989, Band 31 (1/2), A. Müller: Gauquelin und die Folgen - eine Sammelbesprechung

1986, Band 28 (1/2), H. Kunzmann: Zur Überprüfung der Gauquelinschen Planetentypologie - ein Zwischenbericht

Band 28 (1/2), S. Ertel: Wissenschaftliche Qualität und progressive Dynamik im Gauquelin-Paradigma

Band 28 (1/2) S. Ertel: Interview mit Hans Jürgen Eysenck über die Grenzgebietsforschung

Band 28 (1/2), A. Müller: Läßt sich der Gauquelin-Effekt bestätigen? Untersuchungsergebnisse mit einer Stichprobe von 1288 hervorragenden Ärzten

Band 28 (1/2) M. Gauquelin: "Neo-Astrologie": Ein Überblick über ein vierzigjähriges Forschungsprogramm

Band 28 (1/2), H. Kunzmann: Zur Überprüfung der Gauquelinschen Planetentypologie - ein Zwischenbericht

1972 Band 14, M. & F. Gauquelin: Planeten und Charakterzüge - Methodologische Skizze für die Darstellung einer Temperamentskomponente bei der planetaren Heredität

1966 Band 9 M. Gauquelin: Der Planetarische Hereditatseffekt und der irdische Magnetismus p.69-84.

1962, Band 5, Jung: Ein Brief zur Frage der Synchronizitat 1-9

    Band 5, M Gauquelin, Die planetare Hereditat   168-193.

1960, Band 3 M Gauquelin, Neue Untersuchungen uber den Einflus der Gerstirne 10-

1958, Band 1, Carl Jung: "Ein Astrologische Experiment,' p.81- 92

    Band 1, Arno Müller: Eine statistiche Untersuchung astrologischer Faktoren bei dauerhaften und geschiedenen Ehen p.93-101 (discussing the Jung marriage-synastry article)

    Band 1, M. Gauquelin: Der Einflus der Gestirne und die Statistik 102-123.

OTHER ERTEL PUBLICATIONS   1994-2015

1992: *Mars effect survives critique of Dutch skeptics. A Rejoinder*. Third EuroSkeptics Congress. Oct. 4-5, 1991. Science or Pseudo? The Mars effect and other claims, Amsterdam, Utrecht: SKEPSIS.

1990: Gauquelin contentions scrutinized. *Geocosmic relations. The earth and its macro-environment*. G. J. M. Tomassen, W. d. Graaff, A. A. Knoop and R. Hengefeld. Pudoc, Wageningen, 255-166.

1990: "Scrutinizing Gauquelin's character trait hypothesis once again." NCGR Research Journal Spring Equinox: 27-34.

1989: "Reversed eminence correlations. Comments on an article review." NCGR Research Journal, Spring Equinox: 27-34.

GAUQUELIN DATA PUBLICATIONS

'Series A' gives all of the professional birth data.
Volume 1: SPORTS CHAMPIONS   2088, 1970
Volume 2: PHYSICIANS & SCIENTIST 2552 physicians + 1094 Scientists 1970
Volume 3 MILITARY, 3047 1970 (also lists Aviators as 3048-3439):
Volume 4: PAINTERS &   1473 Painters 1970
MUSICIANS   + 866 Musicians and 383 military musicians
Volume 5: ACTORS, 1409 A1-A1409
POLITICIANS   + 1003 P1410-P2412
Volume 6: WRITERS, 1352 W1-W1352 + JOURNALISTS, 675, J1353-J2027, 1971

Series B: Hereditary Experiment
Volume 1: HERED 1   5018 #   1- 5011
Volume 2: HERED 2   4818 # 5012- 9838
Volume 3: HERED 3   3898 # 9847-13740

Volume 4: HERED 4   3760 #13741-17499
Volume 5: HERED 5   3745 #17500-21243
Volume 6: HERED 6   3710 #21244-24949

Heredity Replication
1972: *Profession - Heredity. Results of Series A & B.* Series C, Vol. 1. (BOURGE 9100 City of Bourge, PARIS14B 17131 Paris 14)
1977 M&FG, Replication of the planetary effect in Heredity, LERRCP

Series C: Psychology
Volume 2: The Mars temperament and sports champions 1973
Volume 3: The Saturn temperament and men of Science 1974
Volume 4: The Jupiter temperament and Actors 1974
Volume 5 The Moon temperament and Writers 1977

1979 Sports Champions a new Replication
1982. Report on American Data.vol. 10. Paris
1984b: *2145 Physicians, Army Leaders, Top Executives.* New birth data series, Vol. 1 Pari.
1984c: 1540 Authors, Artists, Actors, Politicians, Journalists. New Birth Data series Vol. 3, Paris.
Report on American Data, Series D, Vol X 1982; the Gauquelin Book of American charts, ACS 1982.

13 GAUQUELIN BOOKS

L'Influence des Astres 1955 * Les Hommes et Les Astres 1960 * L'Heredite Planetaire 1966 * The Cosmic Clocks 1967 * The Scientific Basis of astrology 1969 * Astrology and Science 1970 * Data-volumes sports, writers etc, 1970-72 * Cosmic Influences on Human Behaviour 1973 * Dreams and Illusions of astrology 1979 * Spheres of Destiny 1980 * The Truth about Astrology 1983 * Birthtimes: A Scientific investigation of the Secrets of astrology 1983 * Written in the Stars 1988 * Neo-astrology, a Copernican Revolution 1991.

INDEX

Abell, George, 59, 68
Academiciens de Medicine, 15
Academy of Medicine, 123, 128
Addey, John, 147, 154, 160, 167, 184
amplitude, 190

Astro-Computing Services, 19, 149, 158
Astrologers in Research', 11
Astrology Science or Superstition, 190
Astrology Under Scrutiny, 10

Astro-Psychological Problems, 7, 76
Babylon, 212
basketball players, 63, 142
Belgian Comité Para, 9, 53, 70
Benski Report, 98, 100
birth times, 224
Cadent houses, 151, 183
Campion, Nick, 190
Case for Astrology, The, 76
Castille, Didier, 197
CFEPP, 94
Character-traits hypothesis, 148
Charles Harvey, 5
Cochrane, David, 26
conjunction, 196
correlation, 187
Cosimo de Medici, 207
CSICOP, 62, 64, 222
CURA archive, 193
Da Vinci Code, 208
Dean, Geoffrey, 19, 138, 222
Dean, Malcolm, 51, 189
Dictionnaire Encyclopaedia des Sports, 112
Dommanget, Jean, 71
Douglas, Graham, 88, 104
drug addicts, 183
dynamism of Mars, 153
ecliptic, 22
Eliot, T.S., 204
Energetic, 147
Ertel, Suitbert, 76, 79, 100, 105, 143, 224
Evening Star, 167
extravert, 188
Eysenck, 3
Eysenck Personality Questionnaire, 182
Eysenck, Hans, 52, 76, 182, 192
Eysenck, Sybil, 183
fourfold-structure, 161
Freud, Sigmund, 203
Galileo, 207
Gauquelin database, 8
gender-bias, 142
geomagnetism, 25

Gingerich, Owen, 70
Gnosis, 74
Great Red Spot, 202
heredity data, 139
Heredity Effect', 134
Hommes et les Astres, 129
Humanist Manifesto, 74
Humanist, The, 57
introvert, 188
Irving, Ken, 132
Jigsaw program, 194
John Addey, 17
Journal for Scientific Exploration, The, 80, 125
Jovial, 161
Joyful, 155
Jung, Carl, 3, 186, 200, 211
Kepler, 209
Key Sectors, 14
Kurtz, Paul, 57, 59, 62, 81
L'Influence des Astres, 15
Les Hommes at Les Astres, 44, 118
Lucifer, 167, 208
Mars Effect', 1
Martial traits, 152
Mather, Arthur, 222
Maudsley clinic, 3
Mayo, Jeff, 190
Michelson, Neil, 149
Moon, 154
Morning Star, 167
moving average', 190
Müller, Arno, 91, 118, 185
Murphy, Ray, 195, 214
Nazi stormtroopers, 144
NCGR journal, 168
New Scientist, 64
Nias, David, 52, 136
Nienhuys, Jan, 100, 102
nycthemeral birth distribution, 27, 30, 118
O'Neill, Mike, 199
Objections to Astrology', 56
Olympic gold, 129
para committee, 51
Paris, 193
Phenomena, 24

physicians, French, 143
Placidus houses, 21, 159
politicians, eminent, 142
Popper, Karl, 71
Pottenger, Mark, 22, 34
Powell, Robert, 214
Prometheus Books, 95
Psychology of the Planets, 171
Rawlins, Dennis, 32, 61, 65
Rob Hand, 58
Saturn, 1, 157
Saturn-keywords, 163
Shanks, Tom, 150, 157
Sidereus Nuncius, 207
Smithers, Prof Alan, 189
Solar Fire software, 219
sTarbaby, 67
suicide, of Michel, 204
Synastry, 193
Tarvanien, Kyosti, 160, 216
Tenacious Mars-Effect, The, 74
Truth about Astrology, The, 135
Venus, 145
West, John Anthony, 76
writers, imaginative, 140
Zeitschrift fur Parapsychologie, 77, 211
Zelen test', 32
Zelen, Marvin, 59
Zetetic Scholar, 54
Zetetic, The, 67
Zeus, 156
zodiac longitude, 190

www.ingramcontent.com/pod-product-compliance
Lightning Source LLC
Chambersburg PA
CBHW040509110526
44587CB00044B/4040